LIGHTING
DESIGN BASICS

LIGHTING DESIGN BASICS

Second Edition

MARK KARLEN

JAMES R. BENYA

CHRISTINA SPANGLER

Illustrations by KATHRYN LYONS

WILEY

JOHN WILEY & SONS, INC.

Library of Congress Cataloging-in-Publication Data:

ISBN 978-0-470-47427-3; ISBN 978-0-470-95101-9 (ebk); ISBN 978-0-470-95118-7 (ebk);
ISBN 978-1-118-28792-7 (ebk); ISBN 978-1-118-28794-1 (ebk); ISBN 978-1-118-28795-8 (ebk)

Printed in the United States of America

10 9 8 7 6 5 4 3 2

TABLE OF CONTENTS

PREFACE

A great deal of change has occurred in the technology and practice of lighting design over the past seven years since the writing of the first edition of *Lighting Design Basics*. The amazingly rapid growth of LED (light-emitting diodes) technology has had a major impact on the lighting design industry and the professionals who make decisions on how we light spaces. And as our world constantly changes, other technical and societal developments have had significant impact on lighting design, not the least of which are the growing concerns for, and innovations related to, energy consumption and the issues of sustainability in general. Design professionals have found that the public, and more specifically, their clients, are increasingly informed about these concerns and expect their designers to be fully informed. Simply said, this second edition is necessary for an up-to-date understanding of lighting design.

The primary focus of this book remains with the design aspects of lighting, rather than the terminology and technology of the field. That focus continues to provide consistent concern for the visual tasks and design quality experienced by the people using those interior spaces. This edition has added a series of very practical "Electrician's Notebooks" that provides additional information related to many of the issues encountered in the construction process. In addition, notes have been made of the changes in lighting design practice created by the growing concerns for sustainability. And finally, this new edition has provided the opportunity for extensive use of color, enhancing both learning clarity and aesthetic quality.

Special note must be made of the important contributions made by Jim Benya in creating the original edition of *Lighting Design Basics*. His participation in the second edition has been taken over graciously by Christina Spangler, a particularly experienced lighting designer and a principal in the Philadelphia and New York–based Lighting Design Collaborative. All of the illustrations in this edition—floor plans, reflected ceiling plans, sections, and perspectives—have been skillfully created by designer Kate Lyons. And a special thanks to Paul Drougas, Wiley's senior editor, whose consistent efforts with editorial advice and coordination have made this second edition possible.

Mark Karlen and Christina Spangler

LIGHTING
DESIGN BASICS

Chapter | # INTRODUCTION:
How to Use This Book

This book is an instructional tool designed to develop the necessary knowledge and skills for solving lighting design problems for typical rooms and spaces and for collaborating with lighting design professionals in solving problems for complex rooms and spaces. The book is directed to students and professionals in architecture and interior design or in related fields such as facilities management, construction management, store planning, and electrical contracting and engineering.

The primary focus is on design, not technology or terminology. Design is the development of a lighting design concept and the selection and placement of luminaires to provide optimal lighting and aesthetically satisfying spaces for the visual tasks at hand. Lighting technology (and related terminology) will be covered in enough depth to serve the design orientation of the book's methodologies. For more information related to these technical factors, the Bibliography identifies the best sources.

This is a how-to instructional textbook, the goal of which is to provide its users with the tools required to function effectively in the many design and construction fields of which lighting is an essential part.

ORGANIZATION

Lighting Design Basics is organized in the following five parts:

Part I: Basics About Lighting. Chapters 2 through 9 provide background for the technical (and related terminology) aspects of lighting design, enough to serve this book's purpose but without unnecessary emphasis on technical issues. More specifically, the technical factors addressed are light sources (and their color implications), luminaires, switching and controls, daylighting, and calculations (including rule-of-thumb techniques).

Part II: Design Process. Chapters 10 and 11 provide a basic approach or methodology for developing successful lighting design concepts and solutions, including the graphic representation tools and techniques used to convey the solutions. In this context, success is defined as meeting functional visual requirements, achieving satisfying aesthetic results, and using lighting design technology (including code compliance) intelligently. To aid in this process, a Lighting Design Criteria Matrix has been included as a predesign tool.

Part III: Applications and Case Studies. Chapters 12 through 19 focus on the typical lighting design problems encountered in the five major building use types: (1) residential, (2) office/corporate, (3) healthcare/institutional, (4) hospitality/restaurant, and (5) retail store. In addition, Chapter 18 provides case studies for commonly used spaces, such as restrooms and corridors; Chapter 19 addresses the issues of exterior lighting; and Chapter 20 deals with the recurring questions related to retrofitting existing conditions. Case studies are provided for many of the typical rooms and spaces found in various buildings. Design problems, their solutions, and the rationales for the solutions are presented in detail.

Part IV: Professional Skills. Chapter 21 provides additional and necessary information about functioning as a designer or design-related professional in matters concerning lighting design. This information is intended to serve as a transition from learning to professional practice.

Part V: Electrician's Notebook. Several chapters have additional technical- and construction-related information in boxed notes called Electrician's Notebook. These notes will be of specific interest for readers who wish to proceed a little further in these areas.

Appendixes

Appendix A is a brief overview of the role of computers in lighting design, including data and research, documentation tools, calculations, digital presentation, and rendering.

Appendix B is a summary of energy codes and how they affect design. Included are Internet references for obtaining the most recent energy code information within the United States.

Appendix C is a basic summary on how lighting can contribute to achieving LEED certification. It lists the general approaches that can be applied.

GETTING THE MOST OUT OF THIS BOOK

The information in this book is meant to be applied, not just read. At the heart of the learning process presented here is putting your newly acquired knowledge to work shortly after reading and understanding the related case studies.

The examples in the case studies represent typical lighting design applications. Beyond these examples, lighting design becomes increasingly complex and challenging, even for the most knowledgeable and experienced professionals. The purpose here is not to prepare the reader for those complex problems but rather to provide understanding of lighting design concepts, techniques, and realistic goals so collaboration with a lighting design professional can achieve the best possible results. One must learn to communicate design intentions in a way that a lighting designer can use. Those communication skills require a conceptual understanding of lighting design, the acquisition of which should be one of the major learning goals in working with this book.

Many technical aspects of lighting design go considerably beyond the scope of this book. Issues such as the fine points of color rendition, code compliance, project budget, and lighting live performance spaces can be extremely complex. Working knowledge of these factors is not expected of broad-based design and built environment professionals. However, general familiarity is required to collaborate productively with lighting designers. To acquire deeper knowledge in these more technical matters, consult the Bibliography.

In a classroom setting, the value of this book is enhanced by an exchange of ideas among students working on the same lighting design assignments, the instructor's critiques, and open classroom critiques and discussion. Beyond the classroom, one should take advantage of every opportunity to discuss lighting design solutions with design professionals, particularly those with extensive practical experience. Such discussion can be invaluable.

Two readily available learning tools should be used concurrently with this book. First is the deliberate observation and critique of existing lighting design applications. Be aware of the lighting in public and semi-public spaces, making note of lamp and luminaire types and, more important, what works well and what doesn't. A great deal can be learned from the successes and failures of others. Second, many architecture and interior design professional publications present enough programmatic, plan, and spatial information about interesting spaces to use as design exercises for enhancing one's skills.

It all begins with working on paper or the computer and trying a variety of lighting design solutions to typical design problems.

While this book prescribes a particular approach to solving lighting design problems, it should be understood that several potentially successful methodologies exist. In the professional community of lighting designers and the other design professionals who work with them, the problem-solving process enjoys many workable variations. It is expected that individual professionals, after repeated experience with actual problems, will gradually develop personalized methodologies.

Chapter 2 BASIC CONCEPTS IN LIGHTING

Lighting is an important part of the designer's toolbox because it completely changes how an occupant experiences a space. If the lighting does not adequately and appropriately illuminate the visual tasks and surfaces, the design will not entirely meet its goals. Most environmental experience occurs through vision, and, without light, we literally cannot see. Lighting leads a person instinctively through a space, and it controls what one sees or doesn't see. It can quickly and simply change the atmosphere of a space and how a person feels while in it. Additionally, the proper level of illumination allows the user to easily complete the tasks required. Ultimately, the lighting determines how successful a design will be aesthetically and functionally.

As a designer, it is important to study lighting even though a professional lighting designer is typically involved with most projects. The designers have the most comprehensive understanding of the space, including the architectural features, programming requirements, furniture and equipment planning, user interaction, and overall design concept. Having a basic knowledge of lighting design, sources, and fixtures gives the designer the opportunity to guide a lighting designer and clearly describe the effects desired. Also, recognizing the importance of lighting allows the designer to make lighting decisions throughout the process instead of at the end.

Developing a lighting approach can be overwhelming for a designer because of rapidly changing technology and the countless choices of luminaires. A designer must first determine what objects and surfaces require lighting and develop a visual composition using multiple layers of lighting.

LAYERED DESIGN

The principle of layering provides a framework for understanding and achieving composition and aesthetics in lighting design. Layering permits judicious choices that ensure that design requirements can be established prior to selecting the type or style of fixture. Generally, using layers of lighting gives the space variety and interest while also providing flexibility for the end user. In addition, because more attention is given to lighting specific surfaces, layered lighting is more efficient than lighting a space uniformly.

The following layers of light are identified in the order of their importance and visual impact. Each layer has unique responsibilities to light certain visual tasks; however, the layers often work together to light portions of the space.

3

LIGHTING LAYERS

Focal Layer

The focal layer is typically used to highlight vertical surfaces and three-dimensional objects including architectural features and details, artwork, retail displays, and signage. Although this layer is often considered aesthetic in nature, it plays an important role in determining the perceived brightness of the space.

To understand the layer's significance, it is important to recognize how humans interact with light. Humans typically see and respond to bright vertical surfaces. A space where the vertical surfaces (walls, furniture, art, etc.) are well illuminated will feel much brighter than a space where only the horizontal surfaces (desktop, tables, floor, etc.) are addressed. Identifying the key vertical elements, focal points, and visual destinations will lead a person through the space intuitively (see Fig. 2.1).

Most often, the focal layer light source is not seen. The intent is to highlight the object or feature and not see the luminaire.

Task Layer

The task layer is used to illuminate specific tasks that are performed in a space. Many work tasks, such as reading, occur on a table or desk. It is common to provide task lights at locations where these tasks occur. Using higher levels of illumination at the

---

Electrician's Notebook

Depending on the complexity of the room and its design, it is possible to have all the layers of light represented. Because each of the layers has a different purpose and should be controlled separately, four or more switches or dimmers could be required in a single space. The layers of light can be used intentionally to create a composition in the space, and often the user may like to create "scenes" that vary throughout the day or for different uses.

Instead of a row of standard switches or dimmers, consider using a preset scene controller. Basic scene controllers fit within a four-gang recessed box and can control up to six groups or zones of light. This type of system is similar to a car radio since it remembers a preset so that it can be recalled repeatedly without manually adjusting. The individual zones can be set at different levels as required and memorized as a scene. This type of system also allows integration into home theater and commercial audiovisual presentation systems. Refer to Chapter 7 for additional information about lighting control systems.

---

task location is more energy efficient than providing that level of light throughout the entire space (see Fig. 2.2).

Daylight Layer

The daylight available in a space should be evaluated so that opportunities to reduce artificial lighting can be realized early in the design process.

Advantages of incorporating daylight into the overall lighting design (see Fig. 2.3) include:

- Energy savings can be captured if fixtures are reduced or controlled properly.
- Daylight reveals true colors in a space.
- Building fenestrations provide views and ventilation.
- Daylight creates a positive effect on people by reducing stress and encouraging positive attitudes,

In addition, the contribution of sun and daylight may require control to reduce glare and unwanted heat gain. Refer to Chapter 4 for a more in-depth look at daylighting.

Decorative Layer

One way to think about decorative lighting is as the jewelry of architecture. Like jewelry in fashion, its primary purpose is as an ornament to the space to catch the eye and make statements about style or wealth (see Fig. 2.4). It plays an extremely important role in interior design and themed environments. Additionally, decorative fixtures can provide a desirable eye-level glow that is missing from spaces only lighted from the ceiling. Generally, because of their decorative nature, such fixtures emit light rather poorly, so it is increasingly common to avoid counting on the decorative light for the purpose of task lighting.

Ambient Layer

The ambient layer provides the background lighting that helps create the mood of the space. Typically low contrast, ambient lighting allows basic visual recognition and movement through a space. It is important to note that often, after all the other layers are considered, lighting specific to the ambient layer may not be required, which is why it should be considered last.

The amount of ambient light is important: If the ambient light level in the space is significantly lower than the focal level, the contrast between focal and ambient light will be high and the space will appear more dramatic (see Fig. 2.5). On the other hand, if the ambient light levels are nearly as high as the focal and task levels, the room will be brighter, and cheerier (see Fig. 2.6). Because of its impact on the mood or ambience of the room, choice of ambient lighting is surprisingly critical.

Fig. 2.1 Focal Lighting Example *(Photograph: Kuda Photography.)*

Fig. 2.2 Task Lighting Example (Courtesy of National Kitchen & Bath Association. Designed by NKBA Member Tricia Bayer. Photograph: 360 VIP.)

Fig. 2.3 Daylighting Example *(Photograph: David Baron, creativecommons.org/licenses/by-sa/2.0/deed.en)*

Fig. 2.4 Decorative Lighting Example
(Photograph: Kuda Photography.)

Fig. 2.5 Ambient Lighting Example with High Contrast
(Photograph: Jeffrey Totaro.)

Fig. 2.6 Ambient Lighting Example with Low Contrast
(Photograph: Ted Moudis Associates Reception Area and Feature Interconnecting Stair.)

One Light, Two or More Layers

Too many lights—especially too many types of lights—can be visually busy. It certainly can add cost. A good lighting designer seeks to minimize the lighting design while maintaining the desired effects. One common design approach is to have one luminaire or lighting system provide two or more layers. Here are some common designs:

- *Use decorative lighting as ambient lighting.* Careful selection of decorative luminaires is required to prevent glare; luminaires with mostly uplight do an excellent job of providing both decorative and ambient lighting, whereas luminaires with bare lamps and other traditional elements are generally poor ambient light sources.
- *Use the same type of luminaire for focal lighting and task lighting.* Recessed adjustable luminaires and track lighting can be aimed at tasks as well as artwork.
- *Use decorative lighting as task lighting.* Table lamps, floor lamps, pendants, and other types of decorative lights make excellent task lights in some applications.

Only One Layer

General lighting is an approach whereby only one luminaire or group of similar luminaires is designed to provide all task and ambient lighting. This single-layer technique is used in many basic lighting designs for offices, classrooms, stores, and many other types of spaces. General lighting tends to be inexpensive and easy to build and use, but it usually lacks the drama and style of designs with more layers.

It is important to note that even very simple general lighting designs could greatly benefit from the addition of focal lighting. For example, focal lighting added at the front of a classroom can help students focus; focal lighting on an office display or bulletin board can inform employees; and focal lighting in a store can lead a person to the sales counter.

A NOTE ABOUT COMPOSITION

Good lighting designs bring together these decisions in harmony with the inherent design of the space. As with architecture and interior design, individual skill in lighting design increases with experience, critique, and practice. Simple single-layer designs are generally not as complex as multilayer designs, but it may be challenging to achieve a good composition with a limited amount of equipment. Energy-efficient lighting designs are especially hard to do because some layers, such as the decorative layer, will either need to do more than one job or be eliminated altogether.

Chapters 3 through 11 provide the designer sufficient technical knowledge to speak intelligently about lighting design. This background allows the designer to make deliberate and educated decisions about the lighting to ensure the clients' lighting needs are met. Then, the case studies in Chapters 12 through 19 illustrate how that information can be translated into a design.

Chapter 3 QUALITIES OF LIGHT SOURCES

The sun, moon, and stars are the most important sources of light for life. But because of the human need for additional light, mankind has learned to create light as well. Understanding light sources begins with the fundamental difference between natural and man-made light.

Natural light sources occur within nature and are beyond the control of mankind. These include sunlight, moonlight, starlight, various plant and animal sources, radio-luminescence, and, of course, fire.

Man-made light sources occur under the control of mankind, more or less when deemed necessary and in the amount wanted. These include wood flame, oil flame, gas flame, electric lamps, photochemical reactions, and various reactions, such as explosives.

Due to their obvious advantages in terms of availability, safety, cleanliness, and remote energy generation, electric lamps have displaced all other man-made sources for lighting of the built environment. However, because man-made sources consume natural resources, natural light sources should be used to the greatest extent possible, which remains one of the biggest challenges to architects and designers.

QUALITIES OF LIGHT SOURCES

In practical terms, light sources can be discussed in terms of the qualities of the light they produce. These qualities are critical to the end result and need to be understood when choosing the source for a lighting design.

How Light Is Generated

Most natural light comes from the sun, including moonlight. Its origin makes it completely clean, and it consumes no natural resources while providing light. But man-made sources generally require some consumption of resources, such as burning fossil fuels, to ultimately convert stored energy into light energy. Electric lighting is superior to flame sources because the combustion of wood, gas, or oil produces pollution within the space being illuminated. Moreover, electricity can be generated from natural, renewable sources of energy, including wind, hydro, geothermal, and solar.

How an electric lamp operates determines virtually everything about the light created by it. The common incandescent lamp generates light through the principle of incandescence, in which a metal is heated until it glows. Most other lamps, however, generate light by means of a complex chemical system in which electric energy is turned into light energy where heat is a side effect. These processes are usually a lot more efficient than incandescence at the cost of complexity and other limitations. For instance, a fluorescent lamp generates light by a discharge of energy into a gas, which in turn emits ultraviolet radiation that is finally converted to visible light by minerals that "fluoresce." This process generates light about 400 percent more efficiently than incandescence and is the reason that various fluorescent lamps are promoted as environmentally friendly. Light-emitting diode (LED) lamps are unique—they are called "solid state lighting" because light is generated by principles of quantum physics derived from the simple electrical diode. LED offers outstanding potential for efficiency, sustainability, and best of all, the ability to generate useful light from simple power systems such as photovoltaic (PV) panels and storage batteries.

How the Eye Sees

To understand the importance of why a quality light source should be selected, one must first be aware of how the human eye works and how it sees color.

The Spectrum of Light

As shown in Fig. 3.1, light is a part of the electromagnetic radiation spectrum. Light encompasses a small portion of that spectrum and has wavelengths in a range from about 380 (blue) to 740 (red) nanometers.

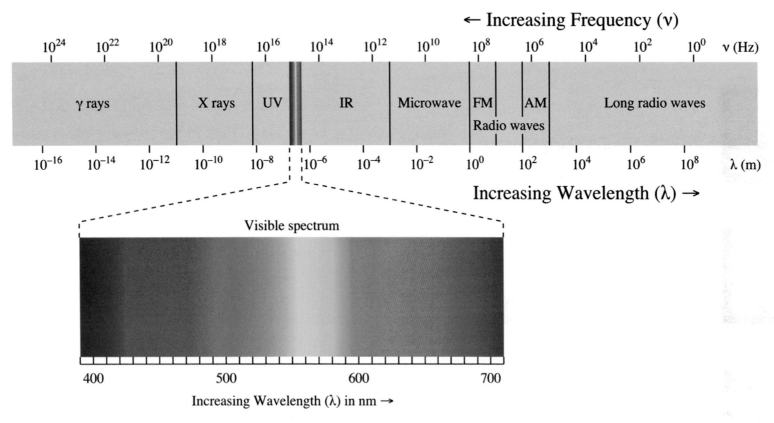

Fig. 3.1 Electromagnetic Radiation Spectrum Diagram with Visible Spectrum Enlarged (Illustration: Philip Ronan, creativecommons.org/licenses/by-sa/3.0/)

The full spectrum of light can be seen in a rainbow or from a prism (see Fig. 3.2), and it includes all of the visible colors. As Sir Isaac Newton discovered through his experiments with prisms, white light from the sun is made up of all the wavelengths combined.

Similar to pigment color, we tend to organize light color into three primaries (red, green, and blue) and three secondaries (yellow, cyan, and magenta). When the three primaries are overlapped, they create white light, as shown in Fig. 3.3.

When white light hits an object, the object will absorb all of the wavelengths that match its own atomic structure and reflect the rest back to our eyes. The eye sees the wavelength or combination of wavelengths and the brain translates it into a color.

Light Source Selection

As one can imagine, the more saturated a white light source is with the full spectrum of wavelengths, the more accurately the eye and brain will be able to interpret the

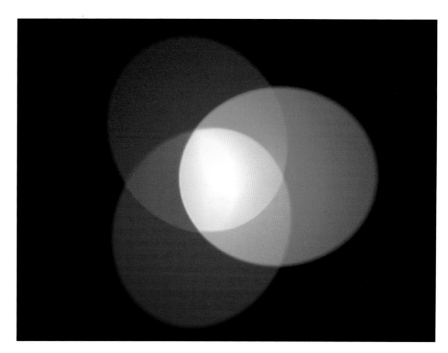

Fig. 3.3 The Three Primary Colors of Light—Red, Green and Blue

Fig. 3.2 A Prism Refracts White Light into the Full Spectrum of Visible Colors *(Photograph: Adam Hart-Davis.)*

true color of an object. Because of this, artificial light sources are measured in two very important ways: Color Rendering Index (CRI) and color temperature.

Color Rendering Index

The CRI describes the quality of the light on a scale of 0 (horrible) to 100 (perfect). This measurement illustrates the light source's ability to render the color of objects correctly, as compared with a reference source with comparable color temperature. Generally, the more wavelength-saturated the source is, the higher the CRI will be. Fig. 3.4 shows the same objects under two different light sources with different CRI values. The higher CRI value renders the colors more accurately, which is important in most interior spaces.

Color Temperature

The color temperature of a light source describes whether the light appears warm, neutral, or cool. The term "temperature" relates to the light emitted from a metal

80+ CRI (3500K)   70 CRI (3500K)

**Fig. 3.4 Objects under Two Light Sources
with Varying Color Rendering Indexes**

A lamp source that is saturated with warm or cool wavelengths will influence how an object appears, and should be selected carefully. Fig. 3.5 takes the same objects used in Fig. 3.4 and places them under light sources with different color temperatures. (Note: All of these light sources contain the same CRI.)

All white light sources can be evaluated by color temperature and CRI. Color temperature is the more obvious of the two; two light sources of the same color temperature but different CRIs appear much more alike than do two light sources of similar CRIs but different color temperatures.

Natural light is defined as having a CRI of 100 (perfect). The color temperature, however, varies a great deal due to weather, season, air pollution, and viewing angle. For instance, the combination of sun and blue skylight on a summer day at noon is about 5,500 K, but if the sun is shielded, the color of the blue skylight is over 10,000 K. The rising and setting sunlight in clear weather can be as low as 1800 K. Cloudy day skylight is around 6500 K.

When choosing electric light sources, it is best to select source color temperature and CRI according to what is shown in Tables 3.1 and 3.2. Note that even if daylight enters the space, it is usually not a good idea to try to match daylight with electric light, as daylight varies considerably.

object heated to the point of incandescence. The higher the temperature, the whiter or cooler the light source appears. Fig. 3.6 shows many typical light sources and their available color temperatures measured in degrees Kelvins (K). As an example, the color temperature of an incandescent lamp is about 2700 K, appearing like a metal object heated to 2700 K.

Color Consistency and Stability

The color consistency of a light source references how reliable the light source is when compared with other lamps that are installed at the same time. The stability of a light source relates to its color over a period of time. All light sources reduce

INCANDESCENT (2,700K)   3000K   3500K   4100K

Fig. 3.5 Objects under Four Light Sources with Varying Color Temperatures

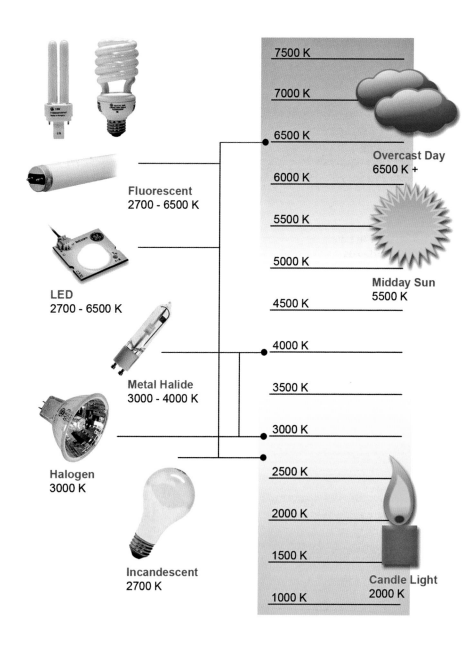

Fig. 3.6 Light Sources and Their Typical Color Temperatures

Table 3.1 Color Rendering Index Applications

Minimum Lamp CRI	Applications
<50	Noncritical industrial, storage, and security lighting
50–70	Industrial and general illumination where color is not important (uncommon for interior spaces)
70–79	Offices, schools, and recreational spaces where color is not important
80–89	Hotels, restaurants, offices, schools, hospitals, and retail where color quality is important
90–100	Retail and museum/gallery display where color quality is critical

Table 3.2 Color Temperature Applications

Color Temperature (Measured in Degrees Kelvin)	Application
<2500	Bulk industrial and security lighting
2700–3000	Residences, hotels, restaurants, themed environments, and some commercial office spaces
2950–3200	Display lighting in retail and galleries
3500–4100	Offices, schools, hospitals, some retail
5000–7500	Special applications where color discrimination is critical; uncommon for general lighting

intensity over time, but some sources also shift in color. For applications like high-end retail, museums, and wherever else image and color matching is critical, this would need to be considered.

Dimmability

Dimming is the process by which lamps are operated at less than full light, often as an energy-saving or mood-creating method. With incandescent lamps, dimming is simple and inexpensive; however, with other types, dimming can be considerably more complex, and, in some cases, not advisable.

Directionality

Light sources vary in shape. The three basic shape types are point sources, line sources, and area sources. Each radiates light differently and thus causes unique effects. Slightly different, LED consists of many tiny point sources that are typically combined to form pseudo point sources, line sources, or area sources.

Initial Cost vs. Operating Cost

The initial cost is the amount that the client will spend to purchase and install the lighting. The operating cost includes the electricity to run it, and the cost to purchase and replace the lamps. Generally speaking, the initial cost is minor compared to the cost of the energy required to operate the lamps over the life of the system. If a complete life cycle cost analysis is completed, the efficacy of the lamps becomes very important.

Efficacy

The energy efficiency of a light source is called its efficacy and is measured in lumens per watt. As with miles per gallon, a higher number is better. Efficacy does not take into consideration the directionality of the lamp.

Low-efficacy lamps, like incandescent lamps, are less than 20 lumens per watt. Good colored light sources, such as metal halide, fluorescent, and LED lamps, can achieve up to about 100 lumens per watt.

Operating Temperature

Some lamps are sensitive and/or optimized by the ambient temperature surrounding it. If the lamp will be in conditions other than room temperature, special consideration may need to be given to the selection.

Auxiliary Equipment

In order to operate correctly, many electric light sources require an auxiliary electric device, such as a transformer or ballast. This device is often physically large and unattractive and can create an audible hum or buzz when operating. LEDs require an electronic circuit called a driver that operates them correctly. What makes LEDs different is that one driver can operate a large number of LEDs while ballasts are often limited to one, two, three, or four lamps.

Throughout the world there are also many types of low-voltage lamps, operating at 6, 12, or 24 volts. Transformers are used to alter the service voltage to match the lamp voltage. In the case of LEDs, the actual LED operates at about 2.5 to 3 volts; a low-voltage DC power supply (often part of the driver) is needed for any LED system.

Ambient Temperature

The bulbs of most lamps can get quite hot. The bulb temperature of incandescent and halogen lamps and most high-intensity discharge (HID) lamps is sufficiently high to cause burns and, in the case of halogen lamps, extremely severe burns and fires. Fluorescent lamps, while warm, are generally not too hot to touch when operating, although contact is not advised. The LED is different—it is usually no more than warm, as an LED hot enough to cause discomfort or burning is probably being damaged as a result of operating too hot.

Life

The life of a lamp is the total operating time at which 50 percent of a large group of lamps are expected to fail. Lamp life for LEDs is measured differently because they do not typically fail, but continue to lose output over time. Their lamp life is measured when they lose 70 percent of their output. Lamp life varies greatly between the different sources, and often becomes an important factor in lamp selection.

Lumen Maintenance

Over a lamp's lifetime, the light that is produced by all sources is reduced. The lumen maintenance evaluates how much of that light is lost by the end of the lamp's life.

Starting Time

Some lamps start operating as soon as power is applied, but most others require a high-energy pulse. This process takes time and the lamp needs to warm-up to reach its full intensity. In addition, if power is lost, some lamps need to cool down before they can be restarted. As the lamp warms up, it first glows faintly, then, after a modest warm-up time, finally gives off full light. Obviously, these considerations can dramatically affect design when safety or security might be compromised by a long warm-up or restart time.

When selecting light sources for a project, it is important to understand what attributes mentioned previously are the most important. Once the requirements are prioritized, it is much easier to select the most appropriate source. Chapter 5 evaluates the major lamp families using the criteria established here.

Chapter **4** DAYLIGHTING

Before one can select the appropriate artificial light source, it is important to consider how daylight can be used effectively. Daylight is highly desirable as a light source because people respond very positively to it. Also, with the proper design, daylight can significantly reduce the amount of electric light required throughout the day.

PSYCHOLOGICAL AND PHYSICAL EFFECTS OF DAYLIGHT

In the 1973 book *Health and Light,* John Nash Ott attributed his better health to "full spectrum lighting," triggering a worldwide debate that continues today. Meanwhile, doctors studying sleep disorders and Seasonal Affective Disorder (SAD), or winter depression, documented improvements in patient health using light as medicine—certain amounts, taken at certain times, helped treat or even cure malady.

Today, widely accepted evidence-based science now exists to explain what really caused Ott to feel better and what cured many SAD patients. The essential "vitamin" is natural light and its daily rhythms of light and darkness. In short, being exposed to natural light and following nature's rhythms reinforces and strengthens the entire body, especially the immune system. This is called the circadian rhythm—the word *circadian* means "about a day."

Morning
The rhythm starts with the early morning light that penetrates the eyelids and causes melatonin levels in the blood to drop sharply. The color of the light—especially the short wavelength blue light—is critical as it signifies the difference between daylight and other sources of light. On a sunny day, the high light levels and high color temperature of the light raises alertness and attentiveness. On a cloudy or rainy day, the body's internal clock takes over and helps provide at least a minimum level of alertness.

Daytime
Daytime light levels are high, and the color temperature of light is still high. Exposure to ultraviolet light, only present during the middle of the day, causes the skin to generate vitamin D, an essential nutrient for the immune system as well as many other needs throughout the body. Alertness is maintained by the relatively high light levels. As the day progresses, the change of light level and lower color temperature signal the coming evening. This begins the tiring and sleeping cycle.

Night
The falling light levels and warmer tones of light cause melatonin levels in the bloodstream to rise. Melatonin causes drowsiness and sleep. The body temperature drops, and muscles and organs get vital rest. In fact, just about every part of the body, even

an infection, slows and sleeps. The immune system is an exception as it seizes the opportunity to kill disease in its sleep. About 30 minutes before sunrise, the cycle starts anew.

The Body's Natural Clock

Left without daylight, the body has an internal clock that will keep the daily cycle going. But it will get off of the natural cycle over time. In the Pacific Northwest, where short days are often accompanied by sunless days for long periods, the misalignment of body clocks to the time clock is a probable cause of Seasonal Affective Disorder. Bright clear days reset the body and time clocks, but actual readjustment can take at least a day for every hour of misalignment. This is directly related to jet lag.

Designing with Nature

With the invention of electricity, humans began a series of changes in lifestyles that are now seen as interrupting nature's rhythms. Although not immediately deadly, these changes threaten individual long-term health. Some of these include:

- In modern developed nations, humans tend to be indoors more than 90 percent of the time and are often vitamin D deficient.
- By day, darkened interiors (relative to outdoors) can detract from normal alertness and attentiveness, affecting productivity and learning.
- At night, high indoor light levels and video screens effectively extend the daylight periods, slowing the onset of melatonin and sleep.
- Exterior lighting disrupts the rhythms of plants and animals and can interrupt the human cycle as well.

Many of the remedies for health issues related to light are personal decisions and lifestyle issues. For example, vitamin D supplements in food can mitigate or prevent problems associated with vitamin D deficiency, and at night, turning off one's television and computer screens earlier than normal can help the body to stay "on time" better.

Nonetheless, we should expect growing awareness and a gradual increase in design-related standards and regulations involving health and light. For everyday projects, the simplest way to reinforce health and light is through daylighting.

DAYLIGHT IN INTERIOR SPACES

Daylight is an excellent light source for almost all interior spaces. It is best for offices, schools, and workspaces that require a lot of light and for public spaces such as malls, airports, and institutions. It is important to note that light directly from the sun is less desirable since it creates deep shadows and causes glare. Daylight, or light from the sky, is the most beneficial for interior lighting.

Daylighting is the practice of using windows, skylights, and other forms of fenestration to bring light into the interiors of buildings. Below are considerations that should be taken into account when designing a building to optimize the amount of usable daylight:

- *Siting* the building—that is, orienting it for optimum solar exposure
- *Massing* the building—that is, presenting the optimum building surfaces toward the sun
- Choosing *fenestration* to permit the proper amount of light into the building, taking into account seasons, weather, and daily solar cycles
- *Shading* the façade and fenestration from unwanted solar radiation
- Adding appropriate operable *shading devices*, such as blinds and curtains, to permit occupant control over daylight admission
- Designing *electric lighting controls* that permit full realization of the energy savings benefit of daylighting

Because daylighting practice involves fundamental architectural considerations, it is difficult to undertake once the building has been designed, or, in the case of an interior design project or tenant improvement, almost impossible to carry out. For this reason, daylighting design is not dealt with in detail in this book. (See the bibliography for a number of excellent references, both modern and traditional.)

The primary issue is introducing a modest amount of daylight: Too much daylight has negative side effects including increased energy to cool the space and photo degradation of interior materials, such as bleaching out the colors in fabrics. Daylight has a relatively high ultraviolet (UV) light content, so extreme care must be exercised when using daylight in places such as museums where damage causes bleaching of pigments and other harm to irreplaceable art and antiquities.

INTEGRATING DAYLIGHTING AND ELECTRIC LIGHTING

The amount of available daylight varies according to time of day, time of year, weather, and/or pollution levels. The maximum amount of daylight is about 10,000 foot-candles on a sunny summer day. For energy efficiency in buildings, however, only about 5 percent of the daylight, or a peak of about 500 foot-candles, should be allowed into a building; more will generate so much heat that energy will be wasted in air-conditioning.

From an energy perspective, daylight enjoys a significant advantage over electric light. In addition to the direct savings acquired from turning off or reducing electric light, it takes 2.5 times the air-conditioning to cool the heating effect of artificial lights. Essentially, if the lights are not on, the air-conditioning system does not need to work as hard to cool the space.

In order to harvest the energy-saving benefits of daylighting, it is necessary to switch off or dim electric lights. There are several ways this can be designed:

- Adequate manual switching or dimming to encourage the user to turn off or dim electric lights
- An automatic photoelectric device in each daylighted zone that either switches off lights during daylight periods or dims lights in proportion to the amount of daylight
- An automatic, time-of-day control system, preferably with astronomic time functions, that switches or dims lights according to a fixed solar schedule

Each approach has specific merits. It is generally agreed that switching lights is least expensive but dimming lights is most desired. Step dimming has been found disruptive in many situations.

The use of both electric light and daylight has often raised the question of whether the electric light source should be selected to match the natural light. In most cases, choosing an electric light source that is appropriate independent of daylight is probably best. To match daylight, it would be necessary to use a light source of very high color temperature, and the electric source would probably appear unusually cool for interior illumination at night. The color of daylight varies as well. The color temperature of the setting sun is as low as 2000 K, and the normal sun-and-sky color temperature at noon on a sunny day is 5500–6000 K.

TOP LIGHTING

One of the most common ways to introduce daylight is through skylights and other means of top lighting integrated into the roof of a building. Like direct electric lighting, top lighting radiates light downward. Principles commonly used for designing electric lighting systems can also be used for top lighting.

There are several classic prototypes for top lighting:

- The skylight (Fig. 4.1), or horizontal glazing, permits direct solar and sky radiation through a fenestrated aperture. Toplighting is the easiest form of daylighting and is relatively unaffected by site orientation and adjacent buildings. It is common to want to illuminate a skylight to imitate daylight at night, but this concept should

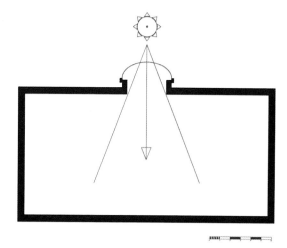

Fig. 4.1 Skylight

be pursued carefully, if at all. Uplighting a skylight, for example, tends to send light through the glass and into the sky, essentially wasting both the light and energy consumed in creating it. What little light is reflected tends to create reflected glare in the skylight. However, illuminating the skylight well and splay can be effective.

- The single clerestory (Fig. 4.2) produces both direct and indirect lighting by introducing light through a vertical clerestory window. Depending on the adjacent

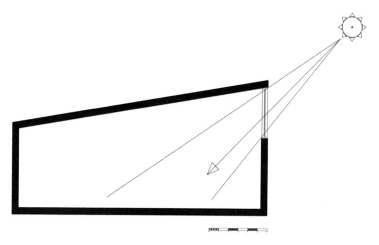

Fig. 4.2 Single Clerestory

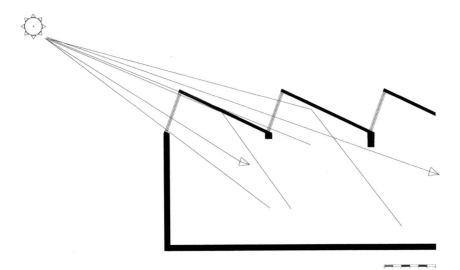

Fig. 4.3 Sawtooth Single Clerestory

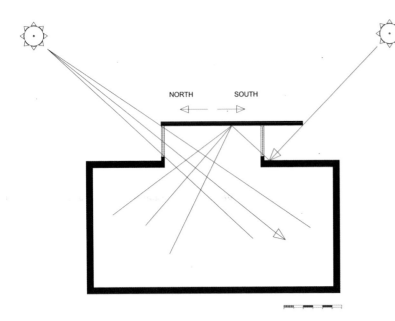

Fig. 4.4 Monitor or Double Clerestory

roof, some of the light may be reflected downward by the ceiling into the space. However, the site orientation can contribute a relatively high percentage of direct light that can be glaring.

- The sawtooth single clerestory (Fig. 4.3) produces both direct and indirect lighting but, by bouncing a high percentage off the adjacent slanted ceiling, increases the amount of downward light and minimizes the amount of direct light. If the sawtooth glazing faces north, it can be an excellent source of natural light for a large interior area.
- The monitor or double clerestory (Fig. 4.4) also produces abundant daylight, especially in buildings where the solar orientation or weather does not permit the sawtooth or other more unusual designs. With proper choice of glazing and overhang, a monitor can produce exceptionally balanced and comfortable daylight.

SIDE LIGHTING

Side lighting employs vertical fenestration (usually windows) to introduce natural light. Unlike top lighting, side lighting tends to introduce light that can be too bright relative to the room surfaces, sometimes causing glare. However, because windows generally provide side lighting, the view is often desirable and the glare is an acceptable side effect.

Many modern commercial windows employ low-e glazing. Low-e glazing employs two or more panes of glass, and one of the panes is coated with a relatively clear material that reflects infrared energy while passing visible portions of the sun's energy. In any climate where there is a cooling season, low-e glass is essential in minimizing solar heat gain. In addition, reflective coatings can also be used, creating a mirrorlike quality to the building while further minimizing solar penetration. Tinting of glass can also reduce solar penetration and glare. Glazing selection is always a compromise between clarity of view and energy efficiency.

Side lighting on east, south, and west exposures can permit direct solar glare and heat gain. One way to increase both efficiency and clarity is to employ solar shading other than within the glass. Solar shading uses building elements to prevent direct solar radiation from entering the space during the cooling season. Common external shading devices include a light shelf (see Fig. 4.5), awnings (see Fig. 4.6), and overhang soffits (see Fig. 4.7).

- Many modern buildings employ a light shelf to shade the lower part of the window, or *view glazing*, permitting a clearer glass. The top of the shelf is reflective, intended to bounce light inward and onto the ceiling, which in turn provides for deeper light penetration and improved interior light quality. The *daylight glazing* is generally darker or more reflective than the view glazing to prevent glare from the bright sky or direct solar radiation. A light shelf is specifically designed

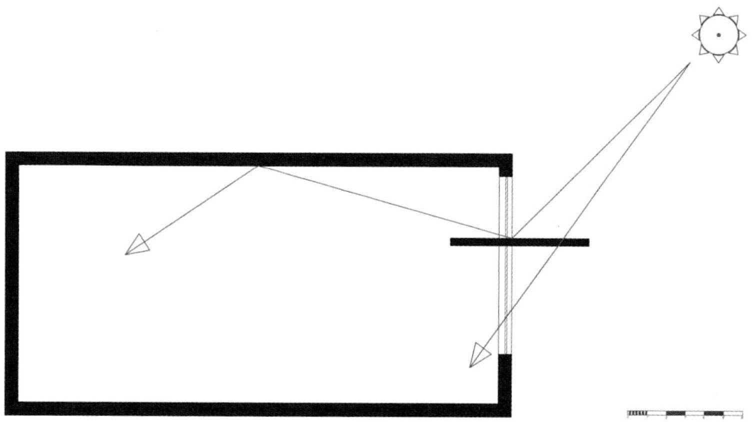

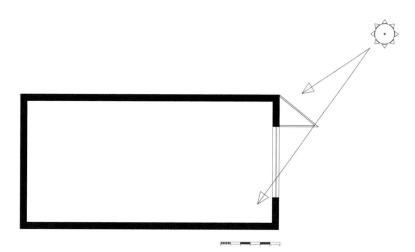

Fig. 4.5 Building Light Shelf

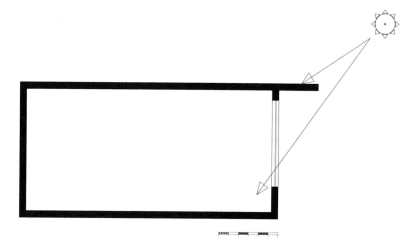

Fig. 4.7 Overhang Soffit

to scoop direct solar radiation into the room and onto the ceiling, where it becomes diffuse indirect light, one of the best types for both work and comfort. A light shelf can increase the depth of penetration of daylight by 100 percent or more, but only when it captures and redirects direct rays of the sun. A light shelf has limited benefit with diffuse light on sunless and cloudy days. In general, light shelves work best on the south side of the building.

Fig. 4.6 Awning

- Awnings or other extended shades offer additional protection and are generally needed on the east and west facades of the building.
- Overhang soffits provide a limited amount of shading and are best employed on the south façade (northern hemisphere) of the building.
- Blinds, curtains, and shades are the most common forms of interior shading. Interior shading devices should be chosen to have a reflective surface so that unwanted light is reflected back outdoors. Dark shades may prevent glare but they can absorb solar energy and become warm, heating the space.

An additional problem caused by side lighting is the limits of penetration into the space. Generally, the effect of the daylight is lost at a distance away from the windows about 2.5 times the window's height. For example, in a room with windows having a height of 8', the maximum useful penetration of natural light is about (8 × 2.5) or 20' (assuming, of course, that no walls are in the way). High windows increase the usable daylight area but can introduce glare.

BASIC PRINCIPLES OF DAYLIGHTING DESIGN AND AWARENESS

While daylighting design can be relatively technical, use the following basic principles to develop designs that address the opportunities of daylighting:

1. Begin by planning the building such that every regularly occupied work or living space has access to a window, skylight, or other source of natural light. Give high

priority to windows that provide a view. Remember that the effective daylit area is only about twice the width of a window and about 2 to 2.5 times its height.

2. Minimize the size of the east and west sides of the building and maximize the south and north sides of the building. Because of the seasonally varying paths of the sun in the sky, it is difficult to design east- and west-facing windows without experiencing glare and heat gain. North-facing windows in the northern hemisphere present no solar heating problems, and south-facing windows are the easiest to protect with passive elements like overhangs, awnings, and light shelves.

3. If a large area of the building is not near a window, investigate top-light skylights in one-story buildings or the top floor of multistory buildings. Simple top-light skylights should occupy 3 percent to 5 percent of the total roof area in order to provide adequate levels of interior lighting.

4. Protect the interior from direct sunlight and an overabundance of daylight. This may include a combination of window glass, exterior shading devices, and/or interior shading devices. Too much natural light is generally 2.5 times (or greater) the amount of electric light that would ordinarily be provided.

5. Provide an electric lighting system and/or automatic lighting controls to permit harvesting of the energy savings. The best way is to dim the electric lights rather than switch them on and off. Modern fluorescent dimming systems allow daylighting controls and fundamentally energy-efficient fluorescent and compact fluorescent lighting.

Chapter 5 LAMPS

There are thousands of lamps to choose from, and opening up a lamp catalog can be a bit overwhelming. This chapter will provide a general overview of the applications, the advantages and disadvantages, and the most commonly used shapes of the major light sources.

Lamp Naming

Lamps come in many different shapes and sizes. All of the lamp types, except for LEDs, are described by size and shape via a simple naming code:

- Letters to describe shape
- The number to represent the size measured by 1/8" increments.

For example, a standard incandescent lamp typically used in a residence is called an A-19 lamp. "A" stands for Arbitrary and the "19" represents the diameter at its widest point: 19 increments of 1/8" of an inch or 2-3/8".

INCANDESCENT LAMPS

Operation

Incandescent lamps generate light when an electric current heats the lamp's tungsten filament until it glows (see Fig. 5.1). The intense heat causes the filament to evaporate, until it eventually breaks and the lamp burns out. The hotter and thinner the filament, the whiter the light it produces, but the evaporation of metal from the filament occurs more quickly. A very dim lamp giving off yellow-orange (2200 K) light may last a long time and a lamp giving off a cool white (5000 K) light may only last for a few seconds. In addition, the evaporated filament material blackens the bulb wall, reducing the light output over time.

Quality

Standard incandescent lamps generate a warm-colored white light (2700 K) and last about 750 to 1500 hours. Even with the warm color, the color rendering index is considered to be 100. Because of these two qualities, incandescent lamps are

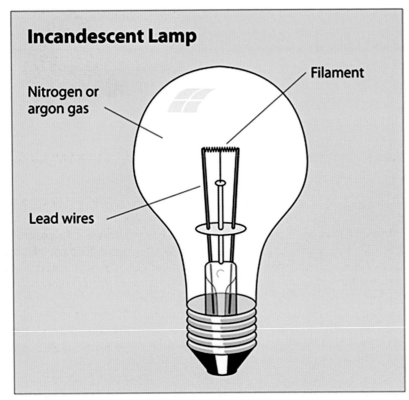

Incandescent Lamp

Nitrogen or argon gas

Filament

Lead wires

The incandescent lamp is the oldest and most common type of lamp. Light is emitted when electricity flows through—and heats—a tungsten filament.

Fig. 5.1 Diagram of an Incandescent Lamp
(Illustration: Office of Energy Efficiency and Renewable Energy.)

generally the preferred light source for residences. Also, newer, more efficient light sources typically try to recreate the qualities of incandescent lamps.

The technology behind incandescent lamps has changed very little in the past 100 years, and because of its simplicity, provides superb consistency between lamps. Also, dimming is accomplished easily by reducing the voltage or power reaching the lamp, providing an even warmer color temperature. This also extends the lamp life because the filament is run at a lower temperature.

Incandescent lamps operate in virtually any position. They start and warm up almost instantly, and can be extinguished and restarted at will. The physical temperature of the incandescent lamp bulb is generally too hot to touch. Underwriters Laboratories (UL) listings of luminaires require the hot lamp to be protected from inadvertent contact, so in general, the lamp's heat is not a problem.

Other than their short lamp life, the biggest shortfall in incandescent lamps is their efficacy. Standard incandescent lamps only generate between 8 and 15 lumens per watt. Generally, the advantages of low first cost, color, and versatility are weighed against the cost of energy and maintenance.

While other source types have some size and shape versatility, no source other than incandescent can range from 1/2-watt peanut lamps to 10,000-watt stage lamps.

Types of Incandescent Lamps

Incandescent lamps are made in thousands of shapes, sizes, and wattages. The shape of the lamp is often arbitrary, but some of the shapes have specific purposes. For example, "R" lamps are designed to reflect light, and "T" lamps are tubes designed to fit into low profile display case luminaires. The most common types are shown here:

- "A" lamps: The majority of incandescent lamps are the popular bulb shape known as "A" (for arbitrary pear-like shape) (see Fig. 5.2). Lamps range from a 15-watt A-15 lamp to a 250-watt A-23. The most popular sizes are 60-, 75-, and 100-watt A-19 lamps.
- "R", "ER", and "BR" lamps: These are lamps that contain an internal reflector coating to direct light in one direction (see Fig. 5.3). The common sizes are R-20, R-30, and R-40. Federal law prohibits manufacture of some traditional "R" lamps, so products have been designed to replace them which include "BR" (bulbous reflector) lamps and "ER" (ellipsoidal reflector) lamps, both of which cost more but use less energy.
- "T" lamps: Often called *showcase lamps*, these tubular lamps were originally developed for lighting inside showcases (see Fig. 5.4). More recently, their small diameter, such as of the 75-watt T-10, lends them to use in wall sconces designed to meet ADA requirements.
- "G" lamps: These are considered decorative lamps often used in bathroom sconces, marquee lighting, and in decorative fixtures (see Fig. 5.5). Sizes include G-16, G-25, G-30, and G-40 and range in wattage from 25 to 150 watts depending on the size.
- "PAR" lamps: These are lamps with a parabolic aluminized reflector (PAR) that are more expensive than "R" lamps but have superior beam control (see Fig. 5.6). Most "PAR" lamps are now in the halogen family; however, higher wattage PAR-38, PAR-56, and PAR-64 lamps are available for special applications.

Fig. 5.2 Standard "A" Lamp   **Fig. 5.3 Reflector Lamp**   **Fig. 5.4 Tubular Lamp**   **Fig. 5.5 Globe Lamp**   **Fig. 5.6 "PAR" Lamp**

HALOGEN LAMPS

Operation

Tungsten halogen (also simply called halogen) lamps are a type of incandescent lamp. The general anatomy and operation is the same, except they contain a small amount of halogen gas within the glass bulb that impedes the evaporation of tungsten. As a result, the filament can be thinner, providing a whiter, brighter light and lasting longer than standard incandescent lamps. The latest products employ a bulb that is coated to keep infrared radiation inside the bulb, reheating the filament and making the lamp much more efficient. It is called an "HIR" or "IR" for (halogen) infrared reflecting.

Quality

Standard halogen lamps have a color temperature of approximately 3000 K, which is slightly cooler than an incandescent, so it appears whiter and crisper. Still being in the incandescent family, halogen lamps also have a color rendering index of 95–100. The improved technology of the halogen lamp compared to incandescent provides a lamp life that typically ranges from 3000 to 5000 hours. For a minor sacrifice in output, there are long-life lamps that can last up to 18,000 hours.

Halogen lamps are more efficient than standard incandescent lamps and can contain 10 to 35 lumens per watt, with the HIR/IR type being the most efficacious. In general, the improved efficiency, longer life, and whiter color make halogen lamps a popular choice for many commercial applications where standard incandescent lamps are not practical, but their qualities are desirable.

Some types of halogen lamps use a quartz glass bulb and get extremely hot. The surface temperature of these lamps can be over 500°F, so they are extremely hazardous. UL listings require most halogen lamps to be protected by glass or wire cage to prevent touching.

Many halogen lamps are intended to be direct replacements for incandescent lamps, and utilize similar shapes and bases. This type can be inserted directly into incandescent luminaires and dimmed with standard incandescent dimmers.

Many common halogen lamps are low voltage and are much smaller than regular lamps, a trait that has numerous advantages for accenting and display. Low-voltage

Fig. 5.7 "BT" Lamp   **Fig. 5.8 Double-ended "T" Lamp**   **Fig. 5.9 Single-ended "T" Lamp**   **Fig. 5.10 MR16 Lamp**   **Fig. 5.11 "T" Lamp**
(Figures 5.2–5.11 courtesy of General Electric Company)

lighting is particularly popular for specialty lights and for display lighting in retail, museums, homes, and other applications.

Transformers are needed to change the primary power, usually 120 volts, to the low voltage. Transformers range from very small electronic types that can fit in junction boxes or inside luminaires themselves to very large, bulky, and heavy magnetic transformers that can power whole lighting systems of many lamps. Luminaires with integral transformers are easiest to install, for they are fed 120-volt power just like any other luminaire. When dimming low voltage halogen lamps, specific dimmers are required. The dimmer type must match the transformer type to work properly.

Types of Halogen Lamps

Here are the most common line voltage (120V) halogen lamps:

- "A", "BT", "MB", and "TB" lamps: Varying slightly in shape, all of these lamps are intended to replace the standard incandescent "A" lamp. They contain a thicker, heavier glass enclosure to protect the halogen capsule inside (see Fig. 5.7).
- "PAR" lamps: Using the same enclosure as incandescent PAR lamps, the halogen PAR lamp is especially suited for employing a small halogen "capsule" lamp inside of the outer PAR bulb. Almost all PAR lamps available today are a halogen lamp-inside-a-lamp. The superior reflector, variety of wattages, and beam spreads has led to an extensive family of lamps. The popular sizes include PAR-16, PAR-20, PAR-30, and PAR-38. Some of these lamps use IR/HIR technology. Lamp watts range from 45 up to 250, depending on the lamp size.
- Double-ended "T" lamps: Commonly used in flood lights and torchiers, these halogen lamps range from 100 to 1500 watts, including some IR/HIR products (see Fig. 5.8).
- Single-ended "T" lamps: These are screw base or bayonet base halogen lamps used in specialty architectural and theatrical equipment (see Fig. 5.9).

Here are the most common low-voltage halogen lamps:

- MR11 and MR16 lamps: Derived from slide projector lamps, MR16 (see Fig. 5.10) and MR11 lamps employ a Mirrored Reflector and are relatively small. Their small size and their extensive selection of wattages and beam spreads have made them very popular for a wide range of lighting solutions in both residential and commercial lighting.
- Compact T-3 and T-4 lamps: These very small halogen "bud" lamps enable very intense lighting from decorative desk lights and other new designs of luminaires (see Fig. 5.11).

Electrician's Notebook

Directional or point source lamps like "PAR" and "MR" lamps are available in many different beam angles. (The beam angle represents the angle where the lamp's cone of light is 50 percent of its maximum intensity.) This variety allows designers to use similar looking luminaires in a space but select a tighter beam for accent lighting and a wider beam for general lighting. Although the lamps may provide a very different effect, they look the same, so it is necessary to read the code on the side of the lamp to distinguish them. Here are typical abbreviations and their approximate beam angles:

VNSP = Very Narrow Spot (3°–9°)
SP = Spot (10°–15°)
NFL = Narrow Flood (20°–25°)
FL = Flood (30°–40°)
WFL = Wide Flood (50°–65°)

Care must be taken during the design, installation, and relamping to ensure the appropriate lamps are provided to maintain the design intent.

FLUORESCENT LAMPS

Operation

The fluorescent lamp was invented in the 1930s and rapidly became accepted as the workhorse light source for commercial and institutional buildings. Fluorescent lamps (see Fig. 5.12) use the principle of fluorescence, in which minerals exposed to ultraviolet light are caused to glow. Inside the lamp is a fill gas that includes a minute amount of mercury. Electric energy "excites" the gas inside the lamp, generating ultraviolet energy, which is absorbed by the phosphor coating on the bulb of the lamp and converted to visible light.

A fluorescent lamp requires a ballast in order to work properly. A ballast is an electrical component that starts the lamp and regulates the electric power flow to the lamp. Some ballasts can operate up to four lamps. There are two types—*magnetic* and *electronic*—of which the electronic ballast reduces lamp flicker considerably and is generally more energy efficient and quiet.

Quality

The inside of a fluorescent lamp bulb is "painted" with a mixture of minerals, called phosphors, which are designated to radiate a particular color of light. Thus, both the color temperature and CRI of a lamp can be chosen from among many variations.

Fluorescent Tube Lamp

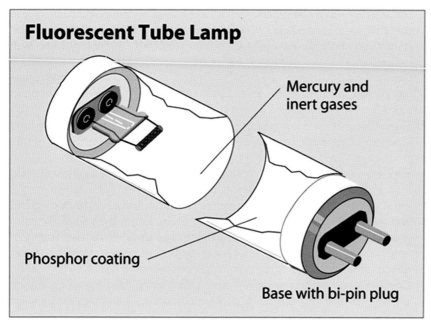

Mercury and inert gases

Phosphor coating

Base with bi-pin plug

In fluorescent tubes, a very small amount of mercury mixes with inert gases to conduct the electrical current. This allows the phosphor coating on the glass tube to emit light.

Fig. 5.12 Diagram of a Fluorescent Lamp
(Illustration: Office of Energy Efficiency and Renewable Energy.)

Using halophosphors, traditional lamp colors are a blend of hues that create a white light, generally with a tint that results in a particular color temperature and CRI. Modern lamps, however, use rare earth phosphors, which generate red, green, and blue primary colors of light to produce white light.

Halophosphor lamps tend to be the least expensive and are commonly used in residences and budget commercial and industrial projects. However, they are rapidly becoming less common. Most halophosphor lamps are known by their color names such as warm white, cool white, and daylight. Most halophosphor lamps have poor color quality; for example, a greenish tint is associated with the cool white color.

Modern "rare earth" lamps are generally known by a color "name" which designates its color temperature and CRI. For example, a lamp having a color temperature of 3500 K and a CRI between 80 and 90 would be known as the color 835. Selecting the appropriate CRI and color temperature is critical in achieving the desired results when using fluorescent lamps.

Electrician's Notebook

There are many electronic ballast types to choose from and depending on how the spaces will be used, a different ballast may be required than what may come standard with a luminaire. Below is a list of the most common types and their uses:

Lamp Starting
- Instant Start: Applies a high voltage across the lamp with no preheating, so it starts instantly. This is typically the most energy efficient ballast but should be used when lights are turned on and left on for at least three hours.
- Programmed Rapid Start: Preheats the lamp while not allowing the lamp to ignite instantly and then applies the voltage to start the lamp. The user may experience up to a one-second delay after turning on the lamps while the pre-heating takes place. This method improves lamp life performance, especially in applications where the lamps are frequently switched on and off.

Control
- Step or Bi-level: Provides two or three levels of light without using multiple circuits.
- Dimming Ballasts: Allows fluorescent lamps to dim down to 10 percent, 5 percent, or 1 percent. Amount of dimming required must be specified.
- Digitally Addressable or "Smart" Ballast: A dimming ballast that contains a microprocessor providing a real time view of the lamp and ballast operation, energy use, and whether maintenance is required. This type of ballast would be connected to an overall lighting management system.

The popularity of fluorescent lamps is mainly attributed to the fact that they are among the most energy efficient white light sources available. T-5 lamps exceed 100 lumens per watt, and compact fluorescent lamps are generally between 50 and 60 lumens per watt.

Dimming fluorescent lamps is possible but requires the use of an electronic dimming ballast. Most electronic dimming ballasts require specific dimmers. Dimming range is typically 100 percent down to 10 percent of light with the best ballasts allowing dimming down to 1 percent. Fluorescent lamps change color slightly when dimmed, tending to appear more purple at lower output levels.

Fluorescent lamps are sensitive to temperature. Bulb temperature is critical for proper light output, and lamps operated in very cold or very warm situations will generally not give off as much light as when operated at room temperature. Also, lamps may not start if they are too cold. The minimum starting temperature of a lamp depends on the ballast; minimum starting temperature ratings are available for ballasts to help choose the right type. Most fluorescent lamps get warm but can be touched while operating without being burned.

Types of Fluorescent Lamps

There are hundreds of variations of fluorescent lamps, but they almost always employ a straight, bent, or curved tube.

Full Size and U-bent Lamps

Most straight lamps, even if they are only 12" long, are called full size (see Fig. 5.13). These are the most common types:

- T-8 standard lamps: These are the standard general lighting lamps since the early 1990s. Standard T-8 lamps are made in lengths of 2', 3', 4', 5', and 8' with lengths of 1', 1'-6", and 2' for U-bent lamps. The T-8 is a model of energy efficiency, good color, and long life.
- T-5 standard and high output lamps: These are relatively new products that became important lamps around 1998. The lamps are made in metric sizes nominally 2', 3', 4', and 5'. The T-5 system is one of the most energy efficient, good-color light source available for general lighting.
- T-12 standard lamps: These are the "old standard" for general lighting with broad applications dating back to the 1950s. Standard T-12 lamps are made in 2', 3', and 4' lengths and in 2' U-bent lamps. It is estimated that over 80 percent of the fluorescent lamps in service are T-12 standard lamps. Future manufacturing of T-12 lamps and ballasts is no longer permitted by federal law.

- T-2 miniature lamps: The extremely small diameter of these lamps makes them useful in tight situations, but as of 2010, there are a limited number of luminaires due to cost and other technical limitations.

Compact Fluorescent Lamps

Deciding which compact fluorescent lamp to use depends on the application. All compact fluorescent lamps require a ballast. The ballast can be local to the lamp or remote, but still within the luminaire.

There are three major types of compact fluorescent lamps:

- Screw base: These lamps are designed to directly replace incandescent lamps in incandescent lamp sockets (see Fig. 5.14). Lamps with screw bases are typically large because the ballast is part of the lamp. Screw base compact fluorescent lamps dim poorly, and the color rendering and color temperature can vary greatly between manufacturers. Care must be taken when replacing incandescent lamps to ensure the new compact fluorescent lamp will fit within the luminaire. Also, important to remember is that compact fluorescent lamps are four times as efficient as incandescent, so the lamps selected should contain comparable lumens so it is not visually too bright. As a general rule, screw base lamps should be limited to residences and for portable commercial lighting.
- GU-24 base: This base permits compact fluorescent lamps to operate directly from line voltage power and allows the interchanging of lamp types and wattages (see Fig. 5.15). Lamps with GU-24 bases are like screw base lamps, but the socket prevents incandescent lamps from being used, assuring an energy efficient luminaire.
- Pin base: This base is designed to fit into sockets in luminaires designed specifically for compact fluorescent lamps with hardwired ballasts (see Fig. 5.16). Pin base lamps have separate ballasts, making the lamp smaller and allowing the use of

Fig. 5.13 Typical End View of a Full Size Fluorescent Lamp

Fig. 5.14 Screw Base Compact Fluorescent Lamp

Fig. 5.15 GU-24 Base Compact Fluorescent Lamp

Fig. 5.16 Twin Tube Compact Fluorescent Lamp

(Figures 5.13–5.16 courtesy of General Electric Company)

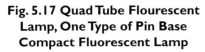

Fig. 5.17 Quad Tube Flourescent Lamp, One Type of Pin Base Compact Fluorescent Lamp

Fig. 5.18 Triple Tube Compact Fluorescent Lamp

Fig. 5.19 Long Twin Tube Compact Fluorescent Lamp

Fig. 5.20 "2D" Compact Fluorescent Lamp

(Figures 5.17–5.20 courtesy of General Electric Company)

better ballasts, including dimming ballasts. The CRI and color temperature of pin base lamps is typically of higher quality than screw or GU-24 base lamps. For most commercial lighting, the pin base lamps are used because of superior performance.

Among pin base lamps, the following are the most common types:

- Standard Twin Tube: The twin tube compact fluorescent lamps were the first ones that were widely used (see Fig. 5.16). The standard sizes are 5, 7, 9, and 13 watts. Twin tube lamps are often used in pairs in fixtures that do not have a lot of depth, like wall sconces.
- Standard quad tube: The quad tube places two twin tube lamps together on a single base (see Fig. 5.17). The standard sizes are 10, 13, 18, and 26 watts.
- Standard triple tube: The triple twin tube or "hex" lamp incorporates three twin tubes on one base (see Fig. 5.18). It has become an extremely important lamp because its size and light output nearly matches some popular incandescent lamps. Standard sizes are 18, 26, 32, and 42 watts.
- Long twin tube: Long twin tube lamps are available from 18 to 55 watts. The most popular lamps are 40, 50, and 55 watt lamps at a length of 22.5", each generating about the same amount of light as a four-foot straight lamp in a much smaller package (see Fig. 5.19).
- "Flat" compact lamps: There are several other important types of compact lamps: circline lamps, made for many years by a variety of companies, up to 40 watts; 2D lamps, up to 55 watts (see Fig. 5.20); and F lamps, from 18 to 36 watts. All of these lamps are relatively flat, making them useful in a number of fixture types that require a low profile.

Fluorescent lamps provide good energy efficiency, good to excellent color, dimming, and many other features expected of modern light sources. The improvements in fluorescent lighting since 1980 have made it useful in homes, businesses, and for almost every other type of lighting application.

But the challenge of the designer remains to determine the best light source to meet the user's expectations, and fluorescent lighting is still not a *direct* replacement for incandescent lighting. There are many places where fluorescent or compact fluorescent can be used; however, it is important to develop expertise in using these energy efficient sources.

HIGH-INTENSITY DISCHARGE LAMPS

Operation
High-intensity discharge (HID) lamps generate light by passing an electric current through a gas containing the vapors of certain metals. The current produces an arc or discharge of light contained within a high temperature, high pressure enclosure called an arc tube (see Fig. 5.21). The light created by an HID lamp depends on the metals used in the arc tube. Almost all modern lamps combine various metals in order to produce the "whitest" light possible.

Quality
HID lamps are designed to emit a great deal of light from a compact, long-life, energy efficient light source. HID lamps are most often used for street and parking lot lighting, and for large indoor spaces like gymnasiums and industrial work floors.

As with fluorescent lamps, a ballast is required to start and regulate the amount of power flowing into the arc. Magnetic ballasts are generally used for most HID lamps, although electronic ballasts are becoming increasingly popular. Ballasts can be bulky, heavy, and noisy, but to minimize these problems some types can be mounted

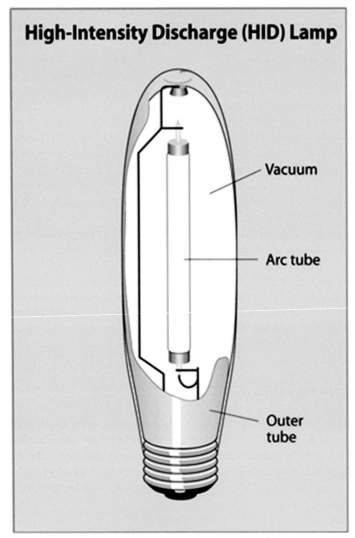

High-Intensity Discharge (HID) Lamp

Vacuum

Arc tube

Outer tube

In a high-intensity discharge lamp, electricity arcs between two electrodes, creating an intensely bright light. Mercury, sodium, or metal halide gases act as the conductor.

Fig. 5.21 Diagram of a High-Intensity Discharge Lamp
(Illustration: Office of Energy Efficiency and Renewable Energy.)

remotely from the luminaire. Although research and development continues, dimming HID lamps is generally not available.

HID lamps can get quite hot and should be protected from direct touch. In addition, some metal halide lamps must be totally enclosed due to a small possibility of lamp explosion. HID lamps start and operate over a relatively wide temperature range, and they are well suited to both indoor and outdoor applications. Because the metals in the arc tube are affected by gravity, the operating position of some HID lamp types can be critical.

HID lamps, like an automobile engine, must be started by an ignition pulse called "striking the arc." Then all HID lamps require time to warm up, getting progressively brighter over several minutes until reaching full light output. During this period, there may be some color shifting, as the various metals heat up and their individual vapor pressures increase. The lamp's true light output and color is often not reached for two to five minutes.

Once the lamp is operating, the temperature and pressure within the arc tube have increased tremendously. However, should power be interrupted, even briefly, HID lamps must cool off before the ignition circuit can restart the lamp. The cool-off period is called the restrike time. Some HID lamps will take over 10 minutes from being extinguished until they can restrike and warm back up.

Types of HID Lamps

There are three families of HID lamps:

Metal Halide Lamps

Among HID lamps, only metal halide lamps produce a good color quality in white light. Metal halide lamps range from compact lamps that can be used in track lighting to huge lamps for lighting stadiums. To some extent, it is possible to choose the color temperature and CRI of metal halide lamps, similar to fluorescent.

Standard metal halide lamps tend to have a color temperature of 3700 to 4100 K and appear cool and slightly greenish. Their CRI is typically 65 to 70. Standard metal halide lamps are used where color is not critical, such as in lighting sports arenas, parking lots, landscape lighting, and building floodlighting. Due to their inefficiency, many types of standard metal halide lamps are now banned by federal law.

Instead, the preferred metal halide lamps are called ceramic metal halide because the arc tube is ceramic rather than glass. This results in superior color rendering (80 to 95) and a choice of warm (3000 K) or cool (4000 K) lamps. Ceramic lamps can be used for interior lighting, such as downlighting, display lighting, and wallwashing, as well as for exterior lighting. The warm toned ceramic lamps appear very similar to halogen lamps in color and are 2–3 times more efficient. The lamp life ranges from 9,000–20,000 hours. If dimming is not required, ceramic metal halide lamps are a good alternative to halogen lamps.

The most common types of ceramic metal halide lamps are listed below:

- PAR lamps: Similar in concept to a halogen lamp, metal halide PAR lamps contain the arc tube inside the PAR bulb (see Fig. 22). Sizes include PAR-20, PAR-30, and PAR-38 and range in wattage from 20 to 150 watts depending on size. The metal halide versions of the PAR lamps also have a variety of beam angles available. Although the base is the same for all, the lamp wattage is specific to the ballast, so interchangeability is limited.
- MR16 lamp: Designed to compete with less efficient halogen MR16 lamps, this small profile lamp works well for retail and other accent lighting where an intense non-dimmed source is needed (see Fig. 5.23). Available in 20- and 39-watt versions with an assortment of beam angles.

Fig. 5.22 PAR Lamp   **Fig. 5.23 MR16 Lamp**

Fig. 5.24 Single-ended T Lamps
(Figures 5.22–5.24 courtesy of General Electric Company)

- Single-ended T lamps: Gaining popularity, these compact lamps are used often in recessed downlights and track heads (see Fig. 5.24). As a lamp that emits light in all directions, the luminaire must contain a reflector to control the beam angle. Removing the reflector from the lamp helps simplify maintenance.

Sodium Lamps

The two types of sodium lamps are high-pressure sodium (HPS) lamps and low-pressure sodium (LPS) lamps. Lamps based primarily on sodium tend to be quite yellowish in color. HPS lamps exhibit a golden-pinkish light that tends to create spaces with a distinctly brown or dirty quality. Low-pressure sodium emits mono-chromatic yellow light, creating stark scenes devoid of any color at all.

Although HPS lamps offer very high lumens per watt, their color deficiencies limit use to lighting roads, parking lots, heavy industrial workspaces, warehouses, security lighting, and other applications where light color is not considered important. LPS lamps are even higher in lumens per watt, but their color is so poor that their use is limited to security lighting.

Mercury Vapor Lamps

Mercury vapor lamps are an older type of lamp that remains in common use as streetlights and security lights. However, compared to other HID lamps, mercury vapor lamps have relatively poor color and low energy efficiency. They are almost never used in new construction.

LIGHT-EMITTING DIODES

Light-emitting diodes (LEDs) are the latest and perhaps the most exciting light source yet invented. Thanks to considerable investment from the U.S. Department of Energy and many manufacturers, LEDs have surged to become the most likely light source of the future. However, LED lighting is still in constant development, there are very few standards, and written literature can still be misleading.

Operation

An LED is fundamentally different from all other light sources, in that it does not utilize a filament, a gas, or a fragile glass enclosure. An LED is a semiconductor device that emits visible light (see Figs. 5.25 and 5.26). It is a basic electrical component that is used in virtually every electronic device—in fact, the little red, green, yellow, or blue indicator lights on cell phones, TVs, radios, and computers are all LEDs. But because they are so different from other light sources, LEDs are almost never called lamps.

There are generally two schools of thought on the development of LEDs. The

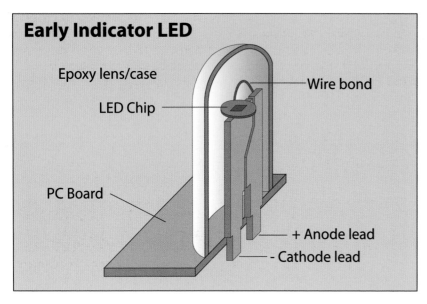

Fig. 5.25 Basic Indicator-type LED (Early, Lower Wattage LED)

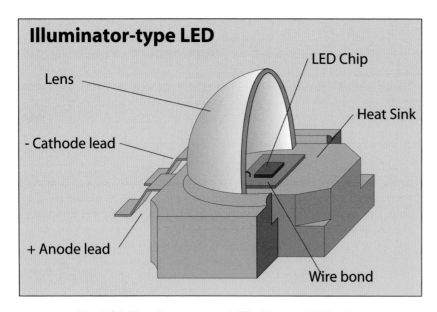

Fig. 5.26 Illuminator-type LED (Newer LEDs Use Larger Chips and Require More Heat Management)

first is to develop lamps that will replace all the other less efficient light sources. These lamps use basic lamp shapes and are designed to be inserted directly into the sockets of existing luminaires (see Fig. 5.27).

Because of their unique anatomy compared to other light sources, the second approach is to develop fixtures around the geometry of the LED. As with compact fluorescent lamps, this approach generally produces superior results, providing increased efficiency and longer life. The problem is that the basic worldwide electrical infrastructure was developed around the incandescent lamp, so both types of LEDs are required.

Quality
Basic LEDs are monochromatic, only emitting light in a single color. The materials used within the LED produce photons at different wavelengths that appear as different colors. Modern materials can produce light in virtually any color except white. Although colored light is dramatic and impactful in spaces, white light ultimately is needed for general lighting, and most recent research has been focused on developing a quality white source.

Fig. 5.27 Examples of LED Replacement Lamps, as of 2011

There are two ways to create white light using LEDs. Because red, green, and blue (RGB) LEDs were some of the first to be developed, they were mixed together to create white light. This is the same process used in computer screens and color televisions. In addition to white light, the intensity of each of the colors can be varied to create virtually any color of light. Although this scientifically creates white light, the color temperature and CRI are low, and it is inconsistent between manufacturers.

The more recent and much more successful approach to generating white light is to create a "white" LED. This is done by taking a blue or ultraviolet LED and applying a phosphor to the lens of the LED to change the color, similar to how a fluorescent lamp functions. This approach provides the ability to select the color temperature. Also, as expected, because a blue LED is typically used, the warmer colors require the most phosphors and end up being the least efficient. Because of the tiny lamps, the minute amount of phosphor, and manufacturing processes, a batch of white LEDs will yield lamps of different color temperatures. At the LED factory, the lamps are separated into bins according to similar appearance, a process called "binning." The more closely matched the LEDs are, the better the binning process. In fact, binning tolerance is one of the most important issues of white LEDs today.

Many manufacturers are using this same approach in a larger scale for their fixture design. They take a cluster of blue LEDs and apply a phosphor lens to modify the color to the desired color temperature.

In addition to their unique method of creating white light, LEDs are very different from traditional sources for many other reasons. LEDs inherently project light in one direction, which generally allows them to be more efficient. However, one of the greatest challenges for LED lamp manufacturers has been to develop an acceptable incandescent "A" lamp replacement. Also, LEDs do not radiate heat, but there is heat produced within the LED that must be removed to ensure it will last as long as expected. This becomes more and more critical as higher output LEDs are developed. LEDs prefer to run cool, and if the LED lamps and fixtures are designed properly, they will be cool to the touch.

Individually, LEDs radiate a small amount of light. That is because they are very small and heat must be conducted away from them. In 2011, the typical LED of one watt generated close to 100 lumens. While their efficiency is phenomenal, the standard 60-watt incandescent lamp generates 900 lumens, so it will take nine 1-watt LEDs to generate a similar amount of light. Clusters of LEDs must be assembled to create functional luminaires.

Basic principles aside, LEDs are a rapidly developing science because of the potential for enormous energy savings and significantly reduced maintenance. Compared to ordinary incandescent lamps, LED lighting could reduce energy use by 50 to 80 percent. Also, they typically last 50,000 hours compared to 750 hours for the incandescent.

LEDs individually are low voltage and need to be powered from a source of DC power that regulates the amount of electricity flowing through the LED. This source is called a driver. Like a fluorescent lamp's ballast, an LED can't operate properly without it. Similar to other sources, the driver can be local to the lamp, within the luminaire, or located in a remote location, depending on the application.

Electrician's Notebook

There are two primary types of LED drivers: constant voltage and constant current. In a constant voltage circuit, the system uses a power supply, typically 8 to 12 volts, that feeds LED circuits in parallel. Each LED has a driver circuit adjacent to the LED, so the LED system can vary the number of LED lamps easily such as in LED strip and string lights. Constant voltage circuits cost more but permit greater flexibility for the installer. Constant voltage systems are almost always for color changing LED systems.

Constant current circuits place a number of LEDs in series so that their total voltage (typically 2.5–3 volts each) matches the power supply voltage. A common system design uses a 24-volt power supply and places groups of eight LEDs in series (3 volts × 8 = 24). Constant current drivers are generally more efficient and can dim more smoothly, but place stricter limits on circuit flexibility.

Dimming of LEDs is possible but requires coordination of the driver with the dimmer. Depending on the LED and driver type, it may dim with a standard dimmer; may require a dimmer used for low voltage lamps; or may require a dimmer typically used for fluorescent lamps. In any case, it is important that the dimmer is tested with the LED product to ensure that it dims smoothly without flickering with an acceptable dimming range.

LEDs have the potential to be an almost perfect light source; they are very efficient, start immediately, can be dimmed, and last an extremely long time. The quality of the light produced from LEDs is good and constantly improving. Unfortunately, standards are still in their infancy, which makes it difficult to evaluate a product simply by reviewing its literature. It is critical to physically see how the product works to ensure it meets the project's requirements. In addition, the technology is still rapidly changing, so a product that is specified may not be available when it is ordered, or it may have changed significantly.

Table 5.1 Light Source Selection Criteria

	Incandescent	Halogen	Fluorescent	Ceramic Metal Halide	LED
Common Applications Design	Residential and Historical	Residential, Hospitality, Retail	Commercial, Institutional, Industrial	Commercial, Retail, Sports, Industrial	Residential, Hospitality, Retail, Commercial
Color Temperature	2700 K	3000 K	To be selected: 2700 K, 3000 K, 3500 K, 4100 K, 5000 K, 6500 K	To be selected: 3000 K, 4000 K	To be selected: 2700 K, 3000 K, 3500 K, 4100 K, 5000 K, 6500 K
Color Rendering Index	100	95–100	75–85	80–95	70–95
Color Consistency	Excellent	Excellent	Good	Good	Varies greatly depending on binning standards
Color Stability	Excellent	Excellent	Good	Good	Good to poor
Dimmability	Yes—easy	Yes—Low voltage fixtures need compatible dimmer	Yes—Coordinate ballast with dimmer	No	Yes— Coordinate driver with dimmer
Directionality	Area	Area and Point	Area and Linear	Area and Point	Area, Point, and Linear
Initial Cost	Low	Low	Low to Medium	Medium to High	Medium to High
Efficacy (Lumens/Watt)	8–15	10–35	35–100	80–125	25–100 (at time of printing)
Physical Environment					
Operating Temperature	Very High	Very High	Cool	Very High	No radiant heat, only conductive
Auxiliary Equipment	None	Transformer required if low voltage	Ballast required	Ballast required	Driver and Transformer
Ambient Temperature	Not affected	Not affected	Sensitive to colder temperatures	Not affected	Very sensitive to higher temperatures
Maintenance					
Life (Hours)	750–1,500	3,000–5,000 (Long-life lamps available with up to 18,000 hours)	8,000–40,000	9,000–20,000	20,000–100,000
Lumen Maintenance	Good	Excellent	Good	Good	Good to Poor
Starting Time	Instant	Instant	Instant on, but warms up to full intensity	+/–5 minutes	Instant
Operating Cost	High	High	Medium to low	Medium	Low

OTHER LIGHT SOURCES

OLED

Organic light-emitting diodes (OLEDs) are nothing at all like LEDs. They consist of sheets of semi-conducting organic material, which generate light on the basis of the composition of the sheets (see Fig. 5.29). In other words, OLEDs will tend to be planar light sources from which evenly distributed light emerges.

In 2011, manufacturers are beginning to design luminaires around OLEDs; however, the development is still in its early stages. Practical OLED fixtures are not expected yet for a few more years. If they prove to be successful and low cost manufacturing is invented, OLEDs could be used as wall coverings, ceilings, or panels, providing soft light in contrast to the harsh light of LEDs. But for practical lighting design they will probably be too expensive and inefficient for some time to come.

Electrician's Notebook

There are a few standards that have been developed to help designers compare LED products. The IESNA (Illuminating Engineering Society of North America) has developed two: LM79–08 and LM80–08.

- LM79–08: This approved method provides standards for manufacturers to test and measure performance, power, and color of LED fixtures.
- LM80–08: It addresses the measurement of lumen maintenance testing for LED light sources including LED packages, arrays, and modules only. The rated life of the LEDs will be at 70 percent of rated initial lumen output for general lighting and 50 percent for decorative and accent lighting.

The U.S. Department of Energy has developed Lighting Facts®, which is a program that allows designers to compare and evaluate LED luminaires using consistent information (see Fig. 5.28).
   The data that is listed includes:

- Light output measured in lumens
- Wattage
- Efficacy (lumens/watt)
- Color Accuracy or Color Rendering Index
- Color Temperature

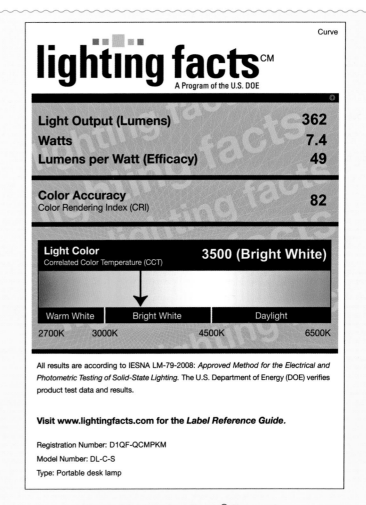

Fig. 5.28 Lighting Facts® Example

Fig. 5.29 Example Application of OLEDs

Induction Lamps

Induction lamps are a type of fluorescent lamp that uses radio waves, rather than an electric arc, to cause the gas in the lamp to give off ultraviolet energy. Induction lamps have most of the characteristics of fluorescent lamps, including 70 to 80 lumens per watt, choice of color, and high CRI. However, because induction lamps have no electrodes, the lamps are rated to last 5–10 times as long as regular fluorescent lamps.

An induction lamp used every day for 12 hours will last more than 20 years. Typical applications include street lighting and lighting in hard-to-maintain locations.

A new type of induction lamp, called a plasma lamp, is entering the marketplace. It is actually an HID lamp that employs induction principles. Its characteristics are very similar to quartz metal halide lamps, but with potentially very long lamp life.

Neon and Cold Cathode Lamps

Neon and cold cathode lamps are the oldest electric discharge lamps. They are closely related to fluorescent lamps in operating principles, but due to other practical limitations, cold cathode and neon lamps have been limited to signs and specialty lighting applications. Both types last 20,000 to 40,000 hours, are reasonably energy efficient, and can be dimmed and even flashed on and off without affecting lamp life.

When thinking of neon and cold cathode lamps, imagine tubular lighting that can be formed into just about any shape and be made to create just about any color of light. Cold cathode lighting is like neon, but generally the lamps are larger in diameter and the light source is used for architectural rather than sign lighting. Cold cathode lamps are also distinguished by having a plug-in base, where neon tubing usually terminates in base wire connectors.

In architecture, neon lighting is most often used for special effects, such as cove lighting, building outlining, and color accents, especially in casinos and retail lighting. Cold cathode lamps produce more light than neon; they are typically used for cove lighting and outlining in conventional building types, such as hotels, convention centers, and office buildings.

Table 5.1 provides a summary of the characteristics described in Chapter 5.

Chapter 6 LUMINAIRES

A luminaire is any device that includes a lampholder and the means of electrification and support for that device. Lighting fixtures are luminaires that are permanently attached to a building. In other words, a table lamp is a luminaire but not a fixture.

Electrician's Notebook

The definition of a "lighting fixture" has significant code implications. As a general code requirement any luminaire must be listed by an accredited testing laboratory for the intended use, which means it has been tested to meet applicable standards. In the U.S., the standards are developed by Underwriters Laboratories (UL) and listed by UL or another laboratory such as Edison Testing Laboratory (ETL). In other parts of the world, there are similar standards and listings.

The choice of luminaire type is fundamental to the overall appearance and psychology of a room and its ambience. Luminaires are characterized by the manner in which light is distributed:

- *Direct* luminaires emit light downward. These include most types of recessed lighting, including downlights and troffers and surface-mounted luminaires. Direct luminaires tend to be more efficient by distributing light directly onto the task area. They generally create dark ceilings and upper walls that can be dramatic but also uncomfortable due to high contrast. Direct lighting is typically used in building lobbies, executive offices, restaurants, and other spaces where the designer wishes to convey a sense of drama. In addition, most task lighting luminaires contain a direct distribution.
- *Indirect* luminaires emit light upward, in turn bouncing light from the ceiling into a space. These include many styles of suspended luminaires, sconces, and some portable lamps. Indirect luminaires tend to create comfortable, low-contrast soft light that psychologically enlarges space. Indirect lighting plays a key role in the task/ambient approach to lighting a space. The indirect lighting provides a diffuse ambient background lighting level, and the addition of a direct task light provides higher levels of light where needed. Indirect lighting is often preferred for spaces in which people spend a lot of time working; however, many people experience totally indirect lighting as bland and dreary. In addition to task lighting, other focal and/or vertical illumination should be considered to add interest and relief from the diffuse nature of a completely indirect design.

Electrician's Notebook

Photometry is the science of measuring light. The candlepower (intensity) of the light from the luminaire can be measured in every angle about the luminaire and reported in a photometric report. Each luminaire has a distinctive manner in which it distributes light, and the photometric report is the luminaire's unique fingerprint.

The photometric report usually includes a polar plot of the luminaire's candlepower. The plot is an easy-to-understand graphic representation of the luminaire's light distribution.

See the following diagrams (Figs. 6.1–6.5) for examples of photometric polar plots for typical luminaire types:

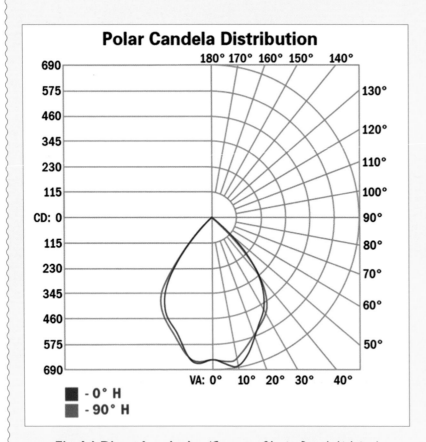

Fig. 6.1 Direct Luminaire (Courtesy of Acuity Brands Lighting.)

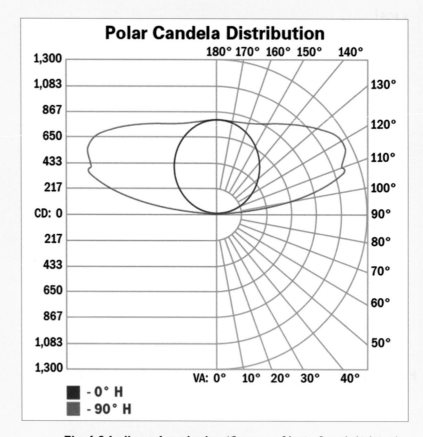

Fig. 6.2 Indirect Luminaire (Courtesy of Acuity Brands Lighting.)

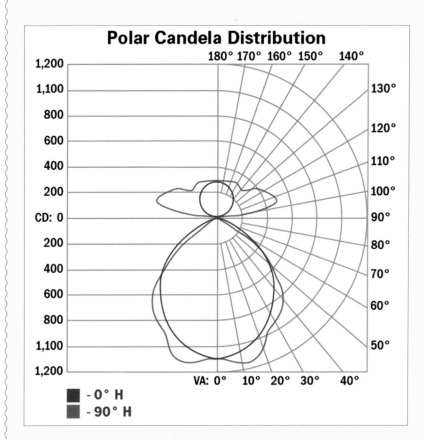

Fig. 6.3 Direct/Indirect Luminaire *(Courtesy of Acuity Brands Lighting.)*

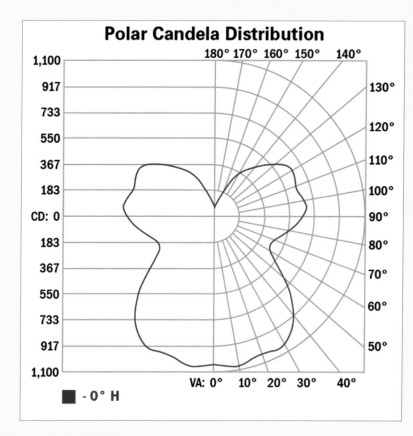

Fig. 6.4 Diffuse Luminaire *(Courtesy of Acuity Brands Lighting.)*

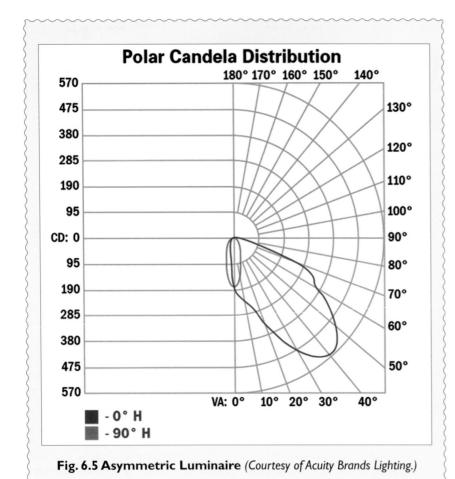

Fig. 6.5 Asymmetric Luminaire (*Courtesy of Acuity Brands Lighting.*)

- *Direct/indirect* luminaires emit light upward and downward but not to the side. These include many types of suspended luminaires as well as some table and floor lamps. Direct/indirect luminaires are a good compromise between the efficiency of direct lighting and the comfort of indirect lighting. The indirect component creates a comfortable, balancing light, while the direct component creates a dramatic light, resulting in comfortable, interesting space.
- *Diffuse* luminaires emit light in all directions uniformly. These include most types of bare lamps, globes, chandeliers, pendants, and some table and floor lamps. Dif-

fuse luminaires tend to create broad general light that often is considered glaring due to lack of side shielding. Most chandeliers and sconces are diffuse luminaires, and they are typically chosen for ornamental reasons or for utilitarian applications. When used carefully, as in a crystal chandelier, diffuse luminaires can create sparkle and interest, but other lighting must also be present. Without other light, diffuse luminaires tend to create a flat, uninteresting light.

- *Asymmetric* luminaires are usually designed for special applications. Asymmetric uplights, for instance, are indirect luminaires with a stronger distribution in one direction, such as away from a wall. Wallwashers are a form of direct luminaire with stronger distribution to one side so as to illuminate a wall. Asymmetric luminaires are chosen when accent lighting of objects or surfaces is desired. For example, choose a wallwasher to illuminate a wall, an accent light to illuminate a painting or sculpture.
- *Adjustable* luminaires are generally direct luminaires that can be adjusted to throw light in directions other than down. These include track lights, floodlights, and accent lights.

COMMON LUMINAIRE TYPES

Recessed Downlights

Recessed downlights are often called cans or high hats. A type of direct luminaire, they are usually round or square and recessed in the ceiling (see Fig. 6.6). Their principal use is general illumination in a wide range of residential and commercial applications, especially in lobbies, halls, corridors, stores, and other finished spaces. Downlights can be equipped with incandescent, halogen, compact fluorescent, HID,

Fig. 6.6 Typical Recessed Downlight (*Courtesy of Acuity Brands Lighting.*)

or LED lamps. Downlights typically consist of two parts: the can or housing above the ceiling, and the trim installed from below the ceiling. The housing must be suitable for the application.

Here are the primary rating types:

- *Thermally protected* (T) luminaires are used in most commercial applications with a dropped ceiling and no nearby insulation.
- *Insulated ceiling* (IC) applications occur where the luminaire is intended to be in contact with insulation. IC housings are typically used in homes, especially in ceilings with attics above.
- *Damp location* luminaires can be exposed to moist air but not to direct water spray or rain. Most downlights are damp rated.
- *Wet location* fixtures can be exposed to direct water spray or rain, including extreme conditions outdoors.
- *Spa or shower* fixtures are designed for use in shower stalls and over spas.
- *Emergency* fixtures are equipped with a backup battery so as to produce light for at least 90 minutes during a power outage (generally, only compact fluorescent and LED luminaires are so equipped).

Most downlights allow for trims that fit into the housing. Among the many choices are open baffles, open reflectors, adjustable accents, wallwashers, and various lensed trims. Trim choice can dramatically affect the light quality generated by the downlight.

Spacing Guidelines

As shown in Fig. 6.7, the spacing of downlights is dependent on the light source being used. Area sources like standard incandescent, compact fluorescent, and some LED luminaire typically should be spaced using a 1.0 spacing criterion. For example, to use compact fluorescent downlights to illuminate a 2'-6" high table in a 9'-6" ceiling, you would need to space the fixtures 7'-0" (9'-6" ceiling height − 2'-6" table height = 7'-0") on center to provide a fairly uniform light level on the table. Note, this does not give you the light level, but provides a starting point for determining a lighting plan.

Point sources, such as halogen, metal halide, and some LED fixtures, should be spaced using a .5"spacing criterion. To light the same table using halogen downlights in a 12'-6"ceiling, you would need to space them 5'-0" (12'-6" − 2'-6" = 10'-0"(.5 = 5'-0") on center.

Generally, area sources should be used in 8'–10' high ceilings and point sources should be limited to ceilings above 10'. As expected, area sources have wider patterns and can be spaced farther apart; however, they do not project light very far, so they do not work as well in high ceilings.

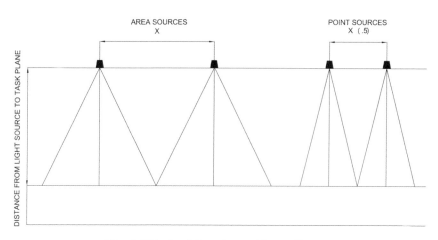

Fig. 6.7 Typical Spacing of Downlights

The previous guidelines are typical recommendations, and manufacturers often provide their own spacing criteria that will give more accurate results. This general information assists designers during the early portion of the design and should be verified with specific information once luminaires are selected. Refer to Chapter 8 for more information about predicting the light level produced.

Adjustable Accent Fixtures

Adjustable accent fixtures allow light to focus on art, signage, and other interior surfaces and features. Because of their purpose, adjustable accent fixtures are designed around point source lamps such as halogen, metal halide, and LED. There are many types of adjustable accent fixtures available, and the selection is mainly dictated by architectural constraints and the design aesthetic:

- *Recessed accent fixtures* (see Fig. 6.11) appear as downlights but internally permit horizontal and vertical rotation of the lamp's light beam. Vertical adjustment is typically limited to 40°.
- *Track lighting systems* allow for flexibility in lamp types and ease of relocation using a single power source. The track is fed at one point and carries the power through the whole length, allowing the track luminaires to be placed at any location and easily changed as the space requirements change. Track luminaires have a great degree of adjustability, much more than recessed fixtures allow. Track

Electrician's Notebook

Light track is available either as a line voltage system (see Figs. 6.8 and 6.9), typically 120V, or a low-voltage system (see Fig. 6.10), typically 12V.

Line voltage track is fed at one location and can operate a full 20 amp circuit of lighting. Many line voltage tracks are available with two or more circuits, so it is possible to load a track with many fixtures. Because of this flexibility, energy codes require that the track be accounted for differently than a single fixture:

- ASHRAE 90.1 mandates that track be valued at a minimum of 30 watts per linear foot.
- California's Title 24 mandates that track be valued at a minimum of 45 watts per linear foot.

There are many times when this may be above and beyond the design requirements of the space, so manufacturers have developed current limiters that attach to the track. A current limiter restricts the wattage of the track, which in turn allows the system to be counted at the designed wattage instead of the maximum wattage. Refer to Appendix B for additional information about Energy Codes.

Low-voltage track requires a remote transformer. Typically a low-voltage track is limited to 300 watts per length, unless the sections are isolated and fed multiple times. Energy codes require that the wattage of the transformer(s) be accounted for even if fewer fixtures are shown during the design. Many low-voltage tracks can be bent to create circles and curving elements at the ceiling (see Fig. 6.10). In addition to track, there are low-voltage systems that incorporate two parallel cables that can be spanned across a room. Although different in appearance, the general concept of the system remains the same as a low-voltage track.

Fig. 6.8 Typical Line Voltage Track (*Courtesy of WAC Lighting.*)

Fig. 6.9 Typical Track Luminaire (*Courtesy of WAC Lighting.*)

Fig. 6.10 Typical Low-Voltage Track Configuration (*Courtesy of Tech Lighting.*)

systems also allow the mixture of different lamp types and fixture styles. For example, in a restaurant, there could be accent fixtures for artwork, and pendants dropped over tables, all hanging from the same track. The track only provides power to the luminaire attached, so if the lamp selected requires a transformer or a ballast, it will need to be a part of the luminaire. Track is popular for retail, restaurant, and museum/gallery applications where the floor plan may change frequently.

- If the flexibility of a track is not required, but the adjustability of a track fixture is needed, or the architectural conditions do not allow for a recessed fixture, a *monopoint* fixture can be used. A monopoint is a track fixture that is attached to a canopy, which is mounted directly to a junction box.

Spacing Guidelines

If an adjustable accent fixture is intended to light art or signage, which is generally located at eye level, or 5'-6" above finished floor, it is important to locate the fixture correctly to avoid shadows from adjacent viewers, and reflected glare from any glossy finish on the focal point. Figure 6.12 shows the 30° aiming angle that will provide the optimum location.

To accurately locate the fixtures in the plan, it is necessary to review the wall in section first. The intersection of the 30° line with the fixture height line indicates how far the fixture should be located away from the wall (see Fig. 6.12). If the art or signage is large, more than one fixture may be required. Generally, the on-center spacing should match the distance off the wall. Ultimately, this will be dictated by lamp selection, but the above guidelines provide a basis to start. Chapter 8 provides more information on selecting an appropriate lamp for accent lighting applications.

Wallwashers

Wallwashers are any type of asymmetric luminaire that is intended to flatly light the wall from the ceiling down to the floor. Wallwashers are available for most lamp types and vary greatly depending on the geometry of the lamp being used. Wallwashers generally should not be used to light a textured surface, as they will visually flatten the material. Wallwashers are available in several types listed below:

- *Downlight-wallwashers* are essentially downlights with a kicker reflector to push light up the wall (see Fig. 6.13). This type of wallwasher is limited to ambient sources like standard incandescent, compact fluorescent, and some LEDs.
- *Recessed lensed wallwashers* resemble downlights but use a cut cone and an angled prismatic lens to spread the light of a point source (see Fig. 6.14). This type of wallwasher is normally used for halogen, metal halide, and some LED lamps.
- *Surface and semi-recessed lensed* and *open wallwashers* throw light onto an adjacent wall using a sophisticated reflector system (see Fig. 6.15). Generally, this style of wallwasher works best, but can be architecturally intrusive. They can also be mounted to a track. Normally, tubular lamps are used for this type of wallwasher including halogen, compact, and standard fluorescent, and metal halide.

Fig. 6.11 Typical Recessed Adjustable Accent Fixture
(Courtesy of Acuity Brands Lighting.)

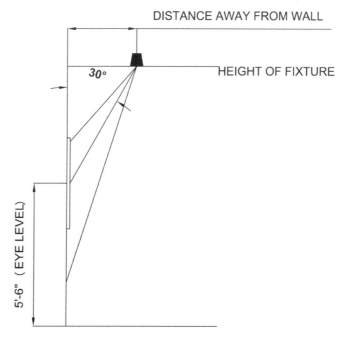

Fig. 6.12 Locating Adjustable Accent Fixtures

Fig. 6.13 Typical Recessed Downlight-wallwasher
(Courtesy of Acuity Brands Lighting.)

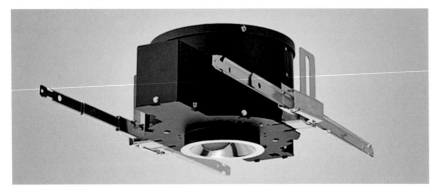

Fig. 6.14 Typical Lensed Wallwasher
(Courtesy of Acuity Brands Lighting.)

Fig. 6.15 Typical Semi-recessed Wallwasher
(Courtesy of Acuity Brands Lighting.)

• *Linear or continuous recessed wallwashers* are small in cross section (2"–4") and contain standard fluorescent lamps or LEDs (see Fig. 6.16). Architecturally, at the ceiling they can provide a continuous line of fixtures parallel with the illuminated wall. They typically are laid into an acoustical tile ceiling grid, but can also be installed into a drywall ceiling.

Spacing Guidelines

As expected, the farther away a light source is from an object, the larger the beam of light will be. This holds true with wallwashers in that the farther away from the wall the fixture is, the farther down the wall it will light. However, a balance must be kept so that the upper portion also remains lighted. In general, wallwashers should be placed 1/4 of the ceiling height away from the wall (see Figure 6.17). For example, if the ceiling height is 12', wallwashers should be located approximately 3' (12 × 1/4) away from the wall.

Since wallwashers are typically intended to light the full height and length of a wall, a grouping of fixtures is needed. Similar to recessed downlights, wallwasher

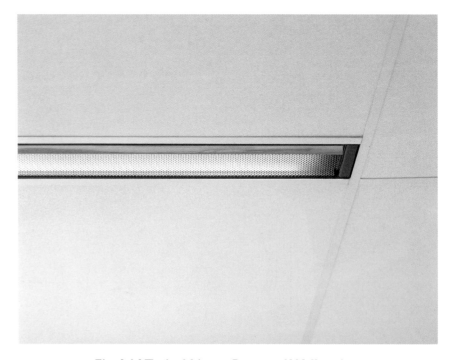

Fig. 6.16 Typical Linear Recessed Wallwasher

on-center spacing is determined largely by the light source. Ambient sources can be spaced 1.5 times the distance away from the wall. For the 12' ceiling mentioned above, ambient source wallwash fixtures could be spaced 4'-6" on center. Point sources should be limited to 1 times the distance off the wall. Using the same 12' ceiling, point source wallwashers would need to be approximately 3' on center.

Again, this information provides general criteria, and manufacturers will provide much more specific data that can be used to ensure that the wall will be evenly illuminated.

Wall Grazing Fixtures

Wall grazing is a technique that places the light source very close to the wall, typically accentuating a textured surface. At one time, this was typically achieved with multiple tight beam halogen lamps in a row. With the advent of high output linear LED fixtures, the halogen lamps are less common because of the wattage used and

heat generated. The grazing effect can be created by placing fixtures into an architectural cove or slot in the ceiling or by installing a continuous finished fixture with multiple lamps.

Troffers

Troffers are widely used in offices, schools, stores, and other commercial and institutional facilities for general lighting in work areas. Troffers are the most common type of fluorescent luminaire. With LED technology improving, many manufacturers are also designing troffers to use LEDs.

• *Lensed troffers* use a plastic lens to refract light and distribute it within the desired area below (see Fig. 6.18). The lens serves to cut off light distribution to minimize glare. The lens can also protect lamps from breaking in food preparation and service areas. Lenses can contain internal RFI shields for use in hospital operating rooms and laboratories. This is the least expensive lighting system for use in suspended ceilings, and it tends to have a low-budget appearance. In general, these

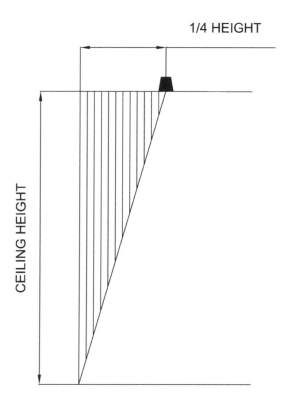

Fig. 6.17 Locating Wallwashers

Fig. 6.18 Typical Lensed Troffer
(Courtesy of Acuity Brands Lighting.)

Fig. 6.19 Typical Parabolic Troffer
(Courtesy of Acuity Brands Lighting.)

luminaires should be specified with two or three T-8 lamps and an electronic ballast.

- *Parabolic troffers* use parabolically shaped aluminum louvers to shield the lamp for improved visual comfort (see Fig. 6.19). The depth of the louver provides sharp visual cutoff, which significantly reduces reflected glare in computer workspaces. Because of the sharp cutoff, supplementary wall lighting is typically needed so that a cavernous effect is avoided. This standard lighting system is appropriate for offices, stores, and many other building types with suspended ceilings. In general, the luminaires should be specified with two or three T-8 lamps and an electronic ballast and the number of rows of cells should equal the number of lamps.

- *Recessed indirect troffers* or "basket" troffers typically incorporate a curving perforated metal shield in the center or the two sides that contain the fluorescent lamp(s) (see Fig. 6.20). The light from the fluorescent lamp is bounced or reflected off the interior box of the troffer. Like other troffers, these are still direct luminaires; however, the reflected light within the fixture provides a softer, more diffuse effect. Although visually much brighter, this style of troffer has become common in office spaces, since most later model computer screens do not have a reflective surface. It is typically specified with T-8 and T-5 straight lamps or high output 2' long compact fluorescent lamps.

- *High efficiency troffers* combine the efficiency of a lensed troffer with the aesthetic quality of the indirect basket troffer (see Fig. 6.21). The lamp shield is typically made from a prismatic lens that conceals the lamp while distributing the light. It is normally provided with T-8 or T-5 lamps.

Fig. 6.21 Typical High Efficiency Troffer (*Courtesy of Acuity Brands Lighting.*)

- *Linear troffers* or *slots* are recessed luminaires that incorporate a straight blade louver or an opal lens diffuser (see Fig. 6.22). They are typically 2", 4", or 6" wide and available in 4' increments. This style has become popular with designers because it is less intrusive than other troffer types and can be used to make patterns and other design statements at the ceiling plane. Also, many manufacturers have the option of including a point source downlight (MR16 or LED) within the housing, which is useful in spaces that require flexibility. It is typically provided with T-8 and T-5 lamps, with LEDs becoming more readily available.

Most troffers are recessed and generally designed to be laid into acoustic tile ceilings, the fixture face aligning with the face of the tile. The most common troffer

Fig. 6.20 Typical Indirect Troffer (*Courtesy of Acuity Brands Lighting.*)

Fig. 6.22 Typical Linear Troffer (*Courtesy of Acuity Brands Lighting.*)

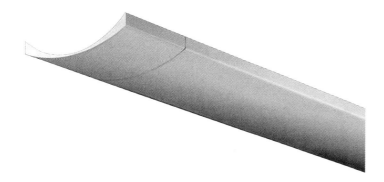

Fig. 6.23 Typical Indirect Pendant *(Courtesy of Acuity Brands Lighting.)*

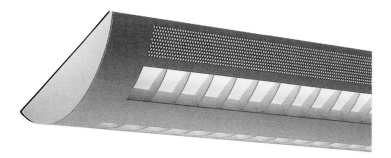

Fig. 6.24 Typical Direct/Indirect Pendant *(Courtesy of Acuity Brands Lighting.)*

sizes are 2' × 4', 2' × 2', and 1' × 4', but other sizes are available. Recessed troffer depth varies from 3–1/2" to over 7", so make certain to coordinate troffers with other elements above the ceiling.

Troffers can be equipped with most fluorescent and LED technologies, including dimming. They can also be equipped with emergency battery packs to power some or all of the lamps during a power outage or emergency condition.

Spacing Guidelines

As an ambient source, fluorescent troffers should generally be used in spaces with ceiling heights of 10'-0" and below. Although influenced by lamping and style, most troffers can be spaced 8'-0" to 10'-0" on center and maintain uniformity. It is important to note, however, that the furniture arrangement below may require the fixtures to be placed closer together. Troffers are often used in offices where workstation panels may obstruct the light from reaching the work plane.

Linear Lighting Systems

Linear lighting systems are fluorescent pendant luminaires having indirect, direct/indirect, and direct lighting distributions. They work well to illuminate offices, classrooms, and other finished spaces. Additionally, they are common in applications where the ceiling is left unfinished and recessing fixtures are not an option. Because the luminaires can be obtained in varying lengths and assembled into patterns, they are called linear systems:

- *Indirect* lighting systems produce uplight only (see Fig. 6.23). They should be mounted at least 18" below the ceiling, with longer suspension lengths improving uniformity of light on the ceiling. To maintain adequate clearance, it is usually necessary for ceilings to be at least 9' high. Semi-indirect systems having a small percentage of downlight (10 percent or less) should be used in the same manner.
- *Direct/indirect* lighting systems are intended to produce both indirect lighting, for its comfort and balance, and direct light, for task lighting (see Fig. 6.24). Suspension length and ceiling height are not as critical as for indirect lighting; however, longer lengths do still improve ceiling uniformity. The ratio of uplight to downlight varies; generally, the higher the ceiling, the greater the downlight percentage should be. These systems are applicable for offices, classrooms, libraries, retail stores, and some medical spaces. They are also considered good lighting for computer workspaces.
- *Direct* linear systems provide downlight only (see Fig. 6.25). They are typically used only in locations where luminaires could not be recessed because of restrictive ceiling conditions, or where an open ceiling is preferred but uplighting is not necessary or desired. Suspension length is not critical; however, the bottom of the fixture generally should not be below 7'-6" if it can be walked under.

Almost all luminaires of this type are for dry and relatively clean indoor locations. They can be equipped with dimming ballasts and battery packs for emergency lighting. Some versions can integrate track or low-voltage downlighting on the bottom

Fig. 6.25 Typical Direct Pendant *(Courtesy of Acuity Brands Lighting.)*

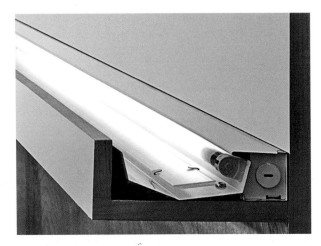

Fig. 6.26 Typical Fluorescent Asymmetric Cove
(Courtesy of Acuity Brands Lighting.)

Fig. 6.27 Typical Adjustable LED Cove
(Courtesy of Acuity Brands Lighting.)

of the luminaire. In addition, many manufacturers can integrate control elements, like a photocell or occupancy sensor, on the bottom of the fixture. (See Chapter 7 additional information.)

Low to moderate cost versions are made of sheet steel, while more expensive and styled versions are made from extruded aluminum. Various combinations of lamps are available, with the most common selections being two or three T-8 or T-5 lamps or one T-5 High Output (T-5HO) lamp across.

Spacing Guidelines

Linear pendants should be used in higher ceilings with a minimum height of 9'-0". For indirect fixtures, the suspension should be a minimum of 18". Generally, linear indirect and direct/indirect pendants can be spaced 10'-0" to 12'-0" on center. Direct pendants should be treated like a troffer, since they do not have an indirect component to fill in areas. In all cases, furniture layouts should be reviewed to ensure that shadows are not created.

Indirect Cove Fixtures

Indirect cove fixtures provide uplighting onto a ceiling plane. Architecturally, they can be within a raised coffer, simply accentuate a change in ceiling plane, or illuminate the ceiling from the wall. Most often, indirect cove fixtures are continuous and concealed within an architectural enclosure, but could be expressed as sconces on the wall. Consideration must be given to the effect that is desired to select an appropriate fixture. Some fixtures are intended to evenly illuminate a ceiling and others are intended to provide just a halo. A few different approaches and fixtures are listed below:

- *Asymmetric fluorescent cove* fixtures contain a reflector that pushes the light out into the space (see Fig. 6.26). To be effective, a minimum of 12" must be maintained from the top of the fixture to the upper ceiling plane. Care must be given to not block the light with the front edge of the cove. The fixtures are normally provided with T-8 or T-5 lamps.
- *Adjustable LED cove* fixtures vary in beam spread, size, and wattage and can be used to illuminate a whole ceiling or simply provide a glow (see Fig. 6.27). Many LED cove fixtures are line voltage, containing integral drivers, and can be easily wired and connected. LED cove fixtures are available in white or color-changing.
- *LED "tape" lights* are very small profile LED strips that typically contain a tape backing (see Fig. 6.28). In addition to indirect cove lighting, LED tape lights are often used as undercabinet task lights and within display cases. Their small size requires that the driver be located remotely.

Task Lights

Task lights are specially designed to illuminate a desk area while minimizing reflections and glare. Task lights can be portable (see Fig. 6.29) or permanently mounted under an upper cabinet.

- Since the invention of the classic architect lamp decades ago, the flexible task light has been a useful and attractive tool. Modern lamp options include low-voltage halogen, compact fluorescent, and LED versions.
- *Undercabinet fixtures* should be mounted under the front edge of a shelf or cabinet and should be as continuous as possible (see Fig. 6.30). Undercabinet fixture

Fig. 6.28 LED Tape Light

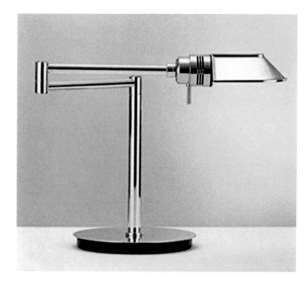

Fig. 6.29 Typical Portable Task Light

Fig. 6.30 Typical Undercabinet Fixture *(Courtesy of Acuity Brands Lighting.)*

using fluorescent lamps are the most common and least costly, but LED versions are becoming more readily available. To assist in meeting more stringent code requirements, many task lights contain integral occupancy sensors.

Decorative Lighting
Decorative lighting is the jewelry of architecture and, in many building types, plays a significant role in building style, period, or motif. Traditionally, most decorative luminaires used incandescent lamping, but compact fluorescent and LED lamps are becoming more common. Generally, if the source cannot be seen, and if the lamp is specified carefully, it is difficult to tell the difference. The key to using a fluorescent lamp in a traditional luminaire is to divide the preferred incandescent watts by 3.5 to determine fluorescent watts.

- *Chandeliers* are ornate luminaires traditionally consisting of many small incandescent lamps that simulate the effect of candle flames (see Fig. 6.31). There are also modern versions of chandeliers that incorporate updated lamping and design aesthetics. Chandeliers are hung from the ceiling and are used for general illumination in hotel lobbies, dining rooms, foyers, and other formal spaces.
- *Pendants* are also ceiling-hung decorative fixtures. In general, the term pendant is used for hanging luminaires less formal than chandeliers that are used in residences, stores, hotels, restaurants, and many other places (see Fig. 6.32). While usually designed to use incandescent or halogen lamps, the increasing number of lamp choices includes hard-wired compact fluorescent and LEDs.
- *Close-to-ceiling* or *surface-mounted luminaires* are similar to pendants but mount closely to the ceiling to allow use in most rooms with conventional ceiling heights (see Fig. 6.33).
- *Sconces* are wall-mounted luminaires and are often decorative (see Fig. 6.34). Sconces exhibit a wide range of styles from crystal fixtures with flame-tip lamps

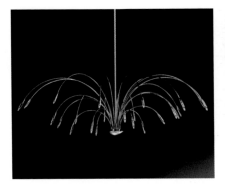

Fig. 6.31 Chandelier Example
(Courtesy of Hampstead Lighting.)

Fig. 6.32 Pendant Example
(Courtesy of Hampstead Lighting.)

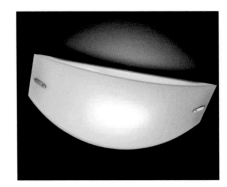

Fig. 6.33 Close-to-ceiling Fixture Example *(Courtesy of Hampstead Lighting.)*

Fig. 6.34 Wall Sconce Example
(Courtesy of Hampstead Lighting.)

to modern designs. They can be used in hotels, office corridors and lobbies, and a wide variety of other space types. Wall sconces can be equipped with incandescent, compact fluorescent, or LED lamping to provide an attractive and effective light at eye level.

• *Table and floor lamps* are portable luminaires (see Fig. 6.35) that are traditionally supplied as incandescent, although versions are now being redesigned to employ hardwired compact fluorescent lamps. Table and floor lamps are used most often in residential applications, but when used in commercial applications, they provide flexibility and desirable eye-level glow.

• *Torchieres* are floor lamps designed specifically for uplighting (see Fig. 6.36). Most use incandescent or halogen sources, although compact fluorescent options should be considered for commercial and hospitality applications.

• *Vanity lights* can be decorative, but they are used as a task light for bath vanity and mirror areas (see Fig. 6.37). They can be mounted horizontally above the mirror or vertically to the sides. Their purpose is to light a person's face and eliminate shadows, so the vanity light needs to be a diffuse source. Fluorescent lamps can be considered as an alternative to incandescent and halogen but should be selected with a high color rendering index and warm color temperature.

Fig. 6.35 Table Lamp Example
(Courtesy of Hampstead Lighting.)

Fig. 6.36 Torchiere Example
(Courtesy of Hampstead Lighting.)

Fig. 6.37 Vanity Light Example
(Courtesy of Hampstead Lighting.)

Fig. 6.38 Typical Fluorescent Wraparound *(Courtesy of Acuity Brands Lighting.)*

Fig. 6.39 Typical Fluorescent Strip Light *(Courtesy of Acuity Brands Lighting.)*

Fig. 6.40 Typical HID Industrial *(Courtesy of Acuity Brands Lighting.)*

Most decorative luminaires can be used in dry indoor spaces only. A few types are wet-labeled, meaning they can be exposed to direct rain.

Commercial and Industrial Luminaires

Commercial fixtures include several types of fluorescent direct luminaires. The most common type is the *fluorescent wraparound*, as shown in Figure 6.38, wherein a lens or diffuser top surrounds the lamps, hiding them from direct view while radiating light downward and to the sides. Commercial luminaires are among the lowest-cost lighting fixtures. They are typically used for general and utility lighting in modest projects.

Industrial luminaires generally have a utilitarian or functional appearance. Fig. 6.39 shows industrial fluorescent *strip lights*. Strip lights can also be supplied with reflectors and be surface-mounted or hung by chains or rods. The typical fluorescent strip light is still often used in architectural details for cove lighting, display cases, sign light-ing, and backlighting translucent materials. HID industrials include *high-bay downlights* and *low-bay downlights* as shown in Fig. 6.40.

Industrial fixtures are generally used in factories, warehouses, and, increasingly, in schools and retail stores where a less finished appearance is desired. Although most industrials are direct lighting, many are semi-direct—that is, having a small percentage of uplight to improve visual comfort.

LUMINAIRE SELECTION

Luminaire selection begins with determining what light source is the most appropriate for the application. Once that decision is made, the designer must evaluate the architectural conditions, design aesthetic, and client budget to determine what type or style of fixture will work best for each project.

Chapter 7 LIGHTING CONTROLS

Since lighting was invented, switching has been essential. Even candles and gaslights were turned on and off and sometimes even dimmed. Lighting controls allow the occupants of a space to adjust the level and quality of light based on their personal preference and needs. In addition to enhancing the ambience of a space, controlling light helps save energy.

PRINCIPLES OF CONTROLS

Controlling Operating Time
First, we control the operating time of lights for convenience and to save energy. By turning lights off, we save both the cost of electricity and preserve lamp life. Of course, we turn lights off when we wish to darken a room for sleep. This is generally called switching.

Controlling Power
Most light sources operate even if their power is varied. This results in a source that is less bright than normal, which we call dimming. Dimming is generally used to cre-

ate a distinct mood, as in a dining room or restaurant. But dimming is being used more frequently to save energy. In many spaces, windows introduce enough light to permit interior lights to be dimmed. The combination of daylight and reduced electric light still provide adequate illumination for the tasks being performed.

Code Requirements
Building codes require lighting controls in two ways:

1. The National Electric Code requires switches by every door in residential occupancies, including private homes, apartments, and condominiums. This is primarily for safety and convenience.
2. Energy codes like the International Energy Conservation Code (IECC), ASHRAE/ IESNA 90.1 (American Society of Heating, Refrigerating, and Air Conditioning Engineers/Illuminating Engineering Society of North America), and various state codes require switching in every nonresidential space but the switching is not required to be by every door. This is primarily to encourage people to turn lights off when they are not needed. For most space types, the switching must ensure that lights are turned off automatically when no one is present, as with an occupancy sensor.

Common Sense

In addition to specific code requirements, switches or other controls for lights are frequently chosen by the designer to enable the proper use of the lighting. Think about how a room is to be used. The best designs anticipate needs and resolve them prior to construction. Where should a light switch or dimmer be located? Should switching or dimming be provided in more than one location? Is dimming rather than switching more suited to the activities that will take place in the room? Once code requirements are met, the best approach is always common sense.

TYPES OF CONTROL

Switching

A switch is a control device that turns lights on and off. Most switches are levers and mechanical devices that open and close electrical contacts in the power circuit directly feeding the lights. One switch is required for each group or zone of lights to be controlled together. If a room has more than one entry, an additional switch must be added at each entry. Multiple switch locations require switches called "three-way" and "four-way" that permit any switch location to turn the lights on and off.

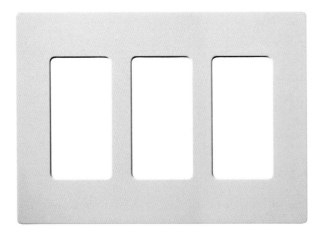

Fig. 7.3 "Ganged" Wall Switch Plate
(© 2012 Lutron Electronics Co., Inc.)

A switch should be located next to the door as you enter a room, preferably on the latch side, and mounted 42" above the floor in order to conform with ADA requirements. Also related, receptacles need to be a minimum of 18" from the floor.

The two most common switch types are toggle and paddle switches as shown in Figs. 7.1 and 7.2. There are many choices of color and plate style. It is possible to use switches that have a finder light (the switch is illuminated in the dark) or a pilot light (the switch is illuminated when the lights are turned on). When there is more than one switch required in a space, the switches can be grouped or ganged together using one wall plate as shown in Fig. 7.3.

Time Control

Many lighting systems are best controlled automatically by time. For instance, the lights in a store with fixed hours of operation can go on and off automatically through the use of a time switch (sometimes called a time clock). Simple clock mechanisms operate a switch by operating a contact closure according to on and off set times. People often use a residential version of a time switch to control lights as a security measure.

Some time control systems can automatically change the set times according to the time of year. This type of control device is called an astronomic time switch.

A timer is a switch that turns lights off automatically after a certain period. Historically, timers used a wind-up mechanical dial, and one of the most common applications is for switching heat lamps in bathrooms. Modern timers use a push button start and a programmable time-out period.

Fig. 7.1 Toggle Switch Example

Fig. 7.2 Paddle Switch Example
(© 2012 Lutron Electronics Co., Inc.)

Fig. 7.4 Wall-Mounted Sensor
(© 2012 Lutron Electronics Co., Inc.)

Fig. 7.5 Ceiling-Mounted Sensor
(© 2012 Lutron Electronics Co., Inc.)

Occupancy Sensing

Occupancy sensors are automatic switches that turn lights on when motion is detected and leave them on until some designated time after the last motion occurs. Occupancy sensors add convenience and save energy. Often, vacancy sensors are being used in an effort to save additional energy. Vacancy sensors require lights to be turned on manually, but turn them off automatically.

It is possible to replace an ordinary switch with an occupancy sensor switch (see Fig. 7.4), making lighting control hands-free and assuring that lights will go off when people are no longer present. Occupancy sensors mounted in the ceiling (see Fig. 7.5) can be connected to a control system, and several sensors can be connected together. This ensures that any motion in a relatively large space, such as a cafeteria or gym, will keep the lights on throughout the space. Also, in spaces such as restrooms where walls or privacy dividers prevent occupancy sensing, multiple sensors make certain that no one is left in the dark.

Sensor placements and their viewing windows are key in guaranteeing the sensor(s) will work properly in the designated space. For example, a sensor in a private office should not read motion in an adjacent corridor.

Dimming

Dimmers are control devices that vary the light level and power to lights. Dimmers almost always combine the dimming electronics with a switch, so they are really switch dimmers. How the switch works is just as important as the dimmer.

In a single-action dimmer, the lights must be dimmed completely before the switch action occurs. In a preset dimmer, the switch is a separate action from the dimmer. Preset dimmers are generally better because they allow three-way and four-way switching, and they permit setting a preferred light level and leaving it there even when lights are switched.

Dimmers need to be selected according to the lamp type and load connected to them, called the "dimmer rating." The most common dimmer ratings are

- Standard dimmers for incandescent lamps. The ratings range from 600 watts to dimmers that are rated up to 2000 watts.
- Dimmers for low-voltage incandescent lights. These dimmers dim the transformer feeding the lights. There are two kinds: dimmers rated for magnetic transformers and dimmers rated for electronic transformers. They are usually rated in volt-amps (VA), which are roughly the same as watts. Magnetic-rated dimmers are rated at least 600 VA; and electronic rated dimmers are rated at least 325 VA.
- Dimmers for fluorescent lamps. To dim fluorescent lighting, it is necessary for the fluorescent lamps to have dimming ballasts. The dimmer needs to be designed to operate with the specific dimming ballast being used.
- Dimmers for neon and cold cathode lights.
- LED lighting requires special dimming circuits, but most are designed to connect to a low-voltage incandescent or fluorescent dimmer. Color changing LED lights require specialized controls, many of them designed to connect to theatrical lighting control systems.

Electrician's Notebook

Manufacturers use a variety of technologies within the sensors to ensure that lights remain on when a space is occupied, even if the motion is very slight:

- Passive Infrared—A passive infrared sensor measures infrared (IR) light radiating from objects in its field of view. The motion is detected when an IR source with one temperature, such as a person, passes in front of an IR source with another temperature such as a wall.
- Acoustic—An acoustic sensor "hears" sounds typically made by a person in the occupied space.

Dual Technology incorporates both passive infrared and acoustic technology.

Electrician's Notebook

Fluorescent dimming ballasts are becoming a very important part of commercial lighting because they are extremely effective energy savers. Unfortunately, there are five different types of fluorescent dimming ballasts that all dim differently:

- Some ballasts can be dimmed using a regular incandescent dimming circuit with two wires (dimmed hot and neutral). The two-wire circuit should employ specific dimmers listed for this application, but the advantage is being able to add dimming to existing circuits without rewiring.
- Some ballasts are dimmed using a special fluorescent ballast with three wires (switched hot, dimmed hot, and neutral). This style is based on the traditional circuits used by magnetic dimming ballasts of prior years.
- Some ballasts are dimmed using a four-wire circuit (switched hot, neutral, low voltage +, and low voltage −) in which the low voltage (0–10 volts) determines the amount of light. This style is used by many modern energy management–oriented control systems, as well as a number of conventional architectural dimming systems.
- Some ballasts are dimmed using a digital circuit in which power (unswitched hot and neutral) is accompanied by a pair of communication wires. The communication wires can be wired "class 1" so that they can be pulled with power wiring, saving additional low-voltage wiring and raceways. The ballast turns itself on and off and varies power according to signals sent from the lighting control system. Each ballast is addressable, allowing systems to be reconfigured and readily reprogrammed.
- Finally, some ballasts are dimmed using a power line carrier signal. This is a digital signal impressed on the power line that only the dimming ballast can hear.

There are a few combination ballasts on the market. One such ballast has both digital control and can be dimmed by a fluorescent dimmer. Another type will accept either two-wire or low-voltage 0–10 volt dimming.

Otherwise, there is literally no compatibility among fluorescent dimming ballasts. It is extremely critical to make sure ballasts and dimmers are properly ordered to be compatible on each project.

Fig 7.6 Rotary Dimmer Example
(© 2012 Lutron Electronics Co., Inc.)

Fig. 7.7 Slide Dimmer with Rocker Switch Example
(© 2012 Lutron Electronics Co., Inc.)

Fig. 7.8 Slide Dimmer with Push On/off Button
(© 2012 Lutron Electronics Co., Inc.)

Fig. 7.9 Paddle Switch with Slide Dimmer
(© 2012 Lutron Electronics Co., Inc.)

There are several styles of dimmers, but the most common are the rotary dimmer (see Fig. 7.6) and the slide dimmers (see Figs. 7.7, 7.8, and 7.9). In the rotary dimmer style, the preset dimmer often has a push-on, push-off dial. In the slide dimmer style, the preset dimmer may have a rocker switch, a push-on, push-off switch, or a touch switch with a separate dimmer slide.

Daylighting

Automatic daylighting controls feature photoelectric sensors that turn lights off or dim them when there is sufficient daylight. In exterior applications, photoelectric switches turn off parking lot lights and streetlights during the day. For interior spaces, photoelectric dimmers reduce the energy used by electric lights in spaces where windows or skylights provide most of the light actually needed in the space, then

Fig. 7.10 Photoelectric Sensor *(© 2012 Lutron Electronics Co., Inc.)*

increase interior electric light levels at night and on dark days. See Fig. 7.10 for an example of a photoelectric sensor.

Lumen Maintenance

Lumen maintenance controls are designed to take advantage of the fact that lighting systems are overdesigned so that as lamps age and luminaires become dirty, designed lighting levels are maintained. This means that for the period right after construction or maintenance, lighting systems can often be dimmed 20–30 percent and still provide the desired maintained light levels. Systems to perform this function use a special type of interior photoelectric cell that measures the light level on the task surface and raises the light level as needed.

Adaptation Compensation

Adaptation compensation is intuitive—it dims lights at night. Especially in commercial buildings like grocery stores, lights can be dimmed considerably at night because shoppers' eyes are already accustomed to darkness. Adaptation compensation can be performed by a photoelectric eye but it can also be programmed into a computer according to the known sunset and sunrise times at the location.

CONTROL SYSTEMS

In large facilities, it is often a good idea to connect lighting control devices so they work as a system. Systems enable building operators to control lights better. In some very large and complex facilities, like stadiums and arenas, lighting controls are essential.

Relay Systems

It is possible for a low-voltage control system to remotely control lighting through the use of relays. Relays are devices that control the 120 or 277 volt lighting power by mechanically opening or closing according to signals sent from low-voltage rocker switches, time clocks, or computer-based energy management systems.

In a relay control system, each group of lights that are switched together must be connected to the same relay. Many relays are located together in a panel, usually next to the circuit breaker panel. Relay systems are best for large commercial and institutional facilities with big rooms that do not require dimming, such as high-rise offices, airports, and schools.

Energy Management Systems

In larger buildings computerized energy management systems operate relays but have the advantage of computer control, centralization, and convenience. These systems may have many different time schedules for the various lighting systems in the building. Major buildings employ this type of control so a single building engineer can effectively manage the facility.

Energy management systems control many relay panels as well as mechanical motors, dampers, and so on. The primary difference between a relay system and an energy management system is that the latter controls all energy use in the building.

Preset Dimming Systems

Preset dimmers permit the light level from each dimmer to be set and memorized. Then, when a button is pushed, the dimmers respond by fading to their preset level.

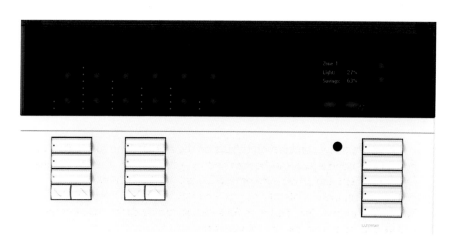

Fig. 7.11 Preset Dimming Controller Example
(© 2012 Lutron Electronics Co., Inc.)

Electrician's Notebook

Computerized lighting control systems are becoming common, even for moderately sized projects, because their ability to reduce energy waste is superior.

There are three major system types:

- A totally integrated lighting control system based on the international DALI (Digital Addressable Lighting Interface) standard in which the switching and dimming of lighting occurs within the ballast or driver. Proprietary communication systems and/or proprietary ballasts are often used.
- A zone-based lighting control system employing Ethernet/TCP/IP or RS485 communications, distributed zone control modules and data gathering nodes, and generic DALI or 0–10 volt ballasts and drivers.
- A conventional central panel system architecture consisting of racks or panels having relays and dimmers or dimming modules capable of controlling conventional incandescent, halogen, fluorescent, LED and/or HID sources loads, and/or DALI or 0–10 volt ballasts and drivers.

All three approaches can achieve similar results but virtually none of the systems is compatible with others, and there are very few generic components. It is a good idea to work with a manufacturer or systems integration specialist.

creating a lighting scene. Preset dimming can be provided as a small local system or as a large-scale system for an entire building.

The most common preset dimming device is a six zone, four scene controller (see Fig. 7.11), typically used to control light in large residential living rooms, meeting rooms, and small restaurants. This is common where scenes are used for different times of day or for different functions. Each of the four scenes is memorized and by pressing the proper button, the scene is recalled and the lights fade from one scene to the next.

Large preset dimming systems have a number of dimmers, usually in cabinets, which are designed to work together to create scenes of light. These more complex systems are used in hotel function spaces, convention centers, casinos, and other facilities where a number of rooms or spaces are controlled from a central computer-based preset controller. These systems are especially powerful and include the following features:

- Dimmer setting of each zone of lighting included in all scenes
- Groups of unique lighting scenes for each room
- Ability to manually choose scenes, and in many cases, change scene settings in each room
- Partition switches, which enable the lighting control system to operate in conjunction with the various positions of movable partitions, as in hotel ballrooms
- Completely programmable automatic operation based on time of day, astronomic time, motion, daylight, or manual override

Computer Controlled Lighting Systems

Among the most powerful lighting control systems today employ a central computer to control the lighting in an entire home or building in a coordinated manner. For example, in a large home, the homeowners can press a button in the car that turns on a scene of lights throughout the home to welcome them. In a commercial building, the lighting systems can be coordinated with solar shades to harvest daylight to the maximum amount, dimming or turning off lights to match the exact amount of available daylight.

Chapter 8 QUANTITY OF LIGHT

It is often desirable to calculate the amount of light that will result from a design. While seldom required in residential design, lighting calculations are critical to the success of lighting designs in schools, offices, stores, and most commercial and institutional building types. In this section, we will describe the various ways lighting calculations can be performed, and provide you with basic tools for predicting lighting results.

In modern design, it is common to talk about foot-candles of light (or *lux*, if working metric) rather carelessly. It is important to remember that, when stating the required number of foot-candles for a space, it is generally inferred that the requirement is for the average light level measured in the horizontal plane at desk height. However, sometimes the criterion is for light only at the task, or for light measured in the vertical plane (as for artwork).

Although the light level is important to consider, the perceived brightness of a space cannot be completely evaluated by looking at foot-candle levels alone. As noted in Chapter 2, humans see and are attracted to illuminated vertical surfaces. A space with light- to medium-toned walls that are illuminated with minimal horizontal illumination will generally be perceived as brighter than a room with higher horizontal level without wall illumination. Calculations are only one piece of the design solution.

DETERMINING THE APPROPRIATE LIGHT LEVEL REQUIRED

Standards for recommended illumination levels are set by the Illuminating Engineering Society of North America (IESNA). Illumination is generally measured in the horizontal plane 30" above the floor. The units of illumination are foot-candles or fc (lumens per square foot) or lux (lumens per square meter). Foot-candles are still used in the United States, but in countries already converted to the metric system, lux is the proper measure.

The IESNA categorizes light level criterion recommendations based on three aspects: complexity and difficulty of the visual tasks being performed in the space, the priority of the task relative to others, and the age of the user. The categories are:

Category A: Public spaces 3 fc/30 lux
Category B: Simple orientation 5 fc/50 lux
Category C: Simple visual tasks 10 fc/100 lux
Category D: Tasks of high contrast and large size 30 fc/300 lux
Category E: Tasks of high contrast and small size 50 fc/500 lux
Category F: Tasks of low contrast and small size 100 fc/1000 lux
Category G: Visual tasks near threshold up to 1000 fc/10,000 lux

For these light level recommendations, it is assumed that more than 50 percent of the occupants are between the ages of 25 and 65. If more than 50 percent of the users are over 65, it is generally recommended that these levels be doubled to compensate for their aging visual systems. In addition, as expected, if more than 50 percent of the users are under the age of 25, the levels can be halved.

To choose an appropriate level for each visual task, use these values or refer to the *IESNA Lighting Handbook*, 10th ed., for further explanation.

Here are points to remember about recommended criterion illumination levels:

- These are recommendations, not codes. However, specific lighting levels may be set by codes, such as life safety code and health code. For instance, NFPA 101 (Life Safety Standard) specifies 1 fc (10 lux) minimum along a path of emergency egress.
- The designer is expected to adjust the criterion level based on project needs. For example, if workers are old, the tasks are small, or the task involves low contrast, the designer may choose to set a higher level.
- The design criterion chosen is an average light level for task lighting. Some tasks may be lower and some higher.

The uniformity of lighting levels is also subject to IESNA recommendations. For interior lighting, IESNA generally recommends the following ratios of illumination:

Task proper: 67–133 percent of criterion value
Immediate surround: 33–100 percent of criterion value
Surround: 10–100 percent of criterion value

By designing light to maintain these relationships, the human eye will be in a constant state of proper adaptation and can respond quickly to visual stimuli.

Initial Versus Maintained Light Levels

When lamps are new and luminaires clean, the lighting system is operating at its peak called *initial lighting level*. As lamps age and luminaires get dirty, light levels drop. The amount they drop depends on several factors, including the type of lamp and its age, the relative dirtiness of the environment, and how often lamps are replaced and luminaires cleaned. Generally, a 15–25 percent reduction is used depending on the type of space. In lighting calculations this is represented as a Light Loss Factor (LLF) and should be inputted as .75–.85.

Factors that account for maintenance of light levels are part of all calculations in lighting design. Assume, from now on, that the text refers to maintained light levels unless stated otherwise.

Basic Theory

The science of lighting was invented over 300 years ago, and was, of course, based on candlelight. The foot-candle is the amount of light striking a surface one foot away from a candle (see Fig. 8.1). The intensity of the light is one candela.

We measure light sources in two distinct ways. Most lamps are measured according to the total amount of light they radiate, while luminaires and directional lamps are measured by the intensity of the emitted light.

Lamps

The gross amount of light generated by a light source is measured in lumens.

Here are lumens for common light sources:

Candle	13 lumens
1-watt LED (c. 2011)	100 lumens
Standard 60-watt incandescent lamp	890 lumens
Standard 18-watt compact fluorescent lamp	1,200 lumens
Standard 4-foot-long T-8 fluorescent lamp	2,850 lumens
100-watt high-pressure sodium streetlamp	9,500 lumens
1500-watt metal halide lamp	165,000 lumens

Some light sources use energy more efficiently than others. Note that the 18-watt compact fluorescent lamp generates more light than the 60-watt incandescent, and that twelve 1-watt LEDs generate as much light as the 18-watt compact fluorescent. Use of light sources like fluorescent lamps and LEDs to generate light with much less power than incandescent lamps represents the first foundation of energy efficient lighting.

Lumens are basic data used in several types of calculations and needed espe-

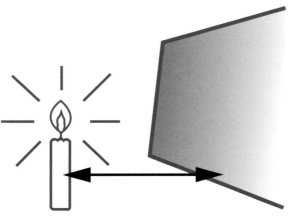

1 lumen = the quantity of light falling on a 1 sq. foot area illuminated to 1 foot-candle

Fig. 8.1 Foot-candle from Candlelight *(Courtesy of GE.)*

cially when designing the general or ambient lighting for a room. The lumens for lamp types can be found in a lamp catalog. Also, many fixture manufacturers list the lumens for the lamps that are used in their fixtures.

Luminaires and Directional Lamps

Luminaires and directional lamps are measured according to the intensity and direction of light emitted from them. This is a complex process involving optical theory. However, there are some basic and useful points that can be readily applied in everyday design.

Electrician's Notebook

For commercial work, computer point-by-point calculations are generally considered standard practice. Software costs are modest, from giveaway software developed by lighting manufacturers to commercially available software ranging in price. Classes are typically available as are on-line tutorials. While it is uncommon for electricians to develop the skills to perform calculations, most electrical contractors now have these capabilities in-house.

Calculations are also commonly provided by distributors, manufacturers, or agents. Especially if the design calls for a number of commercial grade luminaires, it should be possible to obtain free calculation assistance in exchange for an order once the design is set.

As an example, consider a flashlight. An ordinary two-cell flashlight generates a beam of about 200 candlepower. But light is emitted from one end of the flashlight only—not in all directions, like a candle. The flashlight has the intensity of 200 candles, but in a very tight beam.

Candlepower values and distribution diagrams are used in most modern lighting calculations. The most basic calculation is called the distance-squared law, and it works like this:

The illumination equals the intensity or candelas of the light source divided by the distance, in feet, away from the light source.

$$\text{foot-candles} = \frac{\text{candela or candlepower}}{\text{distance}^2}$$

Shine the flashlight mentioned above onto a rock 10 feet away. The illumination in foot-candles is:

$$\frac{200 \text{ candela}}{100} = 2 \text{ foot-candles at the rock}$$

Predicting Lighting Results in Design

When designing lighting, you must make sure you have the proper amount of light. How many luminaires? How many watts? Which lamp type? Keeping in mind that the acceptable light level ranges from about 2/3 to 4/3 of the target, this is the technical part of lighting design that frustrates many architects and interior designers.

PHOTOMETRICS

Photometry derived in accordance with IESNA LM41 procedure. Vertical and horizontal illuminance is calculated with fixture mounted 15" from work surface. Full photometric data available upon request.

Initial Point Illumination on horizontal work surface. (fc)

Coordinates are on 6" centers.

UC 24
Report LTL 6349

	1	2	3	4	5	6
A	7	9	9	7	5	3
B	13	19	18	13	8	4
C	21	30	29	19	10	6
D	26	38	36	23	12	7
E	26	38	36	23	12	7
F	21	30	29	19	10	6
G	13	18	18	13	8	4
H	7	9	9	7	5	

UC 42
Report LTL 6447

	1	2	3	4	5	6
A	22	31	31	21	13	7
B	32	46	44	30	17	9
C	37	54	52	35	19	11
D	40	58	56	37	21	12
E	40	58	56	37	21	12
F	37	54	52	35	19	11
G	32	46	44	30	17	9
H	22	31	31	21	13	7

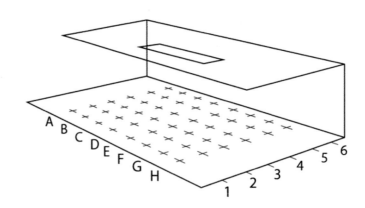

Fig. 8.2 Foot-candle Guide Example *(Courtesy of Acuity Brands Lighting.)*

Predicting General and Ambient Light Levels

General and ambient light levels are almost always average light levels in the horizontal plane. They are the most common calculations of light level.

There are three ways to predict light levels for general and ambient lighting:

1. You can estimate the average lighting based on rough calculations, a procedure explained later in this chapter. While not very accurate, this method works well for many projects. As a minimum, it ensures that a design is not too far off.
2. You can perform lumen method calculations. Lumen method calculations are complex but can be performed on a hand calculator. This method is quite accurate for general lighting, but it does not work well if lighting is designed to be uneven.
3. You can perform point-by-point computer calculations. These require considerable expertise using one of a number of relatively sophisticated programs that run on PCs. Some of the programs are graphically oriented and may be of interest to architects and interior designers, especially those who calculate daylighting. However, most of the calculations are performed by lighting designers, engineers, and lighting sales companies.

Predicting Task Lighting and Focal Lighting Levels

Task light levels and highlights, such as the amount of light on a painting or retail feature display, are relatively hard to predict. In some cases, good data are lacking; in others, the calculations are tedious. Nonetheless, there are four useful ways to predict light levels for tasks and other highlights.

1. Use a guide published by the manufacturer of the luminaire you are planning to use, as shown in Fig. 8.2. This is often the best way regardless of the knowledge level of the designer, especially for task lighting, such as lamps and undercabinet lights.
2. Use the distance-squared law to estimate the light level on a painting or retail display. This is relatively easy to do and an excellent way to estimate highlights for display lighting. The procedure is explained in more detail below.
3. Use a display lighting calculator program. This requires some lighting expertise, but the software is generally free from the lamp companies.
4. Use a point-by-point computer program, as described earlier.

Predicting the exact amount of light at specific points has become important in design, particularly in documenting the path of egress for emergency lighting. Com-

Fig. 8.3 Rendering Example

puter calculations are often used to demonstrate code compliance even if computer calculations are not used for the main lighting systems.

How Will the Space Look?

Ultimately, the deciding factor in completing designs is often the appearance of the space. The advantage held by lighting designers is their ability to envision the appearance of an illuminated space based solely on plans and sections. Even the best traditional renderings typically fail to represent light properly.

Today, many 3-D design programs have rendering engines. Rendering engines use the same technology that is used in lighting design software, and they create renderings of the illuminated space, as shown in Fig. 8.3. Unless the lighting design and requirements are complex, an architect or designer with a modest amount of 3-D computer experience can create and evaluate lighting designs based principally on appearance. Most of the programs will also produce analysis, so a complete lighting design can be evaluated. Of course, a complete lighting design is usually more than just appearance, but for many projects, the design depends on the appearance of the final result and the ability of the architect or designer to establish a strong design direction prior to retaining consultants.

Rough Calculations for Architects and Interior Designers

While it is no longer common for architects and interior designers to calculate lighting levels, it is very common that they produce basic lighting designs and perform lighting layouts. The following methods can be used with reasonable accuracy. Remember, however, that these methods are only estimates and do not replace accurate calculations when they are called for.

The Watts-per-Square-Foot Method

This method works well for many space types. Simply multiply the room area in square feet by watts per square foot using Table 8.1.

area × watts per square foot = total wattage

This will tell you how many watts of either fluorescent or halogen sources you need to achieve recommended average lighting levels. By the way, the table is intended to work in conjunction with all North American energy codes as of January 2000, but other restrictions may further affect your design.

This method works especially well if you follow these rules:

- Apply only to relatively ordinary spaces with white ceilings, medium tone to light walls, and a reasonable number of windows. This method does not work well for dark-colored spaces or spaces with unusual shapes.

- Use common, everyday lighting equipment intended for the space being designed. Avoid custom designs and clever uses of lighting equipment.
- Make sure you understand the different effects of point sources such as halogen lamps and ambient sources such as fluorescent lamps. See examples # 1 and 2.

A Very Simple Lumen Method

The lumen method formula is based on the root definition of a foot-candle, which is

$$\text{foot-candles} = \frac{\text{lumens}}{\text{area}}$$

THE WATTS-PER-SQUARE-FOOT METHOD

Example # 1: Classroom (see Fig. 8.5)

Area: 800 square feet
Average foot-candle level required = 50
Watts per square foot from chart = 1.2
Fixture selected: direct/indirect fluorescent pendant with two 32-watt, 4'-long T-8 lamps (see Fig. 8.4)
Multiply area × watts per square foot:

800 × 1.2 = 960 watts

Divide by wattage per fixture:

960 ÷ (32 watts × 2 per fixture) = 15 fixtures required

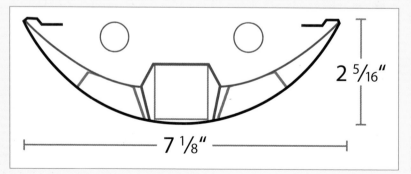

Fig. 8.4 Two-lamp Direct/Indirect Pendant

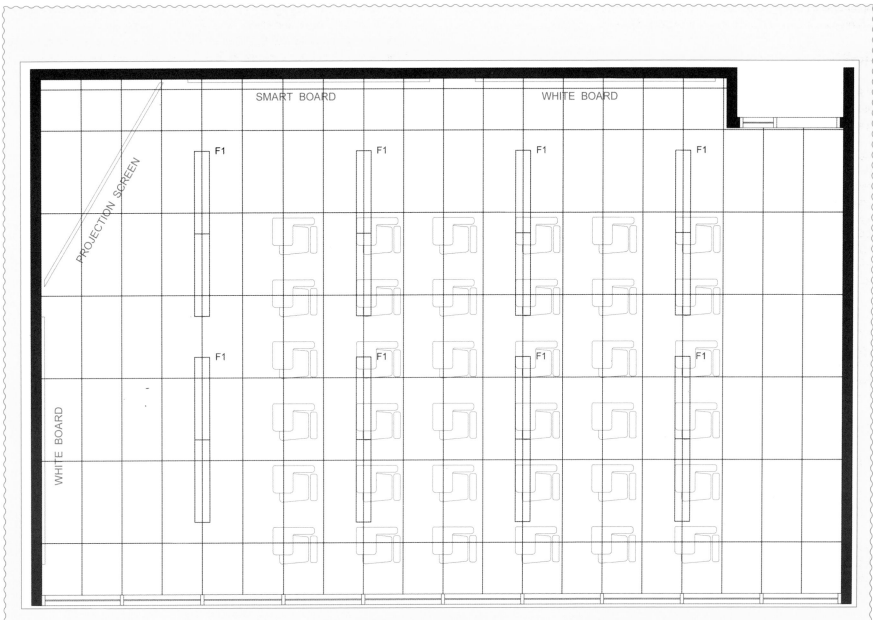

Fig. 8.5 Classroom Example

Example # 2: House Lighting for a Theater (see Fig. 8.6)

Area: 3000
Average foot-candle level required = 10
Watts per square foot from chart = 1.0
Fixture selected: Halogen recessed downlight, either 60 or 100 watts

Multiply area × watts per square foot:

3000 × 1.0 = 3000 watts

Divide by wattage per fixture:

3000 ÷ 60 = 50 fixtures required or
3000 ÷ 100 = 30 fixtures required

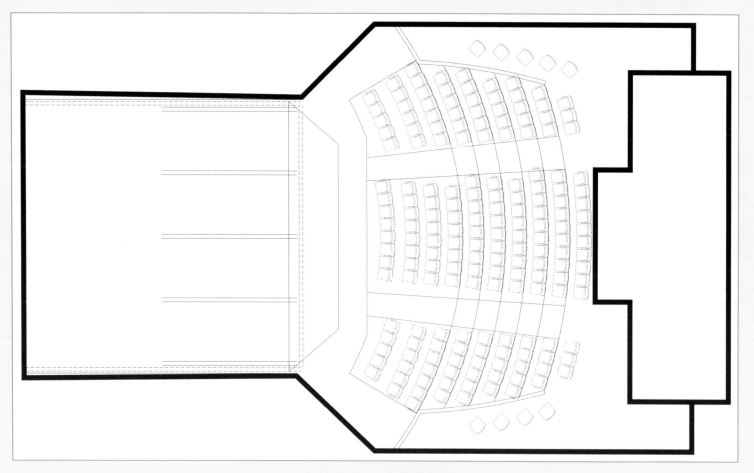

Fig. 8.6 Theater Example

VERY SIMPLE LUMEN METHOD

Example # 3: Classroom

Area: 800 square feet
Average foot-candle level required = 50
Fixture selected: Direct/indirect fluorescent pendant with two 32-watt, 4'-long T-8 lamps. Each 4' lamp has 2850 lumens.
Multiply the desired light level by two:

$$50 \times 2 = 100$$

Multiply the result by the area of the room:

$$100 \times 800 = 80,000 \text{ total lumens}$$

Divide the total lumens by the rated initial lumens of the lamp:

$$80,000 \div (2850 \times 2 \text{ per fixture}) = 14$$

Let's take the same classroom, and assume that a layout has been decided upon, and a fixture has been selected, and you need to verify that there is sufficient light.

Area: 800 square feet
Average foot-candle level required = 50
Fixture selected: Direct/indirect fluorescent pendant with one 54-watt, 4'-long T5HO lamp. Each 4' lamp has 5000 lumens.
Number of fixtures: 16
Divide the total initial lumens generated by the lamps by the area:

$$(5000 \times 16 \text{ fixtures}) \div 800 = 100$$

Divide the result by two:

$$100 \div 2 = 50 \text{ foot-candles}$$

Example # 4: Hotel Ballroom (see Fig. 8.7)

Area: 1200 square feet
Average foot-candle level required = 30 for meeting function
Fixtures selected:

- 10 downlights, each with a 2,000-lumen lamp
- One chandelier with 24 400-lumen lamps
- Cove lighting with 28 3,000-lumen lamps

Determine the total lumens for the entire room:

10 downlights × 2,000 lumens	20,000 lumens
24 chandelier lamps × 400 lumens	9,600 lumens
28 fluorescent lamps × 3,000 lumens	84,000 lumens
Total	113,600 lumens

Divide the total initial lumens generated by the lamps by the area:

$$113,600 \div 1,200 = 94.6$$

Divide the result by 2

$$94.6 \div 2 = 47.3 \text{ foot-candles}$$

Remember that 47.3 represents an approximate value. But you can be confident you will have 35 to 40 foot-candles with all lights on. Also note that if you turn off the fluorescent lights, you will still have at least 10 foot-candles, ((20,000 + 9,600 lumens) ÷ 1,200 ÷ 2 = 12.3 foot-candles), which is plenty for a social event such as a dinner or dance party. (In fact, this is exactly how the layering design method and preset dimming work.)

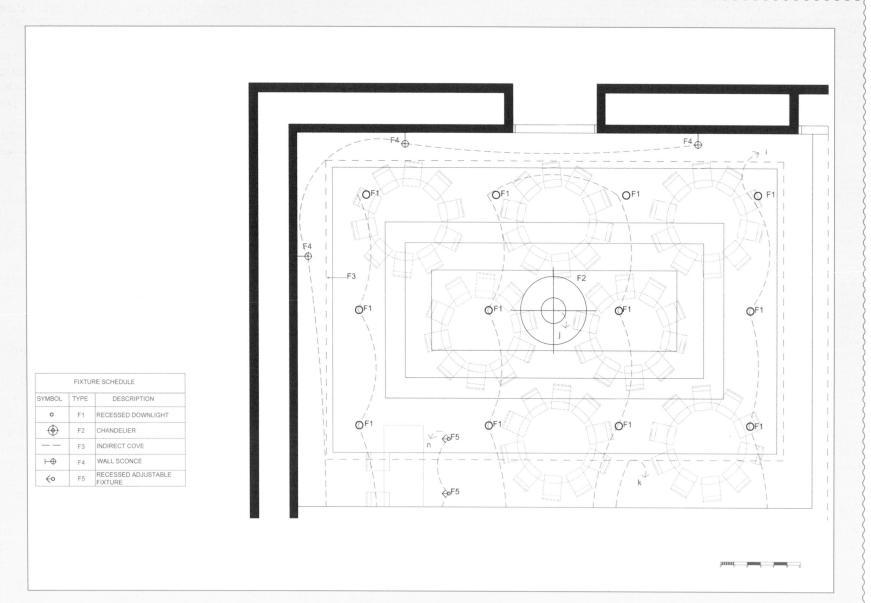

Fig. 8.7 Ballroom Example

FIXTURE SCHEDULE

SYMBOL	TYPE	DESCRIPTION
o	F1	RECESSED DOWNLIGHT
⊕	F2	CHANDELIER
— —	F3	INDIRECT COVE
⊦⊕	F4	WALL SCONCE
⊰o	F5	RECESSED ADJUSTABLE FIXTURE

Table 8.1 Watts Per Square Foot Chart

Average light level desired and typical application*	Watts per square foot of fluorescent, compact fluorescent, or HID lamps	Watts per square foot of incandescent or halogen lamps
2.5–5.0 fc Hotel corridors, stair towers	0.1–0.2	0.3–0.7
5–10 fc Office corridors, parking garages, theaters (house lights)	0.2–0.4	0.7–1.0
10–20 fc Building lobbies, waiting areas, elevator lobbies, malls, hotel function spaces, school corridors	0.4–0.8	1.0–2.0
20–50 fc Office areas, classrooms, hold rooms, lecture halls, conference rooms, ambient retail lighting, industrial workshops, gyms	0.8–1.2	Not recommended*
50–100 fc Grocery stores, big box retail stores, laboratories, work areas, sports courts (not professional)	1.2–2.0	Not recommended*

*Note: These levels are for general or ambient lighting only. It is not good practice to produce high levels of general light using halogen sources. However, you can use halogen sources for accent lighting in these space types.

Unfortunately, this basic formula does not consider the efficiency of the fixture, the geometry of the room, or the finishes of the ceiling, walls, and floor. To make this more accurate, there are two factors that are added to it. First, a Coefficient of Utilization (CU) is included, which takes into consideration how the fixture and room will reduce the number of lumens hitting the work plane. The CU can typically be found on the fixture manufacturer's data sheets. To determine the CU, the Room Cavity Ratio needs to be determined, and the reflectance of the room's surfaces must be understood. Second, as discussed earlier in the chapter, a light loss factor (LLF) is added so that the result represents a maintained value. Now the formula looks like this:

$$\text{foot-candles} = \frac{\text{total lumens} \times \text{CU} \times \text{LLF}}{\text{area}}$$

The Illuminating Engineering Society of North America (IESNA) offers classes that teach the lumen method, or you can teach yourself from the *IESNA Lighting Handbook*.

Although this method can be completed by hand, it is not typical for architects and interior designers to have this level of expertise. To simplify this method for designers, the CU and LLF are removed and the total lumens are simply cut in half. As you can imagine, this is not as accurate, but it does give designers enough information to develop a basic lighting plan.

This method also requires that the rules listed under the watts-per-square-foot method be followed in accord with the kind of lighting and rooms that it will work with. It is based on this principle:

1. Divide the total number of initial lumens generated by the lamps by the area of the space.
2. Divide the result by two to obtain the approximate average light level in the room.

You can reverse the process if you want to find out how many lumens are needed to achieve a desired light level:

1. Multiply the desired light level by two.
2. Multiply the result by the area of the room to obtain the total number of lumens needed from all lamps.
3. Divide the total lumens by the rated initial lumens of the lamp you wish to use to find how many lamps you need.

Let's use the same classroom in Example #1 to test the method (see Example #3). The very simple lumen method works especially well in rooms with several types of lighting systems. For instance, take a look at a hotel ballroom that has downlights, a chandelier, and a fluorescent cove light. See Example #4.

A Very Simple Point Method

In this method, you need to know the distance of a display light from the object being displayed. It works with individual spotlights only; it does not work for wallwashing or other forms of highlighting.

1. Take the distance from the light to the object and square it.
2. Multiply by the desired light level (20–50 foot-candles for homes, hotels, and restaurants; up to 250 foot-candles for feature displays in stores and lobbies) to obtain the approximate candlepower.

LAMP PERFORMANCE DATA

All data was calculated from each lamp manufacturer's published data and is subject to normal lamp variations. Maximum footcandle is usually at the aiming point, but not always on wider spread lamps. Lamp data supplied by manufacturers is approximate, and individual lamp performance may vary.

ACCENT LIGHTING ANGLE PERFORMANCE DATA

DISTANCE LAMP TO LIGHTED SURFACE   2 FEET   4 FEET

DISTANCE DOWN TO AIMING POINT   V1 (FT) 2   V2 (FT) 7

Lamp No.	Watts	Type	MFG.	Beam Width (°) to 50% MBCP	MBCP	Aiming Angle 45° FT-CANDLES	Beam Length	Width	Aiming Angle 60° FT-CANDLES	Beam Length	Width
MR-16											
EZX	20	VNSP	GE	7	8200	725	0.5	0.3	64	2.0	1.0
EZY	20	VNSP	GE	7	13100	1158	0.5	0.3	102	2.0	1.0
ESX	20	NSP	GE/SY/PH	15	3600	318	1.1	0.7	28	4.4	2.1
BAB	20	FL	GE/SY/PH	40	525	46	3.4	2.1	4	19.3	5.8
EYS	42	SP	GE	20	2400	212	1.5	1.0	19	6.2	2.8
EXT	50	NSP	GE/SY/PH	13	10200	902	0.9	0.6	80	3.8	1.8
EXZ	50	NFL	GE/SY/PH	26	3400	301	2.0	1.3	27	8.8	3.7
EXN	50	FL	GE/SY/PH	40	1850	164	3.4	2.1	14	19.3	5.8
EYJ	71/65	MFL	GE/SY	24	4900	433	1.8	1.2	38	7.9	3.4
EYC	71/65/75	FL	GE/SY/PH	36	2100	186	2.9	1.8	16	15.2	5.2
AR-70											
20AR70/8/SP	20	SP	SY	8	7000	619	0.6	0.4	55	2.3	1.1
20AR70/25/FL	20	FL	SY	25	850	75	1.9	1.3	7	8.3	3.5
50AR70/8/SP	50	SP	SY	8	15000	1326	0.6	0.4	117	2.3	1.1
50AR70/25/FL	50	FL	SY	25	2000	177	1.9	1.3	16	8.3	3.5

LOCATION OF ACCENT LUMINAIRE TO PROVIDE AIMING PT. 5.5' ABOVE THE FLOOR

Clg. Ht. (ft)	60° Aiming Angle Out (H)	60° Aiming Angle Down (V2)	45° Aiming Angle Out (H)	45° Aiming Angle Down (V1)
8	1.5	2.5	2.5	2.5
9	2.0	3.5	3.5	3.5
10	2.5	4.5	4.5	4.5

NOTES

1 IES indicates 5.5' above the floor is an ideal viewing height.

2 Tested to current IES and NEMA standards under stabilized laboratory conditions. Various operating factors can cause differences between laboratory data and actual field measurements. Dimensions and specifications are based on the most current available data and are subject to change without notice.

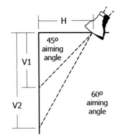

Formula for other distances and aiming angles.

$$fc = \frac{MBCP \times Cos^3 \text{ (aiming angle)}}{H^2 \text{ (distance from wall squared)}}$$

Aiming angle	Cos³	Feet out from wall (H) 6	7	8	9	10
		Feet **down** from ceiling (V)				
45°	.354	6	7	8	9	10
50°	.266	7	8	10	11	12
55°	.189	9	10	11	13	14
60°	.125	10	12	14	16	17
65°	.076	13	15	18	19	21
70°	.040	17	19	22	25	28
75°	.017	22	26	30	34	37

Fig. 8.8 Accent Lighting Lamp Guide

For instance, you wish to light a painting in a living room and you choose 50 foot-candles as the appropriate light level. Given the cathedral-style ceiling, you measure the light to be 20 feet from the painting.

Square this distance:

$$20 \times 20 = 400$$

Multiply by the desired foot-candle level to obtain the intensity of the light source required:

$$(400 \times 50 = 20,000 \text{ candlepower})$$

A lamp catalog (see Table 8.2) lists several 20,000-candlepower projector lamps.

The beam spread is a little harder to decide. This is where experience and a lamp guide come in handy. The PAR38 illuminates a circle about 4-1/2 feet in diameter, the halogen PAR36 illuminates about 2-3/4 feet, and the incandescent PAR36 illuminates about 1-3/4 feet. (All of these values were taken from the lamp guide printed in a major luminaire catalog.) You will choose the actual lamp based on the size of the picture. Many manufacturers provide accent lighting performance data for a variety

Table 8.2 Lamp Candlepower Comparison

Lamp	Candlepower	Beam
60-watt PAR38 IR line voltage spot	20,000	10 degrees
35-watt PAR36 halogen low-voltage spot	20,000	8 degrees
50-watt PAR36 incandescent low-voltage very narrow spot	19,000	6 degrees

of lamps installed within a specific luminaire (see Fig. 8.8), making it easier to select the appropriate lamp for the application.

Making the Leap to Computer Calculations

Using computers to predict lighting levels and to render the lighting effects in rooms has historically been performed by engineers and lighting specialists. However, with the rapid acceleration of 3-D computer technology for buildings, many architects and designers are learning everyday design skills for which detailed lighting and daylighting analysis is an optional extension. Refer to Appendix A for additional information about lighting software.

Chapter 9 QUALITY OF LIGHT

It should be obvious to anyone concerned with lighting design that inherent aesthetic and psychological factors are of great importance to the success of lighting solutions. One can frequently observe well-designed spaces that have been made unsatisfying and unsuccessful with a poor lighting solution. Conversely, ordinary spaces can be made quite satisfying and successful through creative lighting solutions. The aesthetic and psychological factors that must be considered in a complete approach to lighting design are, by their nature, intangible and difficult to categorize. Without exploring the depths of aesthetic and spatial theory, the following factors identify those intangible qualities that are necessary considerations in the lighting design process.

SCULPTURAL QUALITY

The majority of spaces in which we live and work are rectangular in plan and section and have normal ceiling heights. Unless spaces of this kind are spatially modified through unique furnishings or equipment, the value of enhancing their sculptural quality through lighting techniques is questionable. But spaces that have intrinsic sculptural quality, such as a sensuous curved wall, a polygonal shape, or an arched or domed ceiling (see Figs. 9.1–9.3), demand lighting design solutions that enhance their unique shapes. Creating a gradation of light on a curved surface, using shade and shadow to articulate complex angular relationships, and dramatically displaying a collection of medieval armor are just a few examples of the kinds of solutions sought for these special spaces. Many techniques are available to the lighting designer; using them to advantage or enhancing spatial quality is one of the greatest challenges to the designer's creativity.

COLOR AND MATERIALS

As discussed in Chapter 3, white light is made up of all the wavelengths from the visible spectrum. Artificial light sources contain different levels of the various wavelengths, which can be represented graphically on a spectral power distribution chart.

As shown in Figs. 9.4–9.7, lights sources vary greatly and are not nearly as wavelength saturated as natural light. The color and quality of the light source can vastly change how a material or an object is perceived.

In addition to the actual light source, the physical property of the object(s) being illuminated can modify how it is viewed by the occupants. This relationship between the light source and the material of the object is an important part of lighting design. There are two important factors to consider: reflectance and transmittance.

Reflectance

The reflectance of a material represents the percentage of light that reflects or bounces off its surface. Both the quantity of light the material will reflect based on its color and the way in which the light is distributed after it hits the surface can vary. If the material is glossy, the beam of light will remain as a ray and reflect back into the space at the same angle as it hit the surface. This can create unwanted reflected glare, but if done intentionally, can create sparkle and drama as shown in Fig. 9.8. If the material is matte or textured, the light will be scattered in many directions. Fig. 9.9 shows how a wood wall can be softly lighted to create a colorful backdrop.

Transmittance

The transmittance of a material characterizes how much light will travel through the material. The finish and texture of that material will also impact what the light will look like after it has passed through the material. If a material is transparent, like clear glass or plastic, the shape of the beam is not altered but only reduced based on the color or the coating applied to the material. Often glass or plastic lenses are clear, but contain a texture to scatter and refract the light. This will not only reduce the quantity of light on the opposite side, but also spread the light. Translucent materials are diffuse and distribute the beam of light uniformly. Frequently, diffuse materials absorb a large quantity of light, allowing the material to appear as if it is glowing, as illustrated in Fig. 9.10.

How an object is interpreted is also affected by its surroundings. Specific objects are visible because they are in contrast to their environment. This could be provided by a variation of color, texture, or light level. High-contrast lighting provides drama and interest, but is usually limited to spaces where the user is there for a limited period of time and the tasks are not visually critical. In spaces where the occupants spend an extended amount of time, and the tasks are more visually intense, high-contrast lighting can create glare and/or visual distraction that causes discomfort and eye strain.

In addition to glare created by too much contrast on a surface, glare can also be attributed to having too much light in a space. This is normally caused by direct sunlight and can be reduced by providing interior or exterior shading as addressed in Chapter 4.

Fig. 9.1 Sculptural Ceiling Example *(Photograph: Kuda Photography.)*

Fig. 9.2 Polygonal Shaped Ceiling Example *(Courtesy of National Kitchen & Bath Association. Designed by NKBA Member Elina Katsioula-Beall, CKD. Photograph: Suki Medencevic.)*

Fig. 9.3 Curving Bar and Domed Ceiling Example *(Photograph: Kuda Photography.)*

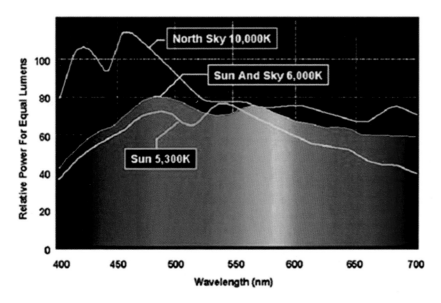

Fig. 9.4 Daylight Spectral Power Distribution
(Courtesy of General Electric Company.)

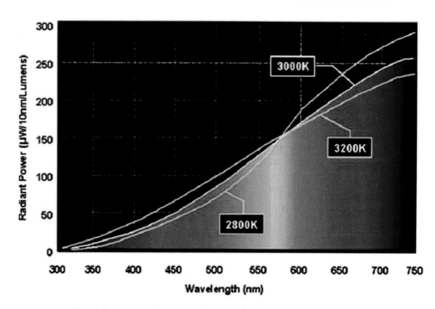

Fig. 9.5 Incandescent Spectral Power Distribution
(Courtesy of General Electric Company.)

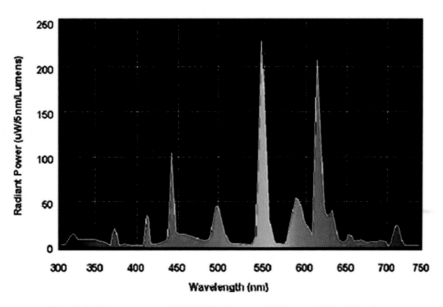

Fig. 9.6 Fluorescent (3500 K) Spectral Power Distribution
(Courtesy of General Electric Company.)

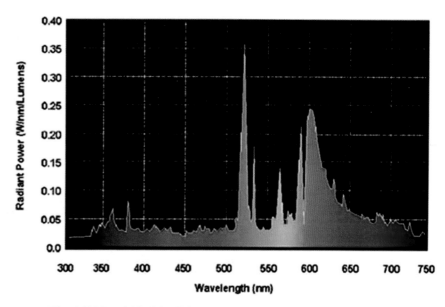

Fig. 9.7 Metal Halide (3000 K) Spectral Power Distribution
(Courtesy of General Electric Company.)

Fig. 9.8 Example of a Reflective Surface Lighted (*Photograph: Kuda Photography.*)

Fig. 9.9 Example of a Matte Surface Lighted

Fig. 9.10 Example of a Translucent Glass Wall
(Photograph: Kuda Photography.)

While eye-level glow is often a desirable quality, glare can also be problematic when a light source is within the normal line of sight. This can be avoided by selecting luminaires that shield the lamps, or provide adequate cutoff, so that the lamp is not visible from the typical seated or standing position required for a specific task.

SIZE AND SCALE

The size and scale of luminaires are important design factors for all spaces. What is appropriate for a living room or a private office is not appropriate for a large and grand lobby or an auditorium. Ceiling height is of particular concern for lighting, where unusually tall spaces cannot rely on standard recessed or surface-mounted luminaires, as is so common with more conventional 8'–10' ceiling heights. The special qualities of residential spaces, in which familiarity and intimacy are normal expectations, have a great deal to do with the traditions of residential scale.

DESIGN QUALITY

The design quality is the most elusive element of these aesthetic and psychological factors. Social norms and expectations play a role in lighting design solutions. Portable lighting (floor and table lamps) is commonplace and appropriate in residential interiors, while their widespread use in nonresidential settings often seems out-of-place and is impractical. Highlighting a decorative wall treatment or richly textured drapery can make the difference in creating a room that is aesthetically satisfying. In general, giving value and paying attention to how a space feels when making lighting design decisions is rewarded with successful lighting design results. Artfulness in lighting primarily means creating perceptible spatial quality. Certain kinds of spaces, such as churches, nightclubs, restaurants and grand reception rooms, seem to demand a special kind of atmosphere, much of which can be created with lighting. However, many less obvious spaces, such as living rooms and conference rooms, similarly benefit from thoughtful and creative lighting. To aid in accomplishing satisfying spatial quality when making lighting design decisions, keep in mind the basic issues presented in this chapter.

Chapter 10 LIGHTING DESIGN APPROACH

The preceding chapters provided an overview of the technical and operational factors involved in lighting design. Intelligently integrating those factors to achieve successful solutions is the heart of good lighting design. When faced with a lighting design problem, one could simply try a variety of hit-or-miss solutions in a trial-and-error approach, but this is clearly not an organized procedure. As is true of any design problem, a rational, efficient, and professional approach to problem solving produces consistently good lighting design. What follows is a prescribed methodology that ensures good-quality, professional results for the vast majority of lighting design problems.

Good lighting design begins with identifying and solving visual functions and task-oriented issues. Contrary to the view of some in the design fields, lighting design is not an art. That view of lighting design implies a mystique connected to creating good lighting. But that mystique does not exist. Good lighting design can and ideally should be artful, in the same way that all design processes involve creative thinking and solutions. Experienced lighting designers bring their richness of background to successfully enhance a room's ambience and spatial character.

Before beginning a lighting design, it is generally a good idea to review and write the criteria to which your design applies. These criteria should include everything you expect from the design, both objective and subjective. The following steps address the basic lighting criteria to meet in a professional design.

SEQUENTIAL STEPS TO SUCCESSFUL LIGHTING DESIGN SOLUTIONS

Step One: Describe

Design Concept

The lighting should look integral to the design of the space and should not appear to be an afterthought. Because of this, the first step in developing the criteria for the lighting design is to review the overall design concept for the space and/or project.

Within this review, it is also important to recognize the environmental feel and ambience that is desired. Most rooms and spaces have a desired ambience, such as a living room that should be warm and inviting, an executive office that expresses competence and success, a healthcare setting that asserts efficiency and professionalism, and a high end hotel lobby that represents luxury. The desired ambience is usually an amalgam of the client's or user's wishes and the designer's vision of the space. Translating that desired ambience in lighting design terms is critical to successful lighting solutions.

This should include describing the general appearance of the light and the psychological effect it will have on the users. This preliminary evaluation will ensure that the future choices made about lighting will help reinforce the early programmatic decisions. Ideally, this assessment should occur during the beginning stages of the design process.

Quality of Light

Additionally, at this point it is a good time to consider more specifics about the quality of the illumination. This does not refer to selecting a light source or a fixture, but rather to thinking about what the lighting should achieve in a space and recognizing what is most important at the beginning. Below is a list of items that should be considered:

*   Color quality and appearance—what should the color temperature and color rendering index be?
*   Intensity of the light—is the space generally a darkened or bright environment?
*   Uniformity—should the lighting be high or low contrast?
*   Control and flexibility—are there multiple uses for the space that have different lighting requirements?
*   Efficiency—does the client have specific energy goals that need to be considered?

Architectural Conditions and Constraints

Finally, within this step it is important to understand the architectural conditions and possible constraints that will influence and potentially limit many of the decisions that follow. The two conditions that most frequently affect lighting design are window size and location and the availability of plenum space. It is not uncommon for the structural system and/or its materials, ceiling heights, partition construction and/or materials, ceiling systems and their materials, and finish materials to have significant influence on lighting solutions.

In the case of an existing building, all of these factors must be surveyed and recorded. Personal observation should be the point of beginning. As-built drawings, when available, can also be invaluable. Discussions with building managers and maintenance personnel usually elicit firsthand knowledge of the property's problems and eccentricities. Regardless of the information-gathering methods used, record the data in an organized manner so it will be of optimum use later in the lighting design process.

With new buildings still in the design phase, particularly when lighting design is given appropriate consideration early in the design process, lighting selections may actually influence building design decisions and improve the finished result. Among the many positive possibilities when lighting factors are taken into account early in the building design process are ceiling systems; the routing of pipes, ducts, and conduits in plenum spaces; and the accommodating of task/ambient lighting systems.

Step Two: Layer

The next step is to evaluate the layers of lighting as described in Chapter 2. Recording the various layers in written form is beneficial as it documents these items early during the design process. This can then be a reference as the design is further developed to make certain that nothing is overlooked.

It may also be helpful to graphically illustrate the layers of lighting in plan and elevation. Visually showing the layers helps identify lighting opportunities and how the layers may overlap.

Step Three: Select

The first two steps have provided enough background information so that a designer can now begin selecting the appropriate light sources and luminaires for the space that will meet the criteria established.

Light Source Selection

Chapters 3 and 5 go into detail about the qualities and specifics of the most common light sources and should be used as a reference when deciding what is appropriate for the project. There are many factors to consider when making these selections, and the goals and objectives of the lighting design will help determine what takes precedence. For example, the color quality of a light source in a gallery is a critical factor; in contrast, energy efficiency may take the lead in an office space.

It is not uncommon for lamp selection criteria to be the dominant factor in luminaire selection when the lamp qualities are critical for economic, code, or color factors. In the great majority of cases, luminaire and lamp selection is an interactive process in which the selection factors for both are considered as a unit.

Luminaire Selection

Achieving the designer's aesthetic vision can involve techniques ranging from the simple to the complex, and the luminaire selection must support the intended approach. While the lighting design professional may have the knowledge and skill to use all of the available technology and techniques, the person with the overall design responsibility must articulately direct that professional to the desired aesthetic result.

The location of the light source is critical. Should light come from above, at eye level, or from below? Should the light be directed or diffuse? Should the light source be visible or hidden? Refer to steps one and two to help make these choices based on the preliminary criteria established.

In addition, the architectural conditions and constraints described in Step 1 often affect these decisions due to lack of plenum space, available ceiling height, or difficulty in getting power to particular locations. In the case studies that appear in Chapters 12 through 19, the details of the architectural conditions are described, and the lighting systems selected for those studies take specific conditions into account.

The details of luminaire construction, shape, and dimension must produce the desired direction and concentration of light as well as fit the details of construction type and the materials with which they are to be integrated. Aesthetic compatibility often plays a major role in luminaire selection; shape, style, materials, and color must integrate with architectural quality as well as the details of interior finishes and furnishings.

Step Four: Coordinate

In this final step, the designer gathers all of the design criteria established in the previous steps and coordinates those items with the team to ensure that the lighting is designed and installed to meet all applicable codes and, ultimately, the clients' needs and expectations.

Quantity of Illumination

Within Chapter 8, lighting calculations and required levels of illumination are discussed in detail, and this information can be used to establish the appropriate level for your spaces.

Once the fixture styles are selected and the required illumination level is determined, developing accurate luminaire placement is the next step. Often, several luminaire-lamp combinations are considered, so the number of luminaires will vary with the lumen output of each combination. In the great majority of cases in which luminaires are placed in, on, or suspended from the ceiling, they should be placed in an orderly pattern, creating an obvious visual geometry. Occasionally, in the case of irregularly shaped spaces or skewed furniture placement, a free-form or non-geometric ceiling pattern is appropriate. As discussed in Chapter 8, for some generic situations, such as classrooms, training rooms, and large office spaces, rule-of-thumb formulas for the spacing of standard luminaires produce commonly accepted levels of general illumination for the intended room function. For most situations, consider each lighting design problem as an individual case and develop solutions specific to it.

Control Needs

This step in the lighting design process is primarily one of logic and common sense. User traffic paths, room usage, and user convenience should be your guides to good switching and control systems. Repeated experience and familiarity with controls technology create workable and user-satisfying solutions. Take into account the opportunities conveyed by the most recent developments in controls that automate energy management or user convenience functions. Refer to Chapter 7 for additional information.

Code Requirements

Finally, to ensure that the lighting meets all safety, accessibility, and energy requirements, there are five types of codes and similar regulations that affect building lighting:

1. *Electric codes* are designed to assure that buildings are safe. These codes are enforced by building inspectors. The National Electric Code (NFPA 70) is used throughout the United States except in a few cities where local codes are used. The NEC has the following major effects on lighting:

   - It requires that electric wiring to lighting is safe.
   - It requires that luminaires are listed for the application. *Listed* means tested and labeled by a testing company such as Underwriters Laboratories (UL).
   - It specifies and limits where lights can be placed in residences, especially in closets and around pools, spas, fountains, hydro-massage therapy tubs, and other water appliances.
   - It limits lighting in industrial applications and other places where explosive vapors or other atmospheric considerations exist.
   - It limits the use of high-voltage lighting, especially in homes.
   - It restricts the use of low-voltage lighting systems, especially those with exposed cables and rods.
   - It restricts the use of track lighting.

2. *Building codes* are designed to ensure that buildings are structurally safe. Their primary impact on lighting is that they require emergency lighting in commercial and institutional buildings to permit safe egress in the event of an emergency.
3. *Energy codes* are designed to ensure that buildings use a minimum of energy to operate. In general, energy codes have less impact on residential lighting but often place significant power restrictions on nonresidential projects (see Appendix B).
4. *Accessibility codes* are designed to ensure that buildings can be used by all persons, including those with disabilities and mobility problems associated with aging. The Americans with Disabilities Act (ADA) requires sconces or other wall-mounted lighting equipment along the path of egress to project less than 4" from the wall if mounted below 80" or above 15" from the floor.
5. *Health codes* are required by some states in hospitals and nursing homes to provide minimum light levels at certain locations. Another type of law requires a protective lens or other covering for lighting in commercial kitchens and cafeteria food service areas.

To Summarize the Four-Step Process:

1. DESCRIBE

   - Overall Design Concept and Environmental Ambience
   - Quality of Light
   - Architectural Conditions and Constraints

2. LAYER

   - Illustrate Focal, Task, Daylight, Decorative, and Ambient Lighting Needs

3. SELECT

   - Light Source
   - Luminaire

4. COORDINATE

   - Quantity of Illumination
   - Control Needs
   - Code Requirements

To assist with this process, a Lighting Design Criteria Matrix has been developed for this publication so that designers can fully study and evaluate the lighting design throughout the design process (see Table 10.1). This matrix is broken into four major headings, coinciding with the four steps discussed above. The matrix can be used by designers to develop lighting design strategies on their own. In addition, it can be used as a tool to clearly illustrate and document the goals of a lighting designer.

One final step in the overall design process is not described in the chart. That is because it occurs long after the first four steps are accomplished. How does a designer know if his or her design efforts are successful? This applies to every aspect of architectural and interior design. Do the results of the finished project properly serve the users' needs? Do the space planning adjacencies work well? Do materials and finishes serve their intended function and wear well? Were furnishings properly selected for ergonomic comfort? Are the lighting design solutions functional, comfortable, and aesthetically pleasing?

Over the past two to three decades, a process called *post-occupancy evaluation* (POE) has been developed to tell designers whether or not what they thought would work well actually does. The POE concept is quite simple: Visit the completed project after it has been in use for some time and, through observation and discussion with its users, find out what works well and what doesn't. The POE process has two purposes for the lighting designer: first, to adjust what doesn't work well so it works better; and second, to learn from experience so successful elements can be repeated or enhanced and, obviously, to avoid or correct techniques that are not successful or workable. Particularly for lighting design solutions, the POE process is valuable because light itself is essentially intangible; the result cannot be touched but only experienced. A fair amount has been written about POE; this book's bibliography will lead you to learn more about its techniques and uses.

Now it is time to get to work and put this methodology to good use. Chapters 12–18 focus on the typical lighting design problems encountered in each of the five major building use types that employ intensive use of lighting design and technology. The case studies present specific lighting design solutions, a rationale for each solution, and the design and construction details required to achieve the solutions.

As is true in all design experience, there are no "correct" or "right" or "perfect" solutions to lighting design problems. In most cases several, and often many, solutions can be successful. The designer should strive for workable solutions that meet the functional, aesthetic, and psychological needs of clients and users.

Table 10.1 Lighting Design Criteria Matrix

Project: ABC Company Headquarters

| Space | STEP ONE: Describe | | | STEP TWO: Layer | | | | |
	Overall Design Concept & Environmental Ambience	Quality of Light	Architectural Conditions and Constraints	Focal (Consider Vertical Surfaces)	Task	Daylight (Harvest and/or Control?)	Decorative (What Styles and Type?)	Ambient
Reception	- Residential feel but still professional and modern - Warm and welcoming	- Warm, soft light - Overall bright feeling, with focus on entry and artwork - Presence at night when closed	- Entry provided by building - Need to incorporate some acoustical ceiling tile - Mechanical equipment above ceiling	- Signage behind desk - Artwork in seating area on east and south wall	- Receptionist's desk—typing, reading, filing, etc. - Light reading by guests	- None available	- Consider table lamps - Simple, modern style	- For basic movement through space
Private Office	- Crisp, clean - Encourage productivity - Personalization	- White, diffuse light - Uniform, bright, focus on artwork, but not too dramatic - Efficiency and automatic controls important	- Acoustical ceiling tile - Large window beside desk puts occupant in silhouette	- Artwork on west and south wall	- Task lighting required on both front and back work surfaces	- Large window on east wall, provide shade and daylight harvesting	- None required	- To supplement task as needed
Executive Office	- Crisp, clean, higher-end than standard office - More residential feel than standard office - Personalization	- Bright, white light - Uniform at tasks, but needs to highlight materials and art - Personal control important, efficiency less critical	- Large window - Preferred GWB ceiling	- Artwork on west and north wall	- Task lighting required on both front and back work surfaces - Light reading by guests	- Large window on east wall, provide shade and daylight harvesting	- Consider table lamps - Simple modern style	- To supplement task as needed
Conference Room	- Professional and modern but can be used for informal or social setting	- Combination of warm and brighter white light to address multiple uses - Flexibility and control important	- Flexibility required for multiple uses of space - Large window requires black-out shades for AV presentation	- Presentation wall - Fabric pin-up wall - Credenza	- Table - Presentation wall	- Large window on east wall, provide shading	- Decorative pendants over table - Simple, modern style	- To supplement task as needed
Open Office	- Crisp, clean - Encourage productivity - Not too corporate, but not too playful	- White, diffuse light - Uniform, bright, focus on graphics but not dramatic - Efficiency and automatic controls important	- Acoustical ceiling tile - Large window	- Large graphic along east wall	- Work surfaces	- Large window on west wall, provide shade and daylight harvesting	- None required	- For basic movement through space

Project: ABC Company Headquarters					
Space	STEP THREE: Select Preferred Light Source	Possible Luminaire Types	STEP FOUR: Coordinate Light Level Required	Control Needs	Code Requirements
Reception	- LED—for focal lighting - Fluorescent—for task and ambient lighting	- Recessed fixtures for focal and ambient - Under counter fluorescent for task - Table lamps	- 30 fc for task - 10 fc for ambient	- General switch at entry - Local switch at task	- 1.1 watts/sf allowed - Emergency egress lighting
Private Office	- LED—for focal lighting - Fluorescent—for task and ambient lighting	- Recessed adjustable fixtures for focal - Linear fluorescent pendant for task/ambient at desk - Under cabinet fluorescent for task	- 50 fc for task - 20–30 fc for ambient	- Occupancy sensor - Photocell - Consider dimmer for personal control	- 1.1 watts/sf allowed
Executive Office	- LED—for focal lighting - Fluorescent—for task and ambient lighting	- Recessed fixtures for focal and ambient - Under cabinet fluorescent for task - Table lamps	- 50 fc for task - 20–30 fc for ambient	- Occupancy sensor - Photocell - Consider dimmer for personal control	- 1.1 watts/sf allowed
Conference Room	- LED—for focal lighting - Fluorescent—for task and ambient lighting	- LED direct cove for presentation wall - Recessed fixtures for focal and ambient - Decorative pendants	- 50 fc for task - 20–30 fc for ambient	- Preset dimming system - Occupancy sensor	- 1.3 watts/sf allowed - Emergency egress lighting
Open Office	- Fluorescent—for focal, task, and ambient lighting	- Fluorescent direct cove for file wall - Linear fluorescent pendants for ambient - Under cabinet fluorescent for task	- 50 fc for task - 20–30 fc for ambient	- Time-clock - Photocell	- 1.1 watts/sf allowed - Emergency egress lighting

11 DOCUMENTING LIGHTING DESIGN

To communicate the lighting design intent to others, it is important to draw lighting in a manner generally recognized by interior designers, architects, engineers, and construction trades and to understand how and why lighting is illustrated the way it is. In this chapter, specific considerations for drawing lighting are presented.

DRAWINGS AND CONTRACT DOCUMENTS

Lighting documents are part of the process of developing working drawings or contract documents, which are the drawings that tell the contractor what to build. The law regulates who can prepare contract documents. Depending on the type of project and its location, an intermediate lighting plan may be used by others. It is common for the initial lighting plan to be drawn by an architect, interior designer, or lighting designer, but the drawing is then passed along to the electrical engineer or

electrical contractor, who must add electrical circuits and other information to the drawing before it can be used for construction.

Lighting Documents

A lighting design can be indicated in a number of ways:

- On the architect or interior designer's plans: The architect or interior designer develops plan drawings and related sections and details. Many of these drawings will help illustrate the intent of the lighting design. Lighting locations, with dimensions, are typically indicated on floor plans and/or reflected ceiling plans. Fixture size, specific mounting information and lighting's relationship to other architectural elements are often shown in sections and details.
- On the electrical plans: Typically developed by an electrical engineer, or contractor, the electrical plans use an architectural base plan (see the following section)

and illustrate electrical information. In addition to lighting, information presented on such plans includes:

- Lighting controls, such as switches and dimmers
- Receptacles, connections to equipment, location of panel boards, and other electrical information
- Telephone jacks, data outlets, fire alarm devices, and other data signaling and communications systems

In a complex building, electrical plans are often separated into lighting plans, power plans, and signal plans as well as legend sheets, detail sheets, and other drawings.

Base Plans

Floor Plans

A lighting design generally begins when the architect or interior designer develops a floor plan (or plans) for a building. The floor plan indicates the footprint of the building; the locations of walls, doors, and windows; and other details that aid in developing lighting drawings. Floor plans especially must be consulted for lighting that is not mounted to the ceiling, such as wall sconces, table and floor lamps, undercabinet lights, and lighting in bookcases, cabinets, and other built-in features.

Floor plans are useful as base plans because they permit lighting to be indicated with respect to walls, furniture, and other details that show up best on plan drawings. See Fig. 11.1 for a typical floor plan with furniture.

Reflected Ceiling Plans

Reflected ceiling plans are used as the base drawing for most lighting plans because lighting is usually mounted on ceilings. Ceiling elements such as HVAC diffusers and grilles, sprinkler heads, and speakers are extremely important for coordination purposes. For complex ceilings with vaults or coffers, the reflected ceiling plan provides critical dimensions (see Fig. 11.2).

Combined Ceiling/Floor Plans

CAD drawings make it especially easy to create custom base plans that incorporate elements of both floor and reflected ceilings plans, as shown in Fig. 11.3. Based on the content of the preceding chapters, it is clear that lighting is very three-dimensional and often relates to specific elements in the space. Because of this, it is important to consider all planes, not just the ceiling where lights are frequently mounted. This

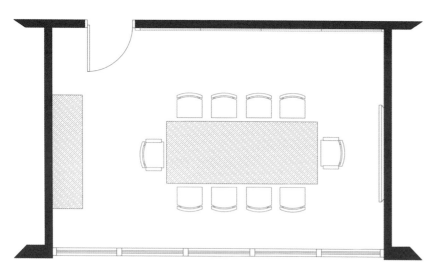

Fig. 11.1 Floor Plan Example

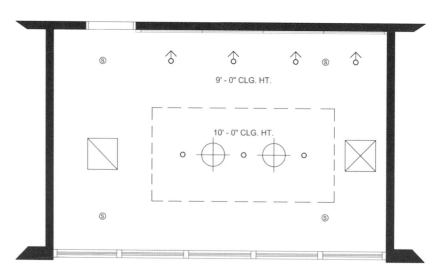

Fig. 11.2 Reflected Ceiling Plan Example

is particularly true when designing spaces with complex layers of light. For instance, in a hotel lobby it may be desirable to have downlights and chandeliers on the ceiling, wall sconces, table and floor lamps, desk lamps, and undercabinet lights, all in the same space. A base drawing showing ceiling details plus a furniture and casework plan makes it easier to show the various kinds of lighting equipment in the right location. Using different layer colors helps to differentiate ceiling elements from floor plan elements, making it easier to draw and check your work.

Creating a Lighting Plan

A lighting plan begins with a base drawing that is usually made less obvious using lighter lines than the lighting symbols.

Lighting Symbols

Luminaires and other lighting equipment are generally indicated by symbols. This approach dates to manual drafting. Symbols indicate the type of luminaire by generic type as shown in Fig. 11.4.

Historically, symbols were not drawn to scale and were often much larger so they could be easily seen on the plan. However, with the use of CAD, it is more

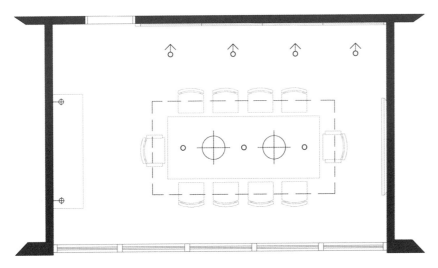

Fig. 11.3 Combined Ceiling/Floor Plan Typically Used for Lighting Plans

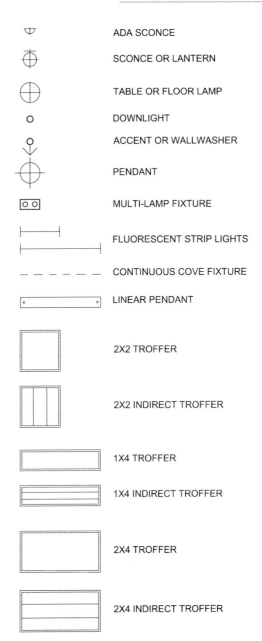

	ADA SCONCE
	SCONCE OR LANTERN
	TABLE OR FLOOR LAMP
	DOWNLIGHT
	ACCENT OR WALLWASHER
	PENDANT
	MULTI-LAMP FIXTURE
	FLUORESCENT STRIP LIGHTS
	CONTINUOUS COVE FIXTURE
	LINEAR PENDANT
	2X2 TROFFER
	2X2 INDIRECT TROFFER
	1X4 TROFFER
	1X4 INDIRECT TROFFER
	2X4 TROFFER
	2X4 INDIRECT TROFFER

Fig. 11.4 Lighting Symbols

common now to scale the symbols. This gives the designer the opportunity to see potential interferences and aesthetic effects. It is smart to take full advantage of layer colors and plotting line weights so the smaller symbols are easily seen as lighting.

Lighting Tags

A lighting tag is an identifier that describes the specific characteristics of luminaires on the plans. The tag is drawn adjacent to a specific luminaire or group of similar luminaires. See Fig. 11.5 for a lighting plan with luminaire symbols and tags. Tag identifiers can be alphabetical (A, B, etc.) or alphanumeric (A1, F1a, etc.) Some tags also show the luminaire type or wattage.

Luminaire tags are generally listed in alphabetic or numeric order, with the most common luminaire on the project being type A, the next most common type B, and so on. On plans for complex projects like hospitals, luminaire types that are identical except for some small detail (such as a different number of lamps) would show as subtypes such as AA, AB, and so on. Note that this system is not hard and fast; the important point is for the tag to match the definition on the lighting schedule.

More recently, and especially because of CAD, tags can be given greater meaning. In the following system, tags contain a substantial amount of information without becoming cumbersome.

F—Fluorescent or compact fluorescent lamp luminaires
A—Incandescent lamp luminaires
H—HID luminaires
L—LED luminaires
N—Neon or cold cathode lighting systems
X—Exit signs
FX—Exterior fluorescent or compact fluorescent luminaires
AX—Exterior incandescent luminaires
HX—Exterior HID luminaires
LX—LED luminaires

This system makes it easy to add and define new families. An exterior exit sign (rare but possible) might be XX1. Sometimes types D are added for decorative chandeliers and lamps; creativity is fine as long as the tags match the lighting schedule.

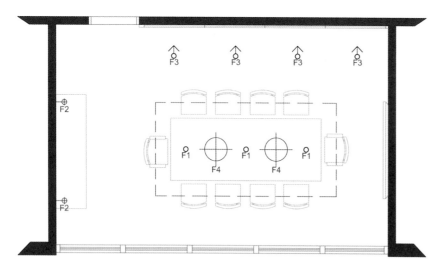

Fig. 11.5 Lighting Plan Example

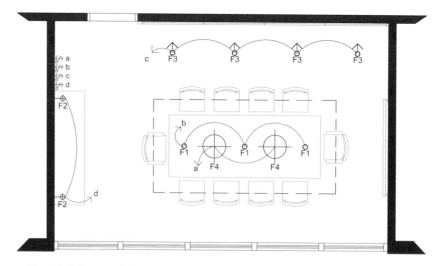

Fig. 11.6 Control Zones Depicted by Connecting Lights with Lines

Control Zones

Illustrating control zones accomplishes two purposes:

1. The designer can communicate the intended switching or dimming zones by connecting lighting groups with lines (see Fig. 11.6) or by indicating common control points by letters (see Fig. 11.7).
2. The designer can indicate how the lighting is to be wired by showing specific connections to control devices, such as dimmers and switches.

Here is where the major difference between lighting design and electrical engineering must be understood. A lighting design does not have to indicate the exact wiring. The lighting designer clearly shows the desired switching or dimming zones but leaves the details of wiring, such as the number of circuits and the specific wiring between devices, to the engineer or contractor. An engineer's or contractor's electrical drawing must illustrate the circuits, wiring, and so on for the design to be constructed.

Switching and Dimming

Switches and dimmers are represented by symbols on the plan. See Fig. 11.8 for conventional symbols. A switch is usually indicated by a standard symbol, which may have subscript modifiers. Dimmers and switches should be shown on the drawings at the intended location. In addition, their connection to the lights being controlled should be illustrated by a line or other obvious means as described earlier.

Details

Lighting details indicate how specific luminaires are to be installed in unusual mounting conditions. The main lighting plan should refer to the details, which may be included on the lighting plan sheet, on a separate drawing containing mostly details, or bound into a project book or manual. See Fig. 11.9 for a few common lighting details.

Lighting Legends and Schedules

Most lighting drawings include a legend and/or a schedule. The legend always appears on the drawings; a schedule may appear on the drawings or be included in a separate project book or manual. In some cases, the legend and schedule are combined.

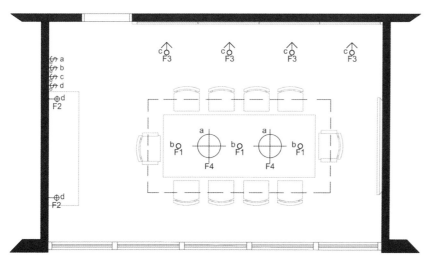

Fig. 11.7 Control Zones Depicted by Letters

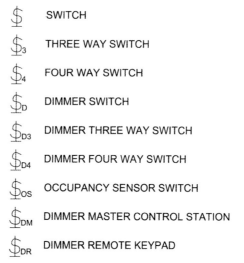

Fig. 11.8 Control Symbols

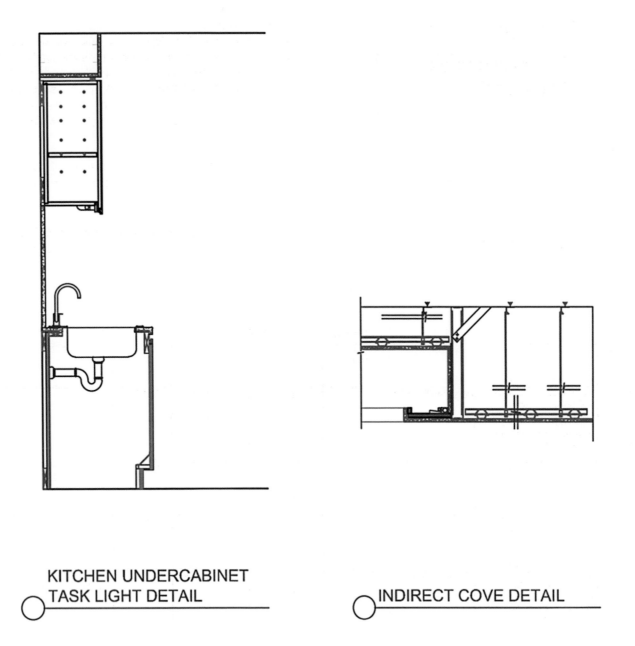

KITCHEN UNDERCABINET
TASK LIGHT DETAIL

INDIRECT COVE DETAIL

Fig. 11.9 Common Lighting Details

LEGEND		
SYMBOL	TAG	DESCRIPTION
o	F1	RECESSED DOWNLIGHT
⊢⊕	F2	WALL SCONCE
←o	F3	RECESSED WALLWASHER
⊕	F4	PENDANT

Fig. 11.10 Lighting Legend Example

Lighting Legends
The purpose of a lighting legend is to generically define each symbol used in the plan, as shown in Fig. 11.10. In the past, only a few symbol choices were used; however, CAD drafting allows much greater detail, so more symbols can be used.

If the symbol is defined as a block in CAD, some CAD programs permit assigning attributes and can aid in counting the number of each tag. This can be of great benefit when estimating the cost of a lighting installation.

Lighting Schedules
The purpose of a lighting schedule is to provide a specification for each tag. The schedule should include all of the following information, as illustrated in Fig. 11.11:

- Tag
- General description of the luminaire including size, materials, and finish
- Lamp(s) to be used in the luminaire including type and wattage
- Mounting
- Manufacturer and catalog number
- Voltage

LIGHTING FIXTURE SCHEDULE									
TAG	DESCRIPTION	MANUFACTURER	CATALOG NUMBER	LAMPS			INPUT VOLT	MOUNTING	REMARKS
				NO	TYPE	WATTS			
F1	HALOGEN LOW VOLTAGE RECESSED DOWNLIGHT WITH 4" DIA. APERTURE, SEMI-SPECULAR CLEAR ALUMINUM REFLECTOR AND INTEGRAL TRANSFORMER.	MANUFACTURER A	XYZ-123	1	MR16	50	120	RECESSED	
F2	FLUORESCENT WALL SCONCE WITH GLASS SHADE, BRUSHED ALUMINUM DETAILS, AND DIMMABLE BALLAST.	MANUFACTURER B	SC-101	1	TRIPLE TUBE CFL	26	120	WALL	1. REFER TO ELEVATIONS FOR MOUNTING HEIGHT.
F3	FLUORESCENT RECESSED WALLWASHER WITH 4" DIA. APERTURE CLEAR ALUMINUM REFLECTOR AND A DIMMABLE BALLAST.	MANUFACTURER A	XYZ-321	1	TRIPLE TUBE CFL	26	120	RECESSED	
F4	FLUORESCENT PENDANT WITH GLASS SHADE, BRUSHED ALUMINUM METAL DETAILS AND DIMMABLE BALLAST.	MANUFACTURER B	PDT-101	3	TRIPLE TUBE CFL	26	120	PENDANT	1. MOUNT BOTTOM OF PENDANT AT 7'-0".

Fig. 11.11 Lighting Schedule Example

Additional information that may be included in a schedule:

- Detail references
- Ballast or transformer specifications
- Special characteristics, such as auxiliary components and lenses

Lighting Specifications

For commercial projects, lighting plans are usually accompanied by written specifications that appear in the project book or manual. Preferably, specifications are developed according to the Construction Specification Institute (CSI) system, in which lighting is generally in sections numbered from 26500 to 26550 and lighting controls from 260933 to 260943. The electrical engineer on the project typically writes this section. Additional information about specifications can be obtained from CSI. Information about lighting specification integrity can be obtained from the IALD. Here are the three major parts of a specification.

1. A general part that introduces the topic (in this case, lighting). It is common to state here requirements for code compliance, published reference standards, shop drawings, storing and protecting materials, and other nontechnical requirements for the lighting installation.
2. A part concerning lighting materials. The specific requirements and approved manufacturers of each lighting product type are discussed. Related topics, such as warranties, are typically included.
3. A part concerning lighting installation. The special installation requirements of the lighting system are discussed.

Today, architects, engineers, and interior designers generally utilize master specifications that are written in the CSI format and designed to be edited by the specifier for project requirements. These master specifications include carefully developed text, called *boilerplate,* that ensures the legal validity of the specification.

Chapter 12 RESIDENTIAL LIGHTING DESIGN

Residential lighting design has unique characteristics. There is a general expectation of personalization in both social spaces, such as living and dining rooms, and private spaces, such as bedrooms and studies. Some of these residential characteristics are comfortably translatable to nonresidential uses, such as small business reception rooms and private professional offices.

Because all of us, by definition, live in residential spaces and are accustomed to conventional residential lighting design solutions, it may be difficult to consider residential lighting from a fresh perspective. This has both positive and negative implications. Understanding most people's expectations of how residential rooms should be lighted is clearly an advantage; on the other hand, an inability to envision creative solutions because conventional lighting design techniques are so entrenched is a disadvantage.

As in all lighting design problem solving, the first step in creating good lighting design solutions for residential spaces is to identify the visual tasks that must be resolved. Because the visual tasks in residences are so commonplace, they may be difficult to recognize and analyze from a fresh point of view. After the visual tasks are identified, the lighting design methodology spelled out in Chapter 10 should be undertaken immediately. Do not assume that conventional residential lighting design techniques are the best or most appropriate, because conventional techniques are often improved upon by new technologies and product development. The most obvious example is the current availability of many new fluorescent and LED lamps and luminaires for residential use.

Residential spaces are usually personal and often intimate in their use, and their lighting design solutions should respond to that aspect of their function. That personalization often relates directly to a desired mood or psychological response, such as a welcoming entrance foyer, the integration of daylight and exterior view, an intimate conversation area, or a festive dining room. The other broad generalization that can be made about residential lighting is that critical visual tasks are usually limited to a few activities and spaces, such as food preparation in the kitchen, grooming in the bathroom, and sewing or desk work in a designated area of the residence.

Of the many conventions related to residential lighting design, the most prevalent is the dominant use of incandescent lamps. With the growing variety and refinement of fluorescent and LED lamps, there is little in residential lighting that cannot be accomplished with these more advanced lamps; moreover, there are a growing number of state regulations that limit the use of incandescent lamps. Despite their energy saving advantage, there remains a persistent conventional aversion to the use of fluorescents in residential settings. Another entrenched convention in residential lighting is the widespread use of portable lighting—that is, table and floor lamps—that offer personal and immediate adjustability. While portable lighting has excellent nonresidential uses as well, its use is generally limited in business and institutional settings, because personal adjustability is often discouraged in many of these settings.

Residential lighting conventions include some generally accepted don'ts, most of which are related to avoiding a nonresidential ambience. For example, it is unusual to find an appropriate use for 2' × 2' or 2' × 4' recessed fluorescent luminaires in a residence despite their prevalent and appropriate use in many nonresidential settings. This is coupled with the inappropriateness of acoustic tile ceilings in most residential spaces. Despite these conventions, however, it is often worth one's time to question or rethink them on the principle that many design conventions have outlived their usefulness. And some of the manufacturers of acoustic ceiling products are now addressing the need to find new solutions for residential settings.

Codes and standards play a limited role in residential lighting. The most significant code impacts are caused by the National Electric Code. However, while energy conservation codes play a major role in all nonresidential facilities, their impact on residential lighting is, as yet, of limited influence. (Note that California's energy code is more stringent than most, requiring major use of fluorescent or LED lighting in kitchens and baths, as well as the use of dimmers and other control devices.) Despite this, it would be socially irresponsible to design residential lighting without attention to energy conservation. Limiting the use of incandescent lamps and employing energy saving control devices are the two major techniques of responsible design. Similarly, Americans with Disabilities Act (ADA) requirements for lighting design have little applicability in residences, although the issue of switch and receptacle placement should not be overlooked.

Compared to other building types, residences have a predictable and relatively limited number of uses and functions. One can usually count on a living/family room function, dining and food preparation spaces, toilet/bathing/grooming functions, and sleeping/dressing accommodations. Homes may have an office, music room, or workshop, but it is unusual to have more than one or two of these special spaces in a single residence.

Residential projects can range from simple and modest to large, complex, and luxurious, with budgets to match. Both ends of this complexity spectrum present problems. Solving lighting design problems for modest residences with limited budgets is as challenging as designing the lighting for a huge house with several specialized spaces, complex control systems requirements, and an unlimited budget. The case studies presented in this chapter fall in the middle of the spectrum, tending toward the modest end. They are intended to be generic in nature, with the thought that the lighting design concepts and techniques presented may be useful in a great variety of floor plan configurations and functional requirements.

CASE STUDY 1—Living Room Lighting

Most living rooms require flexible lighting design solutions because they serve a broad variety of changing functions. The lighting in a typical living room should comfortably serve small group conversation, larger social gatherings that include casual eating and drinking, and more solitary activities such as reading, music listening, and TV viewing. Somewhat less typically, a living room may have a desk or home office corner, a place for card or board games, a major library collection, or an art collection to be prominently displayed.

The visual tasks in living rooms range from basic and simple to complex and highly technical, depending on the size and intended purpose of the room. It is usually safe to assume that ambient illumination levels in all areas of the room are always great enough to comfortably accommodate personal navigation through the space. The typical living room shown in Fig. 12.1, ample but moderate in size and furnished to serve several functions, presents the following visual tasks to be accommodated:

1. Focal light is required for the large floor-to-ceiling bookshelves on the south end of the west wall and the east end of the south wall. Accent lighting is required for graphic material anticipated in three locations: on the north end of the west wall, the center portion of the east wall, and above the fireplace mantel.
2. Task lighting for extended-period visual tasks. In this case, there is one primary reading chair (with ottoman) in the southeast corner of the room and two secondary reading chairs in the northeast and northwest corners of the room.
3. Ambient lighting for conversation and social functions. The furniture arrangement clearly identifies the areas for conversation as well as the general travel pattern for circulation through the space. Illumination levels may vary from low to moderately high depending on the desires of the people involved. More specifically, critical or extended-period visual tasks are not expected to be performed under these lighting conditions.
4. Lighting for television viewing presents unusual lighting requirements because the rest of the lighting in the living room is normally desired at a moderate level. If TV viewing is a frequent function, the lighting design solution should be specifically designed to accommodate it.

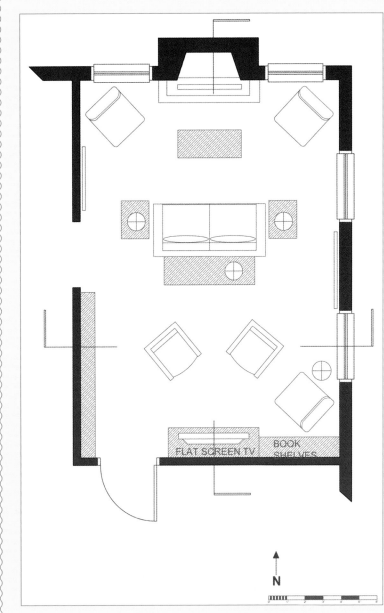

Fig. 12.1 Living Room Floor Plan

The lighting solution shown in Figs. 12.2, 12.3, and 12.4 addresses the visual tasks in the following manner:

1. Focal lighting is provided for the books in the two large book shelf units (south end of west wall and east end of south wall) with the use of continuous linear strips for each shelf. Accent lighting is also provided individually for the three art work locations: north end of west wall, above the fireplace mantel, and the center wall panel of the east wall.

2. The primary reading chair is positioned in the southeast corner of the room, where the floor lamp serves as an appropriate task source. The secondary reading chairs in the northwest and northeast corners of the room will receive adequate task light from the adjacent sconces. Depending on the users' habits, an additional floor lamp can be placed adjacent to the secondary reading chair.

3. The need and desire for ambient lighting is met by several lighting elements. The sconces at the fireplace mantel provide soft illumination for the fireplace area of the room, the intensity of which can be adjusted by the controlling dimmer switch. The portable lighting adds to the quantity and effectiveness of the ambient lighting, provided by the three table lamps, contributing primarily to the area at the north end of the room. The sconces and the floor and table lamps, if their baffles and shades are translucent, can also add much eye-level glow, a desirable quality if a sense of sparkle or warmth is sought. The many fixed and portable luminaires in the room provide for many ways of adjusting the quality of ambient light by selecting those to be turned on as well as by adjusting their output through dimmer controls.

4. Television viewing presents lighting problems in multipurpose spaces such as living rooms, although the now common use of flat screen monitors have made this issue of much less importance. When TV is viewed in a room or space used primarily for that purpose, creating appropriate lighting is simply accomplished. In this example, many of the luminaires could create unwanted reflections on the TV screen. If the sconces on the north wall are dimmed for low output, their negative effect could be quite minor. Adding a floor lamp in the northeast corner of the room would balance the lighting of the room during the viewing period. If daytime viewing is a consideration, window treatments to counteract glare from windows should also be considered.

Because flexibility in lighting is essential in living rooms, most lighting should be controlled with dimmer switches. With this in mind, zoning should be

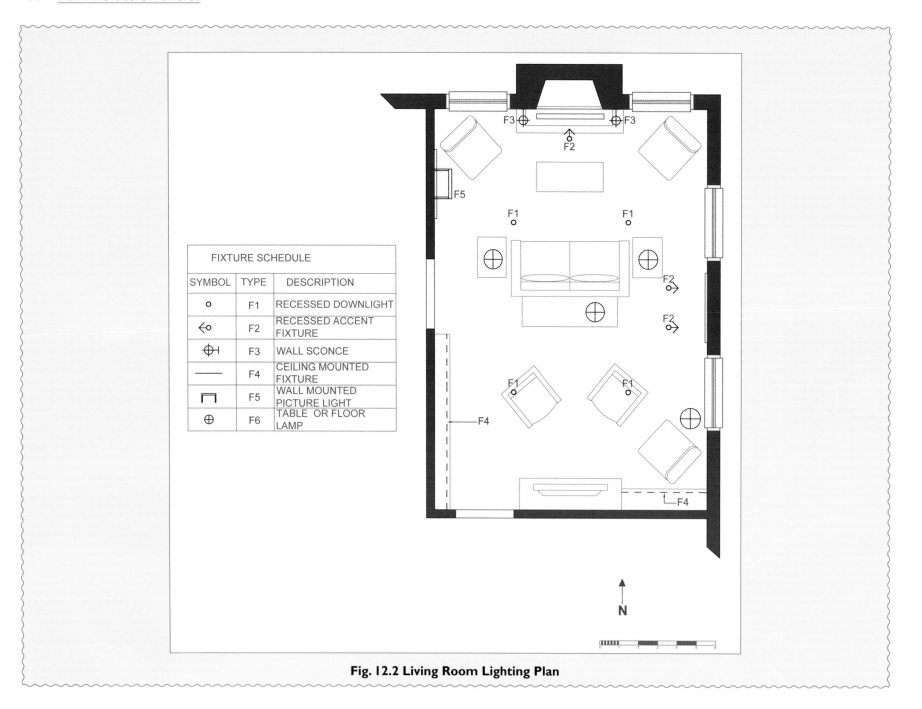

Fig. 12.2 Living Room Lighting Plan

FIXTURE SCHEDULE		
SYMBOL	TYPE	DESCRIPTION
○	F1	RECESSED DOWNLIGHT
←○	F2	RECESSED ACCENT FIXTURE
⊕⊣	F3	WALL SCONCE
——	F4	CEILING MOUNTED FIXTURE
⊓	F5	WALL MOUNTED PICTURE LIGHT
⊕	F6	TABLE OR FLOOR LAMP

Fig. 12.3 Living Room Section

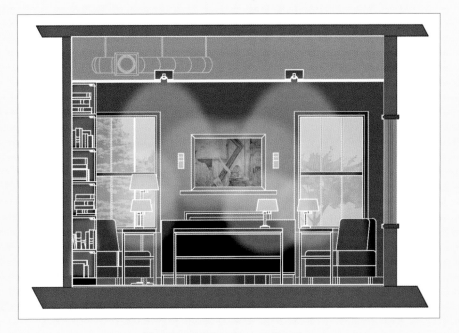

Fig. 12.4 Living Room Section

related to the room's different functions, creating areas of the room in which dimming is controlled. When dimmers are used in this manner, the room can be adjusted to achieve just the right quality for any occasion.

Luminaire and lamp selections should be based on the following considerations:

- Bookshelf lighting: minimal scale linear LED strips mounted at each shelf are used.
- Adjustable accent fixtures: lighting for the artwork on the north and east wall is provided by recessed luminaires with internal aiming mechanism. A point source is required; either low-voltage halogen or LED would be appropriate.
- Lighting for the piece on the west wall is provided by a museum quality wall-mounted picture light.
- Sconces: direct-indirect distribution; task (reading) light for adjacent chairs; eye-level glow and/or sparkle determined by the degree of translucency of the shade and user preference.
- Table lamps: Size and scale of lamp/shade combination to be reviewed in elevation. Direct/indirect distribution with translucent shade to provide eye-level glow and/or sparkle.
- Floor lamp: direct-indirect with task (reading) light for adjacent chair; translucent shade optional if eye-level glow and/or sparkle is desired.

While incandescent lamps are still the standard, in all cases lamp selection can be compact fluorescent or LED with wattage based on personal preference.

The design quality or style of the selected luminaires will be determined primarily by the quality or style of the architectural and interior design detailing and materials, from traditional cut glass (sconces) and fringed shades (portables) to contemporary woods, plastics, and metals to high-tech materials. This element of luminaire selection is difficult to articulate because it deals with the elusive elements of aesthetics, style, and taste. Only long experience in a trial-and-error process over the course of many projects will inform the designer in making intelligent aesthetic decisions.

CASE STUDY 2—Dining Room Lighting

Ambience is vital in dining room lighting. The creation of mood and personal atmosphere must be at the top of the lighting design criteria list, second only to satisfying the visual tasks to be performed in the room. In addition, the desired ambience is subject to change; it is not uncommon to expect a dining room to be bright and formal on one occasion, intimate and romantic on another, and festive yet casual on still another.

The visual tasks in the great majority of dining rooms are basic and relatively simple. For the typical dining room shown in Fig. 12.5, they are as follows:

1. First and foremost, provide light at the table so diners can see their food as well as the faces of the other diners.
2. Assuming that the major wall surfaces will display graphic material (paintings, posters, photographs), focal lighting on these materials is necessary for appropriate visibility.
3. When the buffet is used for serving, provide enough and appropriate light for the server to comfortably perform the task.
4. Ambient lighting is needed for the periphery of the room to avoid the feeling of dimly lighted and empty spaces surrounding the table.

The lighting design solution shown in Figs. 12.6, 12.7, and 12.8 addresses the visual tasks in the following manner:

1. The three recessed down lights placed symmetrically near each end of the table serve the primary visual functions.

   - An alternate solution for lighting the dining table with a pendant luminaire is shown with a dotted line. While downlights are a good and reliable technique, the alternate solution of using a pendant fixture over the center of the table also provides a desirable result. In this case, the downlights are preferred because they will not obstruct the accented artwork centrally displayed over the buffet.

2. The recessed accent fixtures are placed to give visibility to graphic material on the two major (north and south) walls. The south wall is long enough (13') so that three luminaires are needed to provide adequate coverage

if multiple graphics are intended. If a major display of graphic materials is intended for all wall surfaces, including the two sections of the north wall, a track system could be considered for the north, east, and west walls; this would provide maximum flexibility in lighting the graphic works.

3. Wall sconces are placed on both sides of the main entrance to the room as well as on both sides of the buffet on the south wall. They provide ambient light on the west and east sides of the room in addition to the potential for eye-level glow that sconces generally produce. The specific quality of that eye-level glow depends on the design and materials of the selected luminaire. The sconces adjacent to the buffet can provide task light on the buffet surface for serving functions. Because sconces are more visible than ceiling-mounted luminaires, it is good practice to study elevations of walls containing sconces so that good visual composition of those walls is not left to chance. Two recessed accent fixtures are focused on the major art work above the buffet.

4. Specific ambient lighting for the periphery of the room is not required because the three systems described before more than adequately serve that task. Obviously, these luminaires must be selected with their ambient light contribution in mind.

Because ambience is so important in dining rooms, all luminaires must be controlled by dimmer switches so that a great variety of combinations of lighting intensity can be used to create the desired mood for every occasion. Luminaire and lamp selections should be based on the following considerations:

- Downlights: Point source with high CRI and medium spread of light to focus on the table surface. Halogen or high-quality LED would work well.
- Sconces at the buffet: Incandescent or compact fluorescent lamping with direct/indirect distribution providing focus to the buffet surface. The degree of eye-level glow and sparkle determined by shade material and preference.
- Adjustable accent fixtures focused on north and south wall artwork and east wall buffet: Halogen or LED recessed or surface-mounted luminaire with spread of light determined by graphic size. Halogen or high-quality LED preferred for artwork.

The design quality or style of the selected luminaires must be determined by the quality or style of the architectural and interior design detailing and materials, from traditional crystal and cut glass to contemporary natural

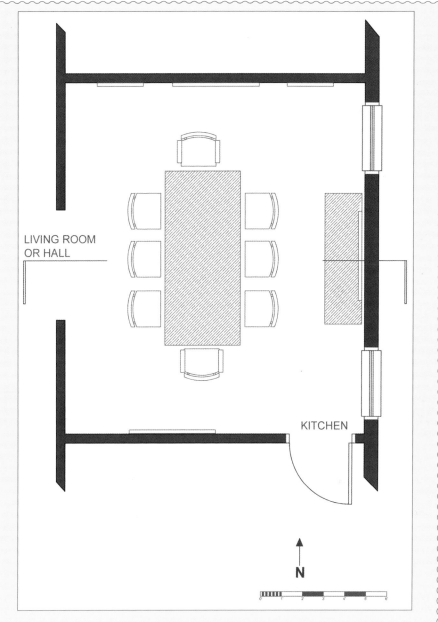

LIVING ROOM OR HALL

KITCHEN

N

Fig. 12.5 Dining Room Floor Plan

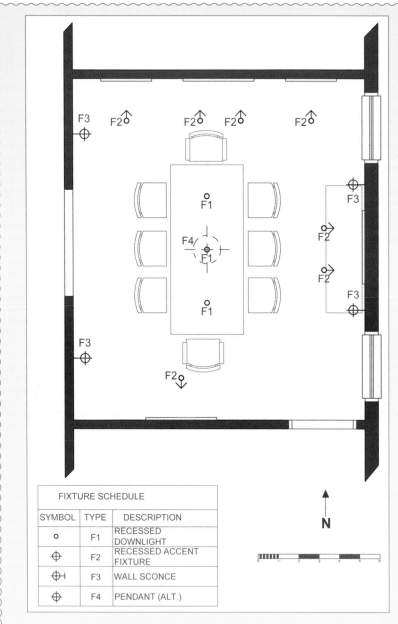

FIXTURE SCHEDULE		
SYMBOL	TYPE	DESCRIPTION
o	F1	RECESSED DOWNLIGHT
⊕	F2	RECESSED ACCENT FIXTURE
⊕⊢	F3	WALL SCONCE
⊕	F4	PENDANT (ALT.)

N

Fig. 12.6 Dining Room Lighting Plan

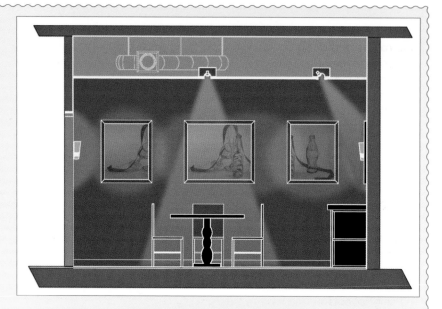

Fig. 12.7 Dining Room Section

Fig. 12.8 Dining Room Perspective

woods to high-tech materials and techniques. It would be quite unusual for the room's detailing and materials to be determined by the lighting design solution, including the selection of luminaires. This element of luminaire selection is the most difficult to articulate because it involves the elusive elements of aesthetics, style, and taste. Only long experience in a trial-and-error process over the course of many projects will inform the designer in making intelligent aesthetic selections.

CASE STUDY 3—Galley Kitchen Lighting

With the possible exception of a home office, day-to-day kitchen functions present the most demanding lighting design solutions of all residential rooms and spaces. Kitchens are workplaces where the critical nature of visual tasks is compounded by the dangers associated with sharp tools, scalding liquids, and burning-hot pots and utensils. The typical small galley kitchen shown in Fig. 12.9 includes most of the functional lighting issues found in all residential kitchens without the complexities of informal dining and the social interaction found in many larger kitchens.

All of the primary visual tasks in the kitchen occur at the counter level, including the work counter surfaces, the sink, and the cook surface. A secondary task involves adequate visual access to cabinets and shelves above the countertop level. While providing visual access to cabinets below the countertop level is also important, kitchen lighting solutions that address that task are rare.

The kitchen requires a modest level of ambient light for general use. Because refrigerators and ovens usually feature an internal light source, tasks related to those kitchen elements are usually not a concern. Avoid casting shadows on the work surface; without strong task lighting aimed directly on the surface, the kitchen's ambient or general lighting source likely will place kitchen users in the position of casting their own shadow on the work counter, making their work difficult.

The lighting solution shown in Figs. 12.10 and 12.11 addresses the visual tasks in the following manner:

1. The task lighting, except for that on the cook surface, is accomplished with the use of undercabinet fluorescent or LED luminaires that illuminate all

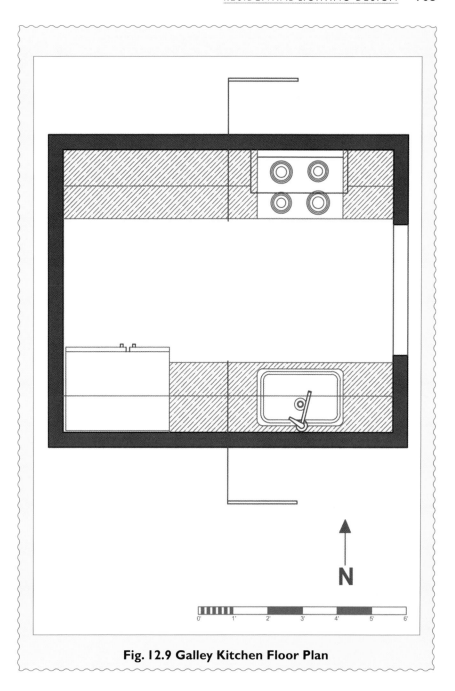

Fig. 12.9 Galley Kitchen Floor Plan

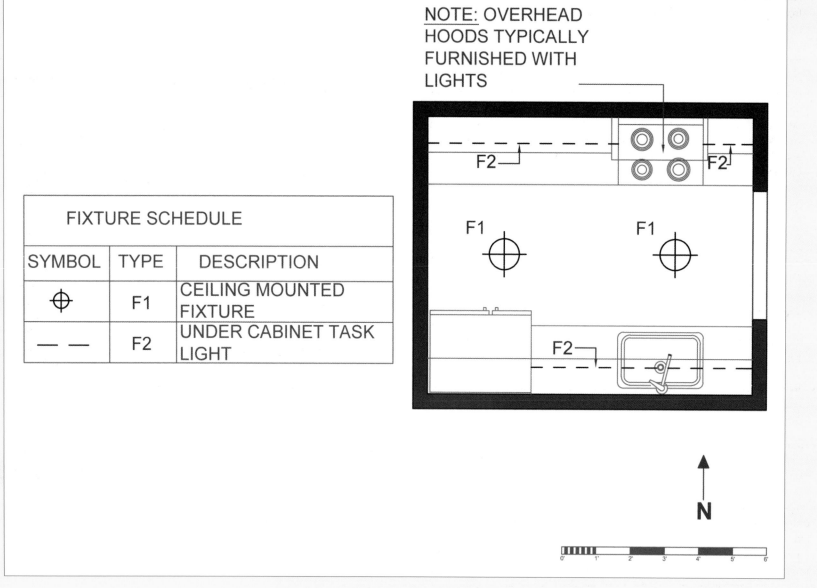

NOTE: OVERHEAD HOODS TYPICALLY FURNISHED WITH LIGHTS

FIXTURE SCHEDULE

SYMBOL	TYPE	DESCRIPTION
⊕	F1	CEILING MOUNTED FIXTURE
— —	F2	UNDER CABINET TASK LIGHT

N

Fig. 12.10 Galley Kitchen Lighting Plan

counter and sink surfaces. Many, if not most, wall cabinets are made with a front lip or fascia to visually conceal the luminaire, providing a smooth and uninterrupted line at the bottom of the cabinet. Exhaust hoods over stoves usually contain their own light source; this automatically addresses the need for task lighting on the cook surface.

2. Ambient light and light for the wall cabinets is accomplished with two recessed downlights with dropped lenses to provide enough horizontal thrust to illuminate the wall cabinets when their doors are open. A decorative alternative to the dropped lens fixtures may be desired; many well-designed sculptural and/or colorful ceiling-mounted fixtures are available that are designed to solve this lighting problem while presenting a less utilitarian appearance.

Standard (non-dimming) switches placed at the entrance to the room are most appropriate in this situation. The light contained in the cook surface hood has its own switch.

Luminaire and lamp selections should be based on the following considerations:

- Undercabinet fixture: fluorescent or LED with direct light focused on the length of the work surface; light source concealed to avoid glare; cover lens to avoid dirt and grease accumulation. Pay particular attention to color rendition because of the focus on food; lamps of 3000 K, 80+ CRI are strongly recommended.
- Recessed downlights: symmetrically placed for even distribution; dropped lens to provide direct light as well as side light for wall cabinets. Lamps at 3000 K, 80+ CRI are strongly recommended.

The design quality or style of the selected luminaires will be primarily determined by the quality or style of the architectural and interior design detailing and materials. Kitchens usually contain standard manufactured equipment (refrigerators, ranges, dishwashers, compactors); the inherent contemporary appearance of these items limits the aesthetic range of luminaire selections.

Even kitchens with a traditional design quality cannot easily incorporate a luminaire appropriate for a period room. Despite this, a broad range of appropriate luminaires for all sizes and design styles of kitchens is available.

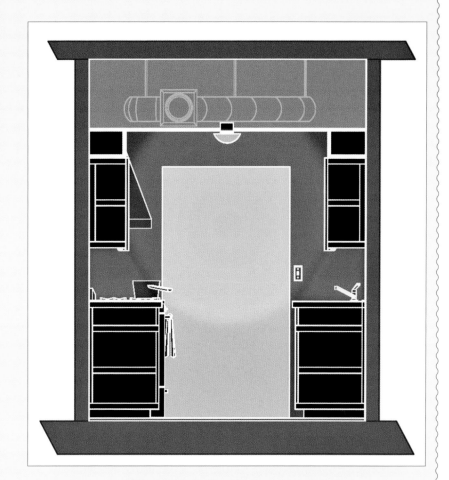

Fig. 12.11 Galley Kitchen Section

CASE STUDY 4—Lighting the Island Kitchen

The typical small kitchen of the previous case study illustrates the basic lighting issues found in all kitchens. But many kitchens incorporate functions that go beyond those of that small kitchen to the point where they become the activity center of the residence. The most frequent use of a kitchen space, after food preparation, is informal dining. The larger kitchen also is often a space for personal and social exchange, where food preparation and conversation are expected to flow in an uninterrupted manner. It is not uncommon for the kitchen to be the hub of all family and social activity such that all living, dining, and kitchen functions flow together in the space. The kitchen shown in Fig.12.12 is a generously sized space that permits more than one person to participate in food preparation, incorporates a small informal dining counter, and provides the opportunity for social interaction with family and guests.

The visual tasks performed in this kitchen are obviously more complex than those in a small kitchen. The increase in complexity is seen in each area of this larger space. The need for strong task lighting on all work surfaces is constant, but the island work surface requires a different lighting design solution. The need for ambient lighting goes far beyond comfortable navigation of the kitchen space to demand an ambience conducive to social interaction. The informal dining counter, while not requiring the flexibility of mood expected in a larger dining setting, still relies on lighting to provide appropriate atmospheric quality conducive for casual dining and conversation.

The lighting design solution shown in Figs. 12.13, 12.14, and 12.15 addresses the visual tasks that are required.

- Task light: Two areas in this kitchen require task lighting.

  1. The perimeter work counter/desk surfaces, which are primarily lighted with undercabinet luminaires, as in the typical small kitchen of the preceding case study, plus the three recessed downlights at the north wall over the sink and the adjacent countertop areas.
  2. The island counter surfaces for work and casual dining, which are lighted with two pendants. These luminaires should be placed to enhance conversation between those seated at the counter and those working in the kitchen, as well as for work functions at the island. In addition, the pendants can also serve in providing adequate illumination for the wall cabinets when the cabinet doors are open.

- Ambient light: The primary technique for providing ambient light is with recessed downlights symmetrically placed around the island. The pendants over the island can also make a major contribution to the room's ambient light and add some eye-level glow and decorative quality. Seen in their totality, the downlights, the pendants, and the undercabinet task fluorescents present a complex and well-orchestrated combination of ambient sources.

Luminaire and lamp selections should be based on the following considerations:

- Undercabinet fixture: Fluorescent or LED with direct light focused on the length of the work surface; light source concealed to avoid glare; cover lens to avoid dirt and grease accumulation. Pay particular attention to color rendition because of the focus on food; lamps of 3000 K, 80+ CRI are strongly recommended.
- Downlight above sink area: basic recessed luminaires with shallow baffle and a medium beam distribution. Halogen or high-quality LED would work well.
- Island counter pendants: direct/indirect ratio, with priority on direct light on counter; degree of eye-level glow to contribute to ambient light; compact fluorescent, halogen, or LED lamps selected for appropriate color rendition.
- Ambient downlights: recessed luminaires with wide beam distribution; incandescent, compact fluorescent, or LED lamps.

This is the only case study in this chapter on residential spaces that has a room with a major glass wall. Daylighting in this kitchen will play a major factor in the room's lighting, at least during daytime hours. In this case, the important lighting issue related to daylighting is switching. The south end of the room will be flooded with natural light during the day. To conserve energy, the downlights adjacent to the south wall should be separately switched (as well as having dimming capability). The same issue is true of the undercabinet fixture at the desk in the southwest corner, but that type of fixture typically has its own switch that is controlled at the desk.

The design quality and style of the selected luminaires will be primarily determined by the quality and style of the architectural and interior design detailing and materials. The pendant luminaires require special attention because they are the only visible luminaires in the space; they could play an important decorative role in establishing the aesthetic character of the room. In contrast to the small kitchen in the preceding case study, the room presented here serves many functions beyond food preparation and has fewer limitations placed on luminaire selection.

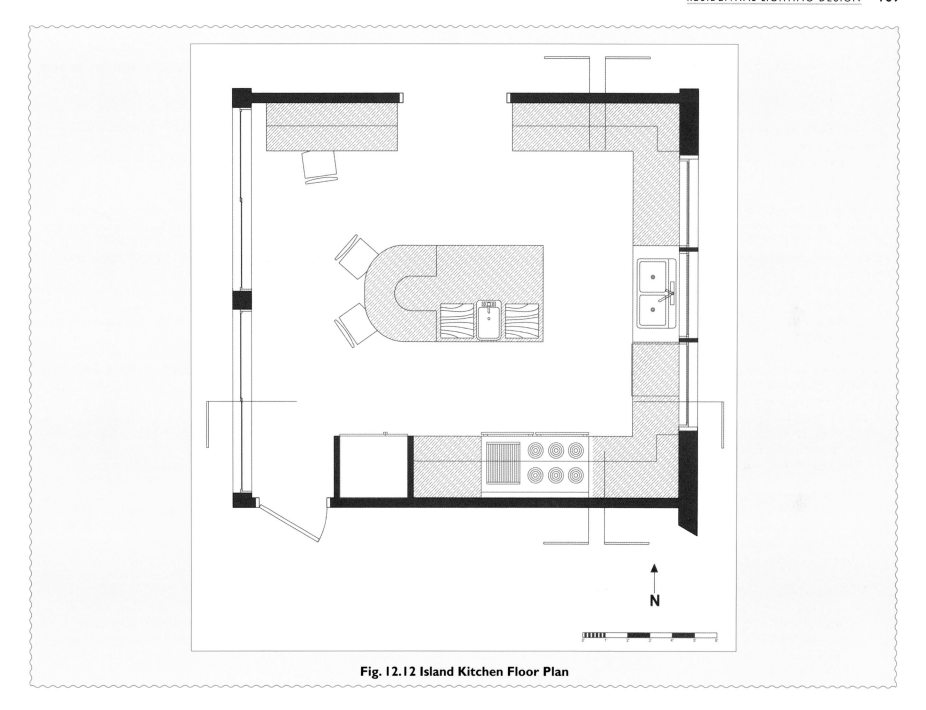

N

Fig. 12.12 Island Kitchen Floor Plan

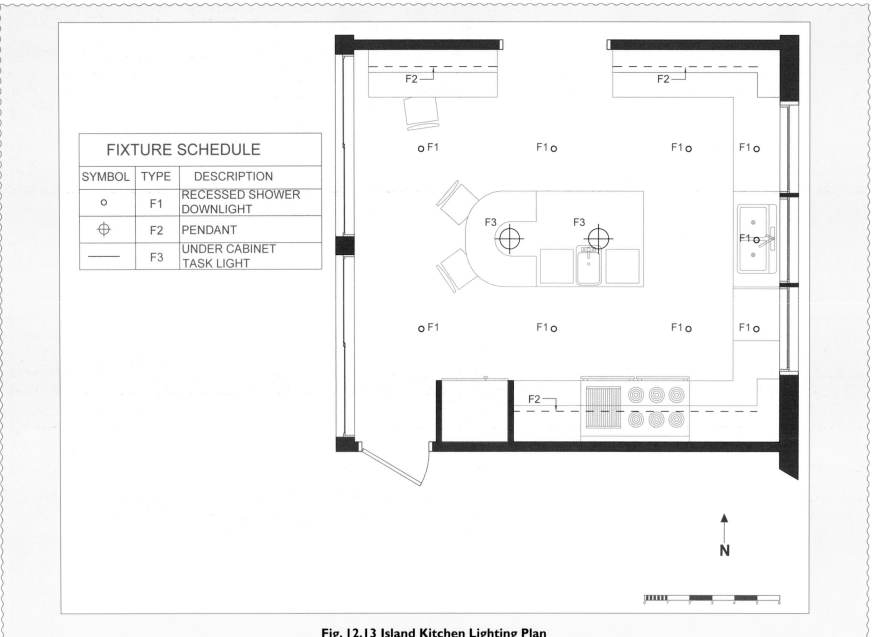

FIXTURE SCHEDULE

SYMBOL	TYPE	DESCRIPTION
o	F1	RECESSED SHOWER DOWNLIGHT
⊕	F2	PENDANT
——	F3	UNDER CABINET TASK LIGHT

Fig. 12.13 Island Kitchen Lighting Plan

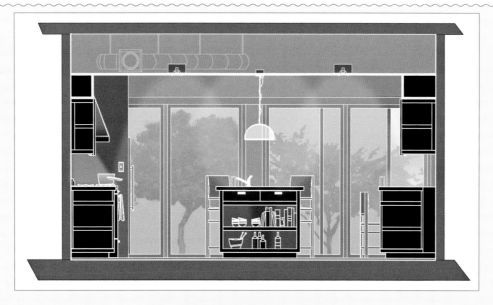

Fig. 12.14 Island Kitchen Section

Fig. 12.15 Island Kitchen Perspective

CASE STUDY 5—Bathroom Lighting

The visual tasks performed in bathrooms are usually basic, predictable, and primarily functional. While ambience and aesthetics are an issue in lighting any space, they are secondary considerations in most bathrooms. Large and customized bathrooms, some of which can include huge whirlpool baths and exercise areas, can require nonstandard lighting solutions; otherwise, task light for grooming and shaving at a mirror and ambient light for showering, bathing, and short-term reading are the only lighting requirements.

The task lighting at the mirror should have certain attributes. First, it should provide enough light for detailed inspection of skin and beard. Second, the lighting effect should be essentially shadowless to avoid sight difficulties and to provide a flattering view of the face. Third, the selected lamp should provide color quality that is flattering to skin tones; lamps at 2700 to 3000 K, 80+ CRI are recommended.

The ambient lighting needs are much more variable. Often, the light emitted from the mirror luminaire(s) is adequate for ambient purposes, particularly if the shower curtain or door is transparent or lightly translucent and the toilet is adjacent to the mirror. Despite this, bathroom shapes, configurations, and fixture locations can sometimes severely limit the mirror luminaire's ability to provide adequate ambient light. Regardless of configuration, and if budget permits, a recessed luminaire rated for shower, spa, or bath use in the shower/tub area ceiling and a luminaire above or adjacent to the toilet are always appreciated. The basic bathroom shown in Fig. 12.16 presents the visual tasks described in the preceding paragraphs.

The lighting solution shown in Figs. 12.17 and 12.18 addresses those visual tasks in the following manner:

1. The grooming/shaving tasks performed at the mirror above the lavatories are addressed by the placement of a fluorescent or halogen bath bar luminaire adjacent to the sides of the two grooming mirrors; this is a common and widely accepted lighting solution for residential bathrooms. This placement of the luminaires provides essentially shadowless illumination, which is not the case when a luminaire is placed above the lavatory mirror.

2. Ambient lighting for the tub and toilet areas is reasonably addressed by the lighting above the lavatories. Despite this, a downlight in the toilet area will brighten the room and provide light for reading when desired. In addition, a recessed and lensed downlight in the tub area is generally helpful

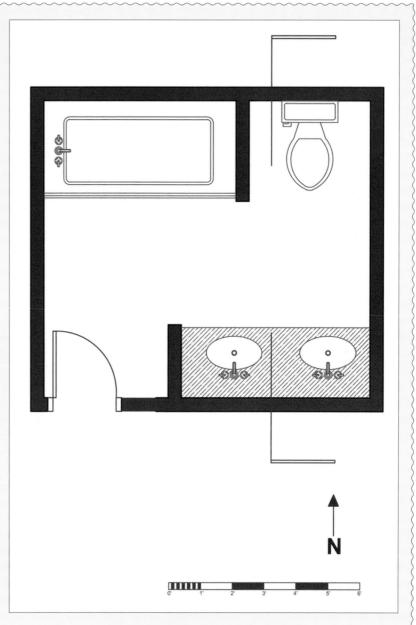

Fig. 12.16 Bathroom Floor Plan

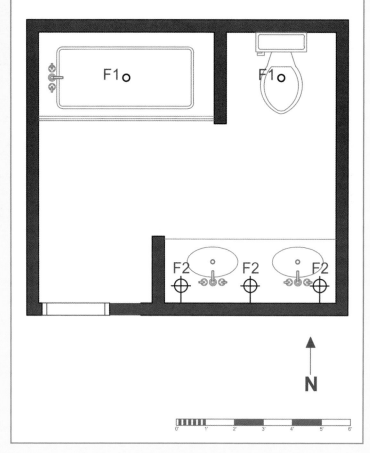

FIXTURE SCHEDULE		
SYMBOL	TYPE	DESCRIPTION
o	F1	RECESSED SHOWER DOWNLIGHT
⊕⊣	F2	VANITY WALL SCONCE

Fig. 12.17 Bathroom Lighting Plan

and sometimes necessary if an opaque or close-to-opaque shower curtain or door is installed. In residential situations, the designer rarely knows in advance the type of shower enclosure that will be used; if the budget permits, specific lighting for the tub/shower area is usually welcome.

Standard (non-dimming) switches are most appropriate in bathrooms. Desired lighting levels are best adjusted in the choice of lamps.

Luminaire and lamp selections should be based on the following considerations:

- Bath bar: vertical sconces of appropriate length, to be placed directly adjacent to the sides of the two mirrors. High-quality CRI and warm color temperature most appropriate to provide flattering, shadowless light for user. Typically, incandescent, halogen, or fluorescent.

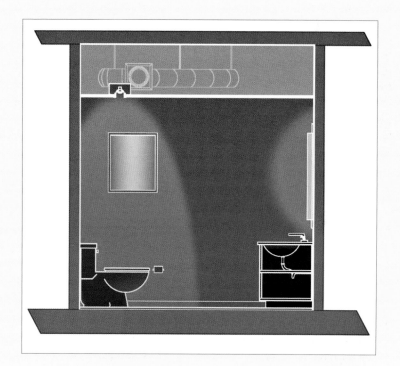

Fig. 12.18 Bathroom Section

- Downlight for the toilet area: recessed luminaire; halogen or LED; narrow beam spread.
- Downlight for shower area: recessed luminaire with lens rated for shower/bath use; with halogen, compact fluorescent or LED lamp, medium beam spread.

Design quality or style is relatively limited in most bathrooms. The presence of moisture places immediate restrictions on luminaire selections. While the room's materials and detailing will influence selections, the range of materials, finishes, detailing, cabinetry, and plumbing fixture color(s) will impose further limitations. Selecting from this relatively narrow band of available luminaire products still requires the same kind of intelligent aesthetic and design judgment that must be applied in all lighting design projects.

CASE STUDY 6—Bedroom Lighting

Two broad generalizations can be made about the design of bedrooms, including their lighting:

1. They should be conducive to sleep.
2. They should be a quiet refuge from the more active or social parts of the residence.

Minimal bedrooms may serve only as a place to sleep and change clothes. More typically, bedrooms also serve as a place to read, watch television, write a letter, or do homework at a desk. When bedrooms are shared, they often serve as a place for intimate relationships. Larger bedrooms may incorporate a sitting/conversation area, a work corner for desk work or sewing, and/or an exercise area. Consequently, bedroom lighting must often serve diverse functions, creating different ambiences, while simultaneously serving the separate needs of two users. The bedroom shown in Fig. 12.19 is planned to serve several functions: sleeping, changing clothes, reading in bed, watching television, doing desk work, intimate conversing, and reading in the large lounge chair. Although it is fairly modest in size, this bedroom requires a lighting solution for several functions.

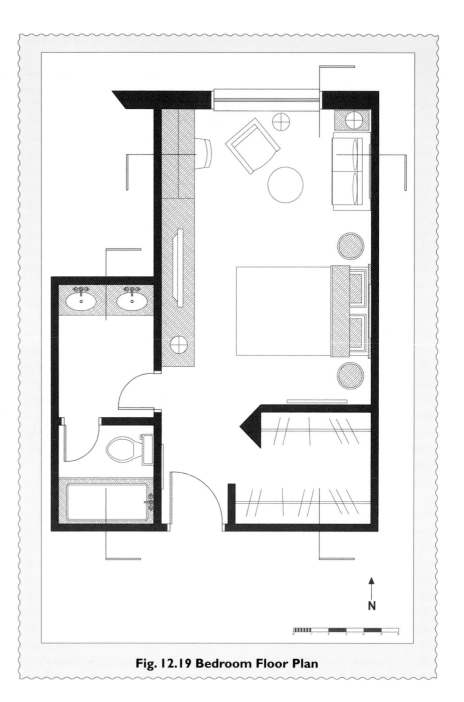

Fig. 12.19 Bedroom Floor Plan

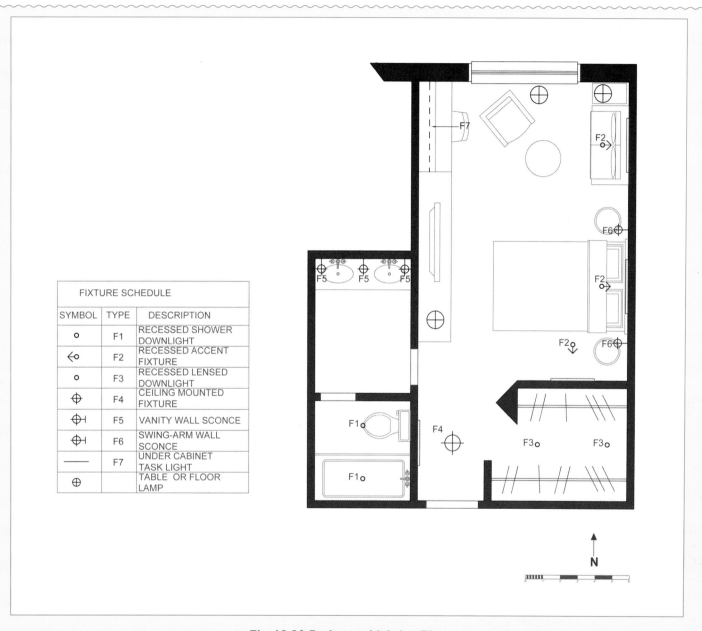

FIXTURE SCHEDULE

SYMBOL	TYPE	DESCRIPTION
o	F1	RECESSED SHOWER DOWNLIGHT
←o	F2	RECESSED ACCENT FIXTURE
o	F3	RECESSED LENSED DOWNLIGHT
⊕	F4	CEILING MOUNTED FIXTURE
⊕⊣	F5	VANITY WALL SCONCE
⊕⊣	F6	SWING-ARM WALL SCONCE
—	F7	UNDER CABINET TASK LIGHT
⊕		TABLE OR FLOOR LAMP

Fig. 12.20 Bedroom Lighting Plan

Fig. 12.21 Bedroom Section

The visual tasks to be resolved in this case are:

1. Focal light: The major art/graphic work(s) anticipated on the south and east walls require focal and/or accent lighting, depending upon the work to be displayed.
2. Task light: In the bedroom proper, three visual tasks must be accommodated: reading in bed, seeing tasks at the desk, and reading in the lounge chair. In the walk-in closet, clothes must be seen in reasonable detail and with color accuracy. Adjacent to the walk-in closet is a full-length mirror, which requires carefully positioned light. The bathroom is where the critical visual tasks of grooming and shaving take place; these were addressed in the preceding case study.
3. Ambient light: Ambient light is needed for several visual functions, including changing clothes, conversing in the sitting area, and watching television in bed or from the sitting area. The bath/toilet compartment also requires a modest level of lighting for bathing and short-term reading.

4. Television viewing: As described in Case Study 1, television viewing presents unusual lighting requirements that often conflict with the room's other lighting needs. If television viewing is an expected function, the lighting design solution for the room as a whole should be adjustable, with minimal effort, for those periods.

The lighting solution in Figs. 12.20–12.24 addresses these visual tasks in the following manner:

1. Focal light: This is provided by the recessed accent fixtures that are positioned to illuminate the anticipated art/graphic work(s) on the south and east walls.
2. Task light: Bedside lighting is provided by wall-mounted swing-arm luminaires; ideally, they should be selected to limit the amount of light that will spill over to the other side of the bed so as not to disturb the bed partner. An often-used alternative to swing-arm sconces is two recessed reading

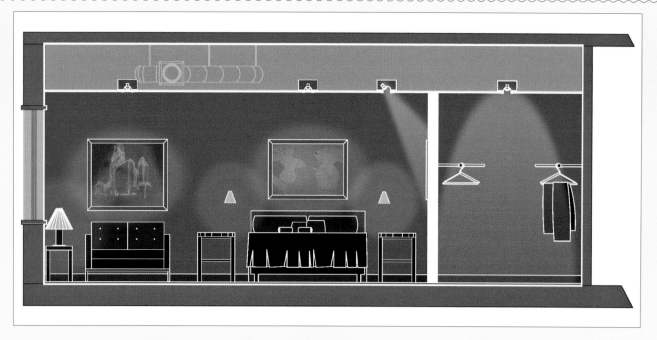

Fig. 12.22 Bedroom Section

luminaires placed in the ceiling above the conventional position for reading in bed. The undershelf fixture provides excellent light for desk work. The floor lamp adjacent to the lounge chair should be selected to provide good reading light and with personalized adjustability in mind. A surface-mounted luminous fixture positioned in front of the full-length mirror can adequately serve the dressing function. The recessed lens' fluorescent downlights in the walk-in closet provide ample light for seeing and selecting the hung apparel while not providing harsh shadows. The grooming/shaving tasks in the lavatory area are satisfied (as they are in the previous case study) by three vertically placed luminaires, which provide even and relatively shadowless light for these tasks and maintain a residential scale and character for the space.

3. Ambient light: These needs are met by several lighting sources. The surface-mounted luminaire in front of the full-length mirror, switched immediately adjacent to the entry door, provides basic navigational light as one enters the room. The two table lamps are strategically placed to provide soft lighting and eye-level glow in the two areas of the room that do not have task-oriented luminaires. All of the task sources (bedside, desk, and lounge chair) can be selectively switched on and off to contribute to the room's quality of lighting, including additional eye-level glow from the bedside sources, if desired. The accent fixtures focused on the south and east walls make an additional contribution to the room's ambient light. A basic dropped-lens downlight in the bath/toilet compartment provides appropriate light for the limited functions in that area.

4. Depending on where the viewers are positioned to watch television, unwanted light sources should be switched off to avoid reflections. Low-level output from the several other light sources can provide a desired dimmed quality.

The diversity of lighting needs and sources in this room requires an equally diverse approach to switching. As noted before, the navigational light provided by the surface-mounted fixture in front of the full-length mirror requires a switch adjacent to the entry door. The three-way switching of the

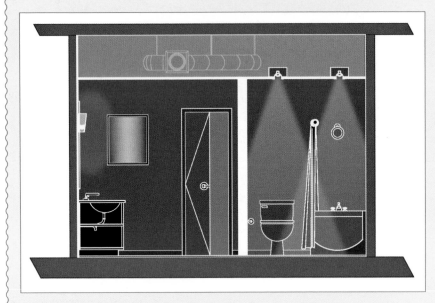

Fig. 12.23 Bedroom Bathroom Section

two convenience receptacles, one convenient to the table lamp adjacent to the television and one in the far northeast corner of the room, allows for a warmer ambient light for the whole of the room and is controllable at its source as well. The National Electric Code (NEC) requires at least one switched receptacle in every bedroom. Except for the recessed accent fixtures, which are switched near their source, all other luminaires are switched directly at their source.

Luminaire and lamp selections should be based on the following considerations:

- Swing-arm sconce: focused reading light; easy personal control and adjustability; degree of desired eye-level glow; compact fluorescent or LED for low heat output.
- The alternative solution for two recessed downlights obviously calls for narrow beam distribution; ideally, a low-voltage MR-16 luminaire should be employed for maximum beam control.

- Undershelf fixture: fluorescent or LED with direct light focused on the length of the work surface; light source concealed to avoid glare.
- Personal viewing at mirror: surface-mounted diffuse fixture; incandescent or compact fluorescent.
- Portable floor lamp: focused reading light; easy personal control and adjustability; compact fluorescent or LED for low heat output. Eye-level glow is not required in this location.
- Closet downlights: recessed incandescent or fluorescent with dropped lens for horizontal thrust; design detail consistent with the bedroom's decorative detail.
- Bath bar: vertical sconces of appropriate length to be placed directly adjacent to the sides of the two mirrors. High-quality CRI and warm color temperature most appropriate to provide flattering, shadowless light for user. Typically, incandescent, halogen, or fluorescent.
- Table lamps: Size and scale of lamp/shade combination to be reviewed in elevation. Direct/indirect distribution with translucent shade for eye-level glow desired.
- Bath/toilet downlight: recessed compact fluorescent or LED with dropped lens for maximum diffusion.

Lamp selection is important for color consistency throughout the bedroom (although a color shift can occur when entering the master bath) as well as for color rendition in a space that should have visually soft qualities rather than crisp and hard lines. Kelvin and CRI values are ideally selected on a personal basis with the client's preferences taken into account.

The design quality of the selected luminaires must be determined by the quality or style of the architectural and interior design detailing and materials, from traditional silk shades to contemporary natural woods to high-tech materials (see Figs. 12.21–12.24). It is rare for the room's detailing and materials to be determined by the lighting design solution, including the selection of luminaires. This aspect of luminaire selection is difficult to articulate because it deals with the elusive elements of aesthetics, style, and taste. Only long experience in a trial-and-error process over the course of many projects will inform the designer in making intelligent aesthetic decisions.

Fig. 12.24 Bedroom Perspective

Chapter 13 WORKSPACE LIGHTING DESIGN

As our work world becomes increasingly service-oriented, more and more people work in office or workstation environments. In addition to the buildings we classify as office buildings, most nonresidential buildings have a significant office area or function.

Because office environments have become so pervasive, typical lighting design solutions in these settings have become simplistic and formulaic in nature. The prevalence of the speculative, multitenant office building has been a major factor in the growing reliance on generic solutions because they must accommodate ever-changing tenants. Most of the design elements of these buildings, including their lighting systems, are geared to serving a great variety of tenants as well as those that regularly move from office space to office space. Hence, there is almost universal use of lay-in acoustic tile ceilings, which permit the easy relocation of 2' × 2' and 2' × 4' recessed fluorescent troffers and access to ceiling plenum spaces for installing and servicing mechanical and electrical equipment. Rarely is this the best lighting design solution for even the most undemanding office design.

In most work environments, productivity and efficiency are high-priority goals, and lighting design solutions are expected to support them. More specifically, visual tasks should be easy and comfortable to perform; fortunately, the growing trend is to increase employee satisfaction in most workplaces, and lighting should contribute to a visually and psychologically satisfying environment. The use of formula lighting solutions provides less than positive results in most workspaces in terms of both user productivity and user satisfaction. Nonstandard and creative solutions can be economically applied in many office settings.

The practicalities of the speculative or multitenant office building do place stringent limitations on the approaches to lighting design that can be successfully employed. Clearly, the rapid turnover and subsequent reconfiguration of tenant spaces demand maximum flexibility and little that is custom-designed, save for reception, conference, or high-level executive spaces in which the company's image is important.

For office spaces designed for more permanent occupancy, such as company-owned business buildings and institutional facilities, the approach to lighting can and should be different. While access to plenum space remains essential, the other elements that affect lighting design decisions can be addressed with greater flexibility. Appropriate and accessible ceiling systems other than lay-in acoustic tile ceilings do exist. Drywall soffits can be employed more freely. Although sconces and other wall-mounted luminaires are used in multitenant buildings, they and other fixed and customized lighting solutions are more practical in owner-occupied buildings.

The relationship between the ceiling system and the lighting system is always critical. In the great majority of office settings, mechanical and electrical equipment and distribution lines are not exposed, primarily because the finished appearance of a suspended ceiling is desired. Typically, office space ceiling heights range from 8'-6" to 9'-0". In small and/or private office spaces, ceiling height can be comfortably reduced to 8'-0", but in any space larger than a conventional enclosed room, 8'-6" should be the minimum ceiling height. The height of the plenum varies considerably depending on the design of the building's structural system. Typically, in high-rise office buildings, they are about 2'-6" from finished ceiling to the underside of the floor above. It is convenient to have a roomy plenum that does not restrict luminaire type or placement, but the tendency is to keep the plenum at a minimum in order to keep the building volume (and therefore cost) as small as possible. While small areas in an office suite can use a drywall or other nonaccessible ceiling, access to mechanical and electrical services is of great importance. Although general schematic lighting design solutions can be conceptualized before the ceiling system is selected, no final lighting design decisions can be made until that selection is made. That architectural decision is best made collaboratively with the lighting designer. Even the specific positioning of the ceiling system as it relates to fixed walls and building core elements is best made collaboratively. More specifically, the final positioning and specification of luminaires cannot be assigned until the final ceiling system details are determined.

In the majority of office settings, traditional 2' × 2' and 2' × 4' grid systems are used. The grid itself can range from the common, low-cost T to visually more discreet (but also more costly) fine-line grids. Myriad tile patterns, textures, materials, and colors are available, as are large-scale 4' × 4' tiles and unique sizes (30" × 30", 2' × 6', etc.).

Variations to the basic lay-in acoustic tile ceiling are limited, but several are viable, even when budget constraints are important. Snap-on aluminum slat systems come in a great variety of colors and finishes. Vertically positioned acoustic baffles present another option, again available in a variety of materials and colors. Suspended or floating panel solutions have been employed, especially in settings requiring a dramatic effect. Translucent or luminous ceilings, employing both plastic and textile surface materials, have been quite successful in many situations requiring diffuse ambient light. And ceiling product manufacturers are now producing additional options, such as wood slats, planks and panels, metal tiles, and decorative coffers. While nonstandard ceiling systems may not always be appropriate, they should be given design consideration whenever possible.

In recent years there has been a resurgence in the use of open or unfinished ceiling techniques in which the floor structure above is exposed and there is not an enclosed plenum space. Without the use of recessed fixtures or a flat ceiling as a reflective surface, major use of pendant fixtures and tracks becomes the generally used lighting fixture solution.

Most design problems respond to many viable solutions. Design students see this regularly in studio classes, when 10 or 20 students each present a different solution to the same design problem. But there is one best approach to solving most office lighting design problems, and that is the use of the task/ambient concept, whereby a generally low level of ambient illumination is employed for most of the space

and strategically placed task lighting luminaires concentrate work-level illumination where critical visual tasks are performed. The task/ambient concept is best because it provides the optimum visual or seeing conditions in the work setting and it conserves energy best by providing high-level illumination only where it is needed. This concept is applicable not only in office work situations but also in kitchens (both residential and commercial), healthcare facilities (as in medical exam rooms and nursing stations), and many retail situations where the lighting task is to draw the customer's eye to specific merchandise.

Of course, some office spaces, such as lobbies and break rooms, do not require task lighting. Likewise, in some office spaces, such as training rooms, visual tasks are performed but the task/ambient approach is inappropriate. But generally, when designing lighting in places where people work, look first to the task/ambient approach for good, workable solutions.

Most office settings house a variety of visual tasks and therefore present a number of lighting design problems. The obvious starting point in solving these problems is with the visual tasks related to the desk, which sometimes means an open or freestanding desk but more often these days means a low-partitioned workstation. Each of these situations presents different lighting design problems. The private office presents additional visual tasks and conditions beyond those at the desk. Reception areas typically require one lighting condition for the receptionist and another for waiting visitors. The primary visual task in a conference room is at the conference table surface, but other activities often occur in these rooms that require additional lighting solutions. This list of office lighting functions and settings could go on to include presentation rooms, exhibit areas, filing centers, training rooms, and more. Regardless of the number of office lighting design problems you encounter, remember that the design solution process begins with identifying the visual tasks related to each function and setting.

It is important to note that office lighting design, as is true of many lighting design problems, is often a compromise between ideal practice and the practical limitations of budget, the lay-in ceiling system, and effective standards of the marketplace. This means that commercial real estate tends to control what is used to light office buildings. In most office buildings, one or two luminaires are identified as building standards. Tenants (and their architects and interior designers) are discouraged from using anything else, unless the tenant is unconcerned with cost. In office settings in other building types, for practical reasons of budget and construct ability, the same design constraints tend to apply. Even in company-owned office buildings, there are standard approaches established to light open and private offices, conference rooms, and other standardized spaces.

Beyond the identification of visual tasks, use the design methodology, which is fully described in Chapter 10, to complete the lighting design process. Despite the primary design focus on employee productivity and the human factors that are part of productivity concerns, don't forget that most people spend more waking hours in their work environment than anyplace else. This fact demands that an intelligent approach to all workplace environments also gives high priority to the human, social, and psychological aspects of those environments. While this is true of all design aspects of workplaces, lighting design plays an important and integral role in the final design result. As discussed in detail in Chapter 4, the integration of daylighting with electric lighting plays a major role in achieving both productive and personally satisfying work environments.

Most of the lighting design concerns in office settings focus on employees, who typically spend many hours there each day. In many business and professional offices, important attention must also be paid to the needs of visitors—clients, customers, colleagues, and vendors. Usually, visitors' access is limited to reception spaces, conference or presentation rooms, and private offices. In some cases, visitors perform specific visual tasks, such as reading and writing in a conference room or reviewing paperwork at a desk. Often, the design intentions in these visitor-accessible spaces include fostering a positive company image that the lighting design solution is expected to support. This may mean highlighting an unusually textured or reflective wall surface, displaying artwork or company products, dramatizing a ceremonial conference room, or showing off the richness and elegance of a chief executive's office. Creating image effects of these kinds is a frequent task of the lighting designer.

Designing office spaces requires consideration for computers and other office equipment. Computers are everywhere; it is rare to find a workstation without one. The widespread use of flat screen monitors has eliminated most of the problems of unwanted reflections on monitors, although that concern should not be entirely overlooked. Indirect ambient lighting, which is rapidly gaining favor, is a more success-

ful technique for avoiding unwanted reflections, and supports the rationale for the use of a task/ambient approach to lighting work environments. Personally adjustable task lighting is a particularly successful approach for the task element of a task/ambient lighting design solution.

The quality of ambient light should not be taken for granted; providing adequate illumination for the casual tasks of personal navigation and conversation does not fully solve the ambient lighting problem. Uniform low-level ambient light, particularly if indirect luminaires are the exclusive source, yields a lifeless and undesirable visual environment. People need both variety and spatial definition in their work environments, and uniform low-level lighting does not create visually satisfying spaces. Varying ambient lighting levels and highlighting wall surfaces at visual termini should be considered and appropriately incorporated to create visually alive and satisfying environments.

Complying with energy codes and employing energy-saving strategies has become a major criterion in all workplace lighting. The primary result is the pervasive use of full-size and compact fluorescent lamps and LED. The expanding development of fluorescent and LED technology has created products that can address all of the needs of workplace lighting, from subtle effects to dramatic creations. HID and low-voltage lighting can assist in office facilities, but the bulk of lighting solutions is accomplished with fluorescents and LEDs.

The case studies presented in this chapter represent five of the most common office spaces and functions. The examples shown are relatively small in order to make the lighting design issues easily understood. These lighting design issues are fundamental and can be translated to larger settings and to varying functional conditions and situations.

CASE STUDY 7—Reception Room Lighting

Reception rooms in office and corporate settings are usually the points of entry to a place of business or professional or institutional office. Typically, the reception room is a place for visitors to be greeted and acknowledged, or perhaps a waiting area to be seen and served. As is the case in all entrances, it is also a symbolic place that creates the first impression of a given environment—one that conveys a professional, corporate, or institutional image and sets the stage for the remainder of the interior space.

Reception rooms range tremendously in size from a few seats and a glass vision panel through which visitors speak to a greeter to a waiting area with dozens of seats and an open reception desk with one or more greeters. The

point of reception can vary from a simple desk that serves only as a point of greeting to a receptionist's workstation that requires a large work surface, files, and storage space. Many business and institutional office reception rooms have an element of display ranging from a simple logo highlighted on a wall to an extensive display of products, certificates, awards, or current work. In general, major entrances, including lobbies and reception areas, present an important opportunity to use lighting to express image and similar ideas.

A few basic visual tasks are served in most reception rooms. Some concentration of light should focus on the reception station in order to visually guide first-time visitors to it. Task light at the reception desk should be geared to the receptionist's work functions, which can be simple reading of paperwork or additional functions such as filing or proofreading. Ambient light is needed for general navigation throughout the space at a level appropriate for personal conversation and the casual reading of a book or magazine. Focal light may be needed to visually accent a company logo, a display of company-related material, or other art or graphics.

The floor plan in Fig. 13.1 indicates a modest-sized reception room, one that might be appropriate to a small- or medium-sized professional firm, such as a law firm, or that could be the entrance to a department within a large corporate or institutional office.

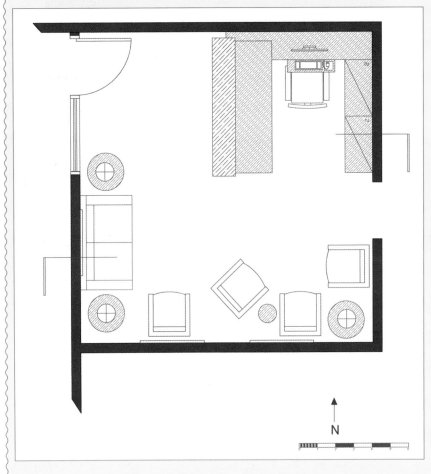

Fig. 13.1 Reception Floor Plan

N

1. The logo on the east wall requires focal light that directs visitors to the reception station and aids in viewing the contents of the file drawers when they are open. Framed art or graphic work is placed on the west and south wall surfaces; it is assumed that they also require focal illumination, but of less intensity.
2. The workstation configuration indicates that this receptionist requires task light for concentrated paperwork, filing, retrieval of paperwork, and other typical desk-related functions, including work at a desktop computer. If thoughtfully selected, that task light can also serve as the concentration of light needed to direct visitors to the receptionist when they enter the room.
3. The seating area requires a modest level of ambient light to serve the typical casual visual tasks of a waiting room—primarily personal conversation and short-term magazine reading.

The lighting solution shown in the lighting plan in Fig. 13.2 and the section in Fig. 13.3 address the visual tasks in the following manner:

1. The focal light required to highlight the company logo is handled simply with three recessed wallwashers focused on the logo area. The recessed accent fixtures are focused on the west and south wall artwork.
2. Task light at the receptionist's workstation is met with undercounter linear fluorescent or LED fixtures that concentrate light on the primary work surface.
3. The ambient light component is resolved with nine recessed downlights in the large central area of the room and three table lamps that are directly related to the waiting area seating. The table lamps, because of their scale and placement at eye level as well as their association with residential lighting, provide a personal and welcoming touch to the room.

For better placement of focal/accent lighting, the ceiling has a band of gypsum board soffit on all four sides of the room. The soffit is at 8'-6" above finished floor (AFF). The remainder of the ceiling is an 8'-8" AFF acoustic tile grid positioned for the placement of the nine recessed downlights.

Because the reception room is critical in setting the tone of the overall interior environment, the optimum level of illumination should be determined when the room is first put into use and not adjusted day to day. For this reason, a single switch is used to control all luminaires, architectural and portable. In situations of this kind, switching may be operated best on a time clock with a manual override because personal control is not necessary and may even be detrimental.

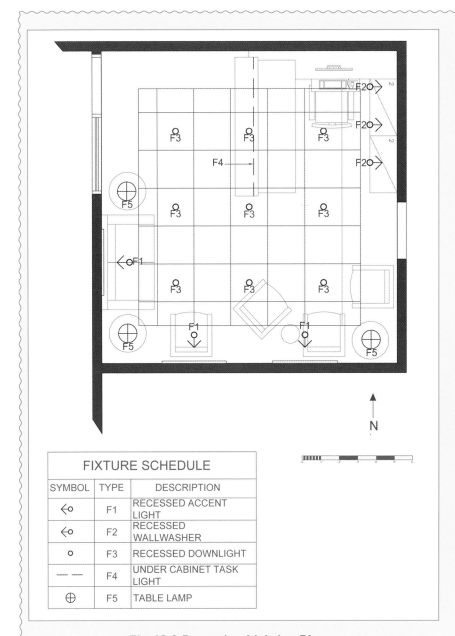

FIXTURE SCHEDULE

SYMBOL	TYPE	DESCRIPTION
←o	F1	RECESSED ACCENT LIGHT
←o	F2	RECESSED WALLWASHER
o	F3	RECESSED DOWNLIGHT
— —	F4	UNDER CABINET TASK LIGHT
⊕	F5	TABLE LAMP

Fig. 13.2 Reception Lighting Plan

Fig. 13.3 Reception Section

Luminaire and lamp selections should be based on the following considerations:

- Downlights: Compact fluorescent is most appropriate, or LED if the budget allows. The lamp should be regressed within the cone so that it is not visible or glaring from normal view. A wide beam spread works well for this ceiling height.
- Table lamps: Size and scale of lamp/shade combination to be reviewed in elevation. Direct/indirect distribution with translucent shade for eye-level glow desired. Compact or circle line fluorescent most appropriate lamp choice.
- Wallwashers: Recessed compact fluorescent or LED with asymmetric light distribution to light full height of logo wall.
- Adjustable accent fixtures: Recessed with internal aiming mechanism. A point source is required, either low-voltage halogen or LED would be appropriate.

The only luminaires that have significant aesthetic impact on the space are the three portable table lamps; their selection should be closely coordinated with the interior design color, finishes, and furniture selections.

CASE STUDY 8—Private Office Lighting

The traditional private office conveys an element of status as well as positive acoustic separation for its occupants. Despite the growing use of open, nonprivate workstations for all levels of office tasks and management, the private office is still widely used where customs of status and/or visual and acoustic confidentiality require it. This case study addresses the issues of the modest-sized office designed for its primary occupant and a maximum of two or three visitors. It is a place for concentrated deskwork and conversation. The larger, status-oriented executive office is dealt with in Case Study 9.

The lighting requirements of the private office shown in Fig. 13.4 are typical of most rooms of this type. The freestanding desk is the primary focus of task light, with the north wall credenza serving as a secondary work surface that requires adequate task light. People's faces on both sides of the desk should be comfortably illuminated for conversation. Some private offices have graphic material on their walls—a tack board, work-related material, or fine artwork—that require focal light. Here, the south and west walls are otherwise unused and could accommodate several kinds of graphic materials. With so many visual tasks to be served, it is assumed that additional light sources will not be required for ambient light in this relatively small room.

The solution shown in the lighting plan in Fig. 13.5 and sections in Figs. 13.6 and 13.7 address the visual tasks in the following manner:

1. Focal light for anticipated graphic material or artwork on the north and west walls is achieved with two wallwashers focused on each wall. Reflected light from the wallwashers also adds desirable ambient light to those two edges of the room, which might otherwise feel a little underlighted in contrast to the concentration of light in the two work areas.
2. Task light for the freestanding desk is accomplished with a 4'-long, direct/indirect pendant fluorescent luminaire that provides relatively shadowless light and avoids disturbing veiling reflections. There are other workable solutions for lighting a freestanding desk, such as the use of two 1' × 4' recessed fluorescent troffers that provide a wash of task-level light on the desk, or the use of a task/ambient approach in which a single 4'-long pendant fluorescent uplight provides a wash of ambient-level light in the desk area, supplemented by a portable adjustable swing arm desk luminaire lamped with a compact fluorescent lamp.
3. The secondary task light on the credenza top is produced by two 4' undercabinet fluorescent or LED luminaires. Because these luminaires are so close to the work surface, a modest lamp output provides a more than adequate level of illumination. This undercabinet light source serves two additional purposes. First, it helps illuminate the contents of the lateral file drawers. Second, it provides eye-level glow behind the desk user in a room that is otherwise lighted only from the ceiling. If the shelf or binder bin above the credenza does not have a fascia to hide the luminaires, it is aesthetically desirable to detail and provide one.

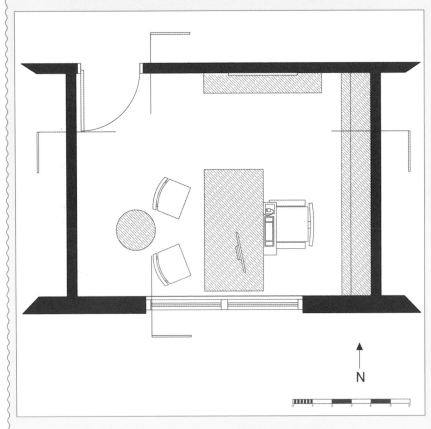

N

Fig. 13.4 Management Office Floor Plan

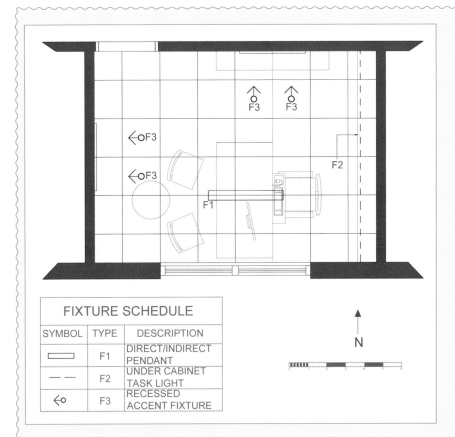

FIXTURE SCHEDULE

SYMBOL	TYPE	DESCRIPTION
▭	F1	DIRECT/INDIRECT PENDANT
— —	F2	UNDER CABINET TASK LIGHT
↙○	F3	RECESSED ACCENT FIXTURE

N

Fig. 13.5 Management Office Lighting Plan

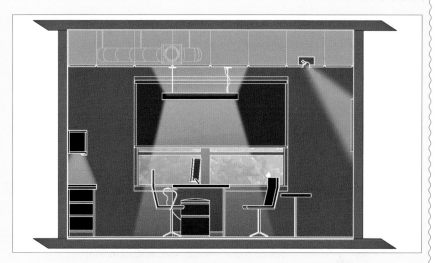

Fig. 13.6 Management Office Section

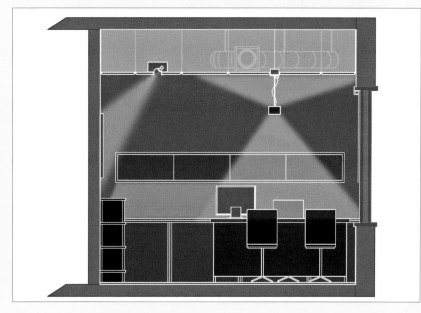

Fig. 13.7 Management Office Section

Switching can be accomplished with a few different approaches. By conventional means, a manual switch is placed at the entry door to control all the lighting in the room. However, this does not provide any personal control or energy savings. In this case, a dimmer is used to adjust the light level to the user's preference, or to manually lower or turn off the lights if daylight is sufficient. An adjacent switch is used to control the wallwashers. An alternative solution uses an occupancy sensor and a photocell to automatically adjust the level of illumination in conjunction with the daylight factor. Note that the undercabinet luminaires are switched from the wall directly below the wall cabinets.

Special note should be made of the uncommon window location in this office. More typically, offices of this kind have the entry door and the window on the short walls. The plan shown avoids the common problem of the office occupant having the window behind them, creating a difficult silhouette view for the visitor facing the person behind the desk. There are no easy solutions if the occupant wants the window uncovered by blinds or shades during daylight hours. Note also that a window shade is shown in the plan. Control of daylight is a critical issue related to lighting, heat gain, and audiovisual (A/V) issues.

Luminaire and lamp selections should be based on the following considerations:

- Pendant: 4'-long, direct/indirect fluorescent or LED placed centrally over the desk.

- Undercabinet fixture: Fluorescent or LED with direct light focused on the length of the credenza work surface; light source concealed to avoid glare.
- Wallwashers: Recessed compact fluorescent or LED with asymmetric light distribution to provide general wash of light on wall surface.

Luminaire design characteristics and style should be consistent with the architectural and interior design qualities of the room, including materials, color, furniture, and detailing. The only visible luminaire is the pendant over the desk. The luminaire could have distinctive design characteristics, but, in most cases of this kind, it should be selected so as to not draw attention to itself.

CASE STUDY 9—Lighting the Large Executive Office

The large executive private office serves two functions in addition to those of the more typical (and smaller) private office described and shown in the previous case study. First, its larger size accommodates more guests; second, it imparts an aura of prestige, status, and importance to its occupant. Some executive offices are immense, often containing a large conversational area and a sizable conference table in addition to a large desk and credenza for its primary user and a few pull-up chairs at the desk. For the purposes of this study, a more modest and typical executive office has been selected.

The lighting requirements for the executive office shown in Fig. 13.8 are typical of those required for most offices of this kind and size:

1. Focal light should be provided for artwork located on the east wall with the seating in front of it. Additionally, large-scale artwork or other graphic material is programmed for the north wall. The bookshelves in the southwest corner of the room also require a soft focal light.
2. The one critical requirement for task light is at the desk, where concentrative work occurs regularly. The credenza on the west wall provides a secondary work surface that also requires adequate task light.

3. Ambient light, for navigation and short-term reading, is required for the conversation area as well as the central space in the room.

The lighting solution shown in Figs. 13.9, 13.10, and 13.11 addresses the visual tasks in the following manner:

1. Strong focal light for the north wall graphics or artwork is provided by the three equally spaced recessed wallwashers, and the two recessed accent luminaires focused on the east wall artwork provide visibility for the occupant's preferred decorative items. The single wallwasher focused on the bookshelves in the southeast corner of the room give better visibility of the bookcase unit itself, and adding the special warmth that a display of books generally brings to a room.
2. Task light for the freestanding desk is provided by the swing-arm portable table lamp placed on the desktop. Its simple and direct adjustability permits the user to place high-level illumination directly on the paperwork at hand. Luminaire and lamp selection can be highly individualized to the style and preferences of the user. Task light for the credenza work surface is provided by a typical undercabinet fluorescent or LED luminaire that blankets the work surface with working-level illumination and creates desirable eye-level glow behind the primary desk. The light source itself should be concealed from view.

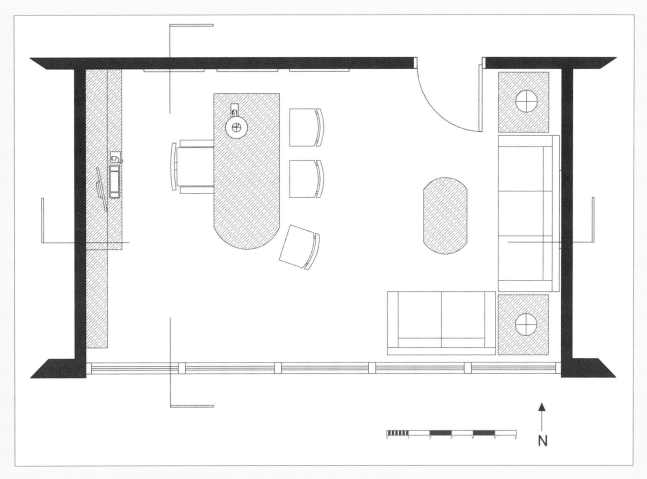

Fig. 13.8 Executive Office Plan

3. Ambient light is provided by three very different sources. The eight downlights cover the central area of the room. Their illumination level should be adjustable to accommodate a variety of desired moods. The focal/accent luminaires add a significant factor to the room's ambient light due to the reflected light from the wall surfaces that they illuminate. In addition to the focal/accent luminaires, the table lamps on the end tables at either side of the three-seat sofa provide an alternative kind of ambient light as well as eye-level glow for the west end of the room.

The large expanse of windows in the east wall plays an important role in switching for this room. All ceiling-mounted fixtures are switched at the entry door. The row of downlights closest to the windows are switched separately so that they can be switched off when the natural light provides adequate illumination for that edge of the room. The remainder of the downlights is switched separately from the focal/accent luminaires. The table lamps and undercabinet luminaires above the credenza are switched directly at their source.

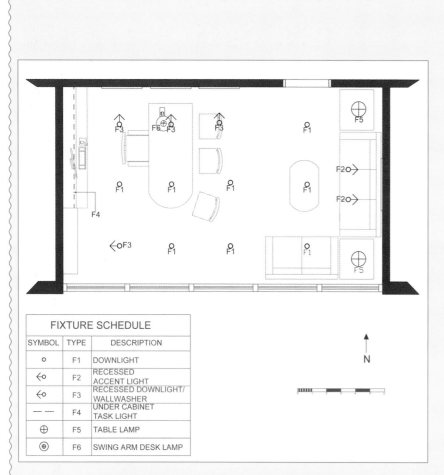

FIXTURE SCHEDULE		
SYMBOL	TYPE	DESCRIPTION
○	F1	DOWNLIGHT
←○	F2	RECESSED ACCENT LIGHT
←○	F3	RECESSED DOWNLIGHT/ WALLWASHER
— —	F4	UNDER CABINET TASK LIGHT
⊕	F5	TABLE LAMP
⊕	F6	SWING ARM DESK LAMP

Fig. 13.9 Executive Office Lighting Plan

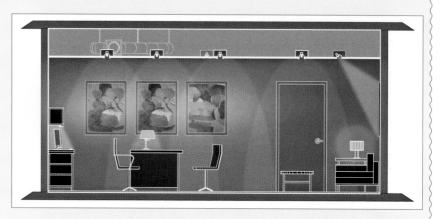

Fig. 13.10 Executive Office Section

Fig. 13.11 Executive Office Perspective

Luminaire and lamp selections should be based on the following considerations:

- Desk lamp: Ease and amount of adjustability important. The luminaire must provide a high-level work illumination with the lamp type and wattage best selected by individual user.
- Undercabinet fixture: Fluorescent or LED with direct light focused on the length of the credenza work surface; light source concealed to avoid glare.
- Downlights: Compact fluorescent or LED is most appropriate. The lamp should be regressed within the cone so that it is not visible or glaring from normal view. A wide beam spread works well for this ceiling height.
- Table lamps: Size and scale of lamp/shade combination to be reviewed in elevation. Direct/indirect distribution with translucent shade for eye-level glow desired. Compact or circle line fluorescent most appropriate lamp choice.

- Wallwashers: Recessed compact fluorescent or LED with asymmetric light distribution to provide general wash of light on wall surface.

Luminaire design characteristics and style should be consistent with the architectural and interior design qualities of the room, including materials, finishes, color, furniture, and detailing. In this case, the three portable luminaires are important to the room's decorative qualities and should be selected as much for their role as furniture and accessories as for their lighting quality. In other words, they are best selected with the furniture after appropriate consultation with the lighting designer. Often, luxurious executive offices are treated as personally as a living room, where the personal wishes of the occupant dominate every design decision.

CASE STUDY 10—Conference Room Lighting

Conference rooms generally serve a limited range of functions in which groups of people meet for verbal exchange. While some conference rooms can accommodate scores of people for large-scale presentations, more typically they contain a central table of a size that permits personal eye contact, conversation, and a limited amount of reading and notetaking. Conference rooms are frequently used for simple discussions or personal and group presentations, which may involve the deployment of a variety of electronic media.

A few basic visual tasks are performed in most conference rooms. The primary visual task is reading and writing at the conference table. Good lighting of the faces of those seated at the table is also important. Personal presentations that include graphic material such as diagrams and charts require focal light on those items. While conference rooms require comfortable navigational ambient light, consideration should be given to adjusting it for video, PowerPoint, and other electronic presentations. A less critical consideration is providing comfortable task light for a surface from which beverages and food are served.

The conference room shown in Fig. 13.12 is typical of many modest-sized conference rooms, including their lighting requirements.

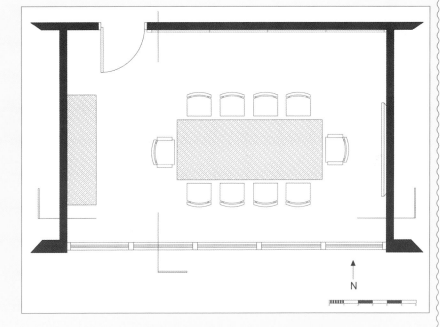

Fig. 13.12 Conference Room Floor Plan

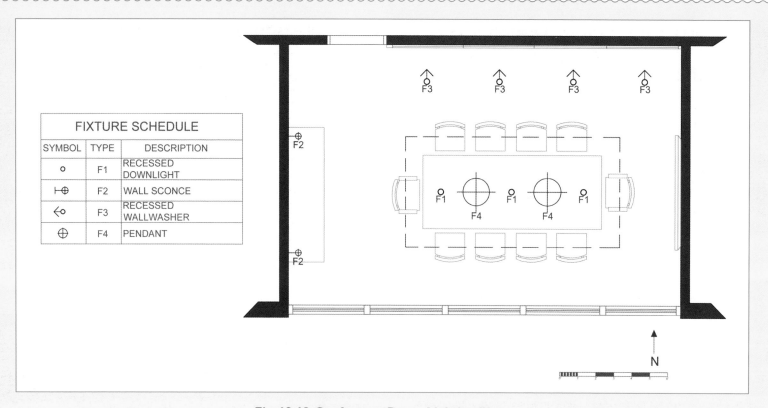

Fig. 13.13 Conference Room Lighting Plan

As indicated in the previous paragraph, the primary lighting requirements are as follows:

1. The presentation wall on the north side of the room requires strong focal light when it is in use, but should be dimmable to provide perimeter light when the focus is not on the presentation wall.
2. Appropriate task light for reading and writing at the conference table is required. That light source should also provide appropriate illumination of the faces of those seated at the table. The credenza surface, used for beverage and casual food service, requires modest task light.
3. The perimeter of the room must receive sufficient ambient light, not just for navigation purposes, but to keep the perimeter edges of the room from seeming visually lifeless or empty. Comfortable viewing of the large

flat screen TV at the north end of the room must be accommodated with appropriate switching and/or dimming.

The lighting solution shown in Figs. 13.13 through 13.16 addresses the visual tasks in the following manner:

1. Focal light for the graphics/presentation wall is achieved with recessed wall-washers centered on the panels. While many types of wallwashers can be used in a situation of this kind, compact fluorescent or LED luminaires have been selected in order to maximize coverage.
2. Conventional task light at the conference table is accomplished with two pendants placed symmetrically on either side of the center line of the conference table, and with three halogen or LED downlights placed along

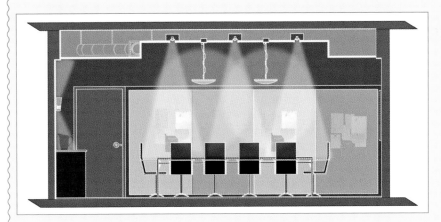

Fig. 13.14 Conference Room Section

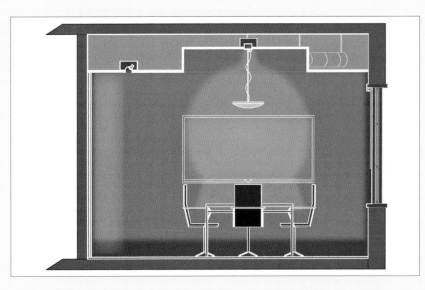

Fig. 13.15 Conference Room Section

that center line for a more direct, punchier task light for reading and writing tasks, especially during audiovisual presentations when the pendants would be off. Secondary task light for the credenza surface is provided by a pair of compact fluorescent sconces.

3. Ambient light for the north and west edges of the room are accomplished with the focal light on the presentation wall and the sconces for the credenza.

Each of the four groups of luminaires is separately switched at the room's entry door. All switches should have dimming capability to accommodate a variety of presentation requirements.

Luminaire and lamp selections should be based on the following considerations:

- Pendants over the conference table have a prescribed direct/indirect ratio. Their degree of decorativeness must be coordinated with the design qualities of the room.
- Downlights over the conference table have a narrow distribution band to serve reading and writing tasks.
- Recessed wallwashers focused on the presentation wall provide an even distribution of light and are of inconspicuous appearance. Lamps shall have a similar color temperature and CRI values as the primary lighting over the conference table in order to provide a unified (undramatic) visual environment.

Fig. 13.16 Conference Room Perspective

- The compact fluorescent sconces at the credenza provide adequate light for the self-service function of the credenza. Their decorative quality must be unified with the design qualities of the room.

The design characteristics and style of all luminaires should be consistent with the architectural and interior design qualities of the room, including materials, color, furniture, and detailing. In this case, the only significantly visible luminaires are the pendants over the conference table. Because of their physical prominence, the decision to make them visually dominant or unobtrusive is a major design decision.

CASE STUDY 11—Open Office Lighting

Lighting the workstation areas of office settings is one of the most common building design challenges. As discussed in some depth in the introduction to this chapter, several factors must be considered and integrated in creating these lighting design solutions. To briefly recount these factors, they are:

- User needs for visual comfort and productivity, utilizing task/ambient lighting concepts for optimum visual conditions, including minimizing CRT reflections.
- Construction practicality and economy, including built-in flexibility, access to mechanical and electrical systems, and development and use of building standards.
- Energy codes that limit energy consumption, which again strongly suggests the use of task/ambient concepts.

In most cases, open office areas do not involve major visitor traffic, making public image of limited concern and allowing the lighting design solution to focus on user needs. The following list presents most of the typical lighting design considerations in work settings like the relatively small open office area shown in Fig. 13.17:

1. Focal lighting for anticipated graphics/artwork/bulletin board on the east north wall is required.

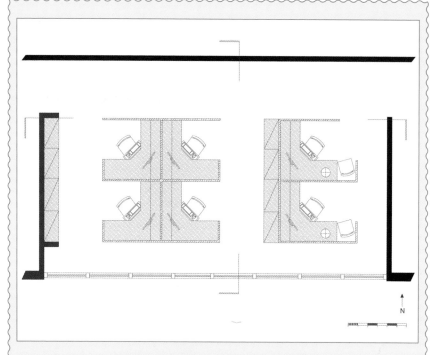

Fig. 13.17 Open Office Floor Plan

2. Of prime importance is high-quality task lighting for each station. Adequate seeing conditions for placing or finding written material in the filing cabinets is required.
3. Comfortable, low-level navigational lighting is needed throughout the space, as is eye-level glow and the lighting of people's faces at the two stations with visitors' pull-up chairs.
4. Ambient daylight is available along the southern portion of the space.

The lighting solution shown in the plan in Fig. 13.18 and sections in Figs. 13.19 and 13.20 addresses the visual tasks in the following manner:

1. Focal lighting for the north wall is accomplished with eight evenly spaced recessed wallwashers providing an even wash of light for graphics, artwork, and other visual material.

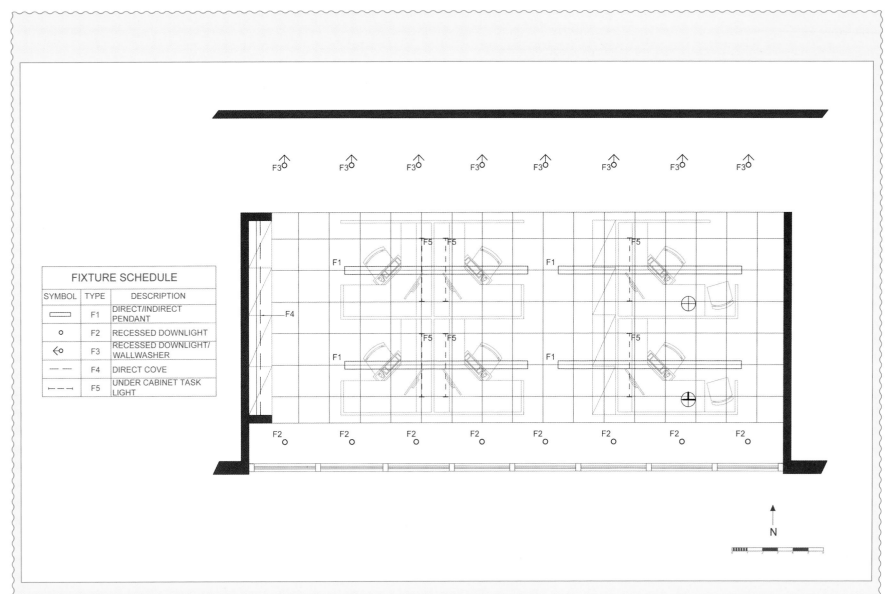

FIXTURE SCHEDULE

SYMBOL	TYPE	DESCRIPTION
▭	F1	DIRECT/INDIRECT PENDANT
○	F2	RECESSED DOWNLIGHT
←○	F3	RECESSED DOWNLIGHT/ WALLWASHER
- - -	F4	DIRECT COVE
⊢- -⊣	F5	UNDER CABINET TASK LIGHT

Fig. 13.18 Open Office Lighting Plan

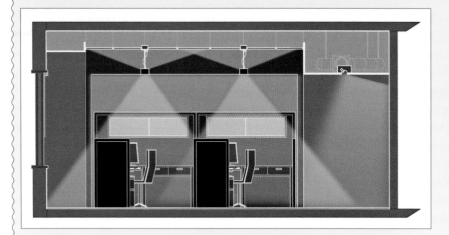

Fig. 13.19 Open Office Section

Fig. 13.20 Open Office Section

2. Task lighting is accomplished primarily with an undercabinet luminaire at each station. The two stations with visitors' chairs also have swing-arm desk lamps adjacent to the chairs to provide eye-level glow as well as illuminate faces when there is a personal exchange. In addition, task lighting for the bank of lateral filing cabinets along the west wall is provided with a built-in trough containing concealed linear luminaires.

3. Ambient lighting is accomplished primarily with four 12'-long indirect fluorescent pendants, which provide an even wash of moderate light for most of the space. The row of luminaires closest to the window wall is separately switched and controlled by a daylight sensor in order to conserve energy when daylighting will provide adequate ambient light. In addition, the focal lighting of the north wall contributes to the ambient light for navigation.

All task lighting is controlled at its source by the employees at the workstations. All other switching is controlled at a nearby panel box because personal choice is not at issue. As noted above, the fluorescent pendants closest to the window wall are controlled by a daylight sensor. All lighting will require an automatic timer shutoff to meet code requirements.

As is always the case, luminaire design characteristics and style should be consistent with the architectural and interior design qualities of the room, including materials, color, furniture, and detailing.

Chapter 14 CLASSROOM LIGHTING DESIGN

Classrooms are the primary design problem for schools, but they also are found in office buildings, corporate headquarters, hospitals, and many other building types. Classrooms vary in their lighting requirements as more of them incorporate digital and electronic techniques and equipment, and distance learning becomes more prevalent.

Traditional classrooms are still common in the majority of primary, secondary, and post-secondary schools. The invasion of computers is not as critical in designing classrooms as once thought. Conventional concerns for illumination of deskwork and vertical surfaces still take priority. The modern challenge is to provide high-quality lighting and low-energy use while remaining within the budget. The psychological benefits of daylighting are especially important; recent studies have shown that daylighted classrooms contribute to improved learning, as measured by standardized tests. Refer to Chapter 4 for additional information.

When designing the lighting for a conventional classroom, a variety of tasks must be considered. In addition to tasks performed at classroom seats, visual tasks occur at the white board, bulletin boards, and other vertical display surfaces as well as in special study areas. Often, general illumination is utilized to ensure that an adequate light level is achieved throughout the classroom. Lighting systems that produce relatively high vertical surface illumination and, if possible, ceiling illumination for comfort and balance of brightness should be used. Most traditional tasks are considered properly illuminated with 50–70 foot-candles of electric lighting. Because this light level is on the higher end, it is important to provide the opportunity to dim or switch lights off based on the needs of the instructor to allow for flexibility and energy savings.

From a lighting standpoint, there are two special types of classrooms:

1. Rooms in which the classic or fine arts, especially painting and sculpture, are taught and practiced.
2. Rooms in which computer arts and sciences are taught and practiced.

137

CASE STUDY 12—Classroom Lighting

The classroom floor plan shown in Fig. 14.1 is consistent with the design needs of many typical contemporary classrooms.

1. The focal lighting issues involve illuminating the two marker boards, the display board at the entry end of the room, and the special focal needs related to viewing the projection screen.

2. The primary task lighting issue is at the students' tablet arms where they typically will be reading and writing.
3. With the amount of light generally provided in the room, ambient lighting does not require specific attention, except when lights are dimmed for viewing the projection screen.

The lighting design solution shown in the lighting plan and sections in Figs. 14.2 and 14.3 address the visual tasks encountered by the classroom's students.

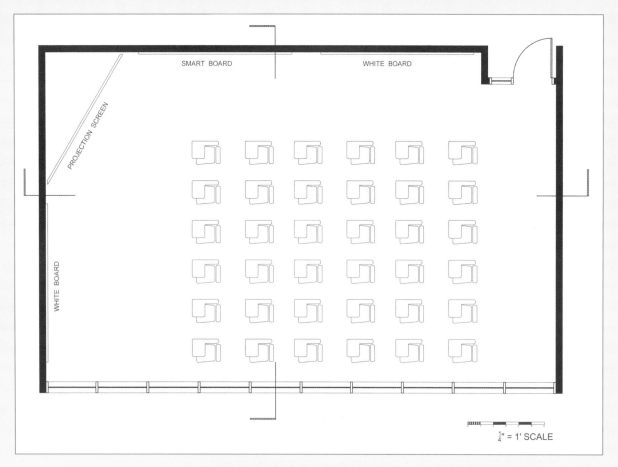

SMART BOARD   WHITE BOARD

PROJECTION SCREEN

WHITE BOARD

¼" = 1' SCALE

Fig. 14.1 Classroom Floor Plan

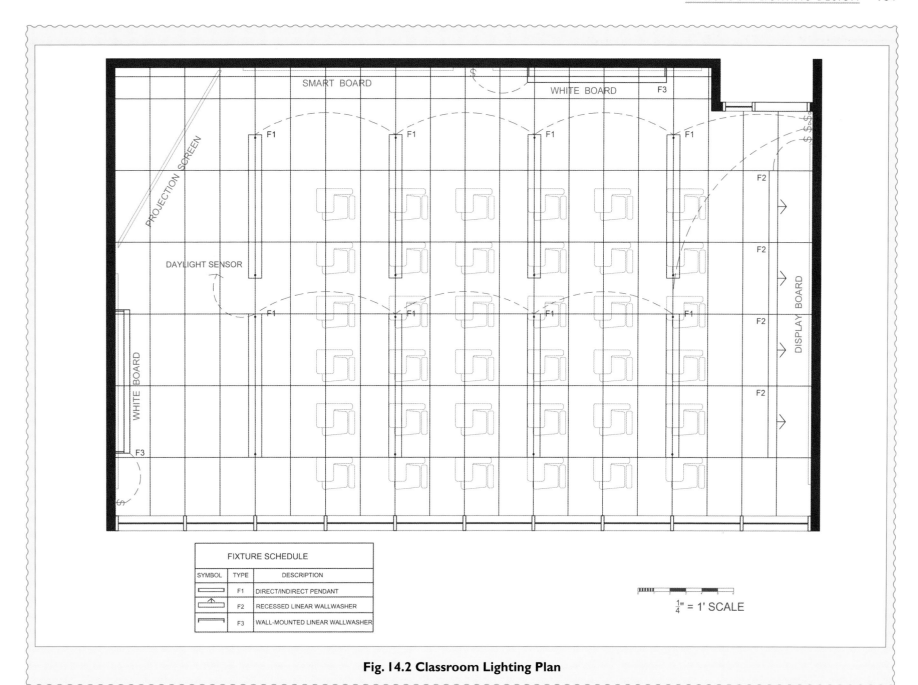

Fig. 14.2 Classroom Lighting Plan

1. Focal lighting for the two white boards is accomplished with the use of wall-mounted linear wallwashers and, for the display board, with recessed linear wallwashers. The viewing of the projection screen depends upon the nature of the material displayed on the screen. For film and video viewing that do not require note-taking, all luminaires will be turned off; for any kind of presentation requiring the students to take notes, the general lighting pendants will be appropriately dimmed.

2. For task lighting, the eight direct/indirect fluorescent pendants will blanket the space with a consistent and workable illumination level to reading and writing. Note that the four pendants on the window side of the room are separately switched so that they will be turned off automatically when the daylight condition provides adequate task light.

3. Adequate ambient illumination for navigational purposes is available throughout daylight hours. When the pendant task luminaires are on, they typically provide more than adequate ambient light for the room. The wall-washer luminaires that are focused on the north, east, and west walls will add to the ambient light quality as their focus on wall surfaces will reflect a great deal of light to the room's periphery.

Luminaire and lamp selections should be based on the following considerations:

- Pendant: 8' direct/indirect fluorescent pendant mounted at 7'-6" above finished floor (AFF), to provide approximately 50 percent uplight and 50 percent downlight.
- Wall-mounted wallwashers: Asymmetric distribution with aiming rotation to focus on the white boards with fluorescent or LED lamping, depending upon budget allowances. Also to be mounted at 7'-6" AFF.

- Recessed wallwashers: Asymmetric distribution to wash east display wall. Fluorescent troffer design allows easy installation into acoustical ceiling.

The two banks of pendant fluorescents are separately dimmed at the entry door. Switching for all three wallwashing luminaires are located adjacent to each fixture. The bank of pendants adjacent to the windows will be dimmed automatically by a daylight sensor. It is also common for an occupancy or vacancy sensor to be utilized to ensure that lights are off when the classroom is not being used.

Specialty classrooms, as noted above, require customized attention. The traditional fine arts classroom, where painting, sculpture, and related arts areas are taught, call for generally higher lighting levels and a higher than conventional CRI figure. Foot-candle readings should be at the high end of the conventional classroom requirement and a CRI of 90 or better should be achieved. Daylight in arts classrooms is a major plus, particularly if windows can face north and/or translucent skylights can provide a wash of natural light over the room. In addition, many arts classrooms contain display or gallery spaces that may require a flexible accent lighting system.

Electronic classrooms, including those for the digital arts, have similarly specific lighting needs. Computer screen displays and projection screens can be affected by room lighting, so that a greater than normal level of lighting controls is necessary. And flexibility in creating varying lighting conditions for specific teaching situations is highly desirable. In general, specialty classrooms demand coordination with relevant educators in order to provide successful teaching environments.

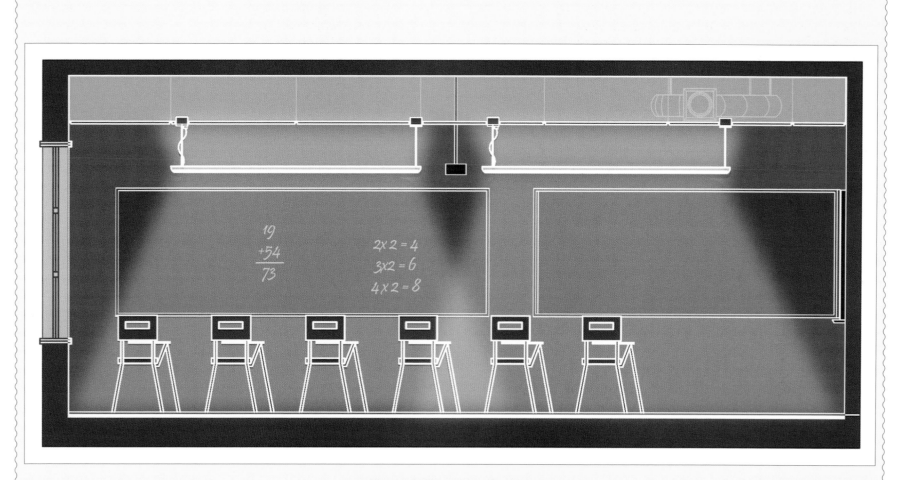

Fig. 14.3 Classroom Section

Chapter 15 HEALTHCARE LIGHTING DESIGN

Healthcare facilities are challenging for the lighting designer because of the wide variety of tasks performed and the constant change and evolution. Perhaps even more challenging is meeting the lighting needs of a wide range of ages, from newborn infants to the elderly. With an increasingly aging population, lighting must be designed with the visual difficulties of an active elderly population in mind. Further, because of the emphasis on health, there is an increased awareness of how lighting design can be either beneficial or problematic in addressing photobiological issues such as Seasonal Affective Disorder (SAD) and changes in circadian rhythms.

The greatest challenge is probably to provide competent, energy efficient, and cost-effective lighting that does not contribute to the institutional appearance traditionally attributed to hospitals and doctors' offices. Low-cost fluorescent lighting systems are increasingly less acceptable and most new hospitals, senior living facilities, and clinics now require lighting design that exceeds the quality standards of office buildings and hotels.

Unlike in hotels, theme and style are generally not important in healthcare facilities. Most hospitals, clinics, and medical offices employ a standard palette of interior finishes that appear modern, clean, and simple, if not a bit bland. Despite this, there is a growing tendency for all healthcare facilities to lose their traditional institutional qualities and adopt a more relaxed and emotionally comfortable environment, in some instances employing the design vocabulary of the hospitality design world. Contemporary architectural and decorative lighting systems are easily incorporated,

giving the lighting designer a relatively wide choice among lighting fixtures that use fluorescent and compact fluorescent, halogen, and LED sources. While codes and standards will play a significant role in the lighting of healthcare facilities, lighting design can and should be creative in addition to properly addressing the visual tasks that must be met.

Senior living and care centers are different from more acute healthcare facilities because they are more like hotels or apartment buildings. A strong design theme is often used for their interiors in order to establish a noninstitutional ambience. Portable lighting, such as floor lamps and table lamps, help reinforce a residential theme. After all, seniors want to live in a home, not an institution.

Healthcare facilities include a number of spaces in which demanding visual tasks are important. Operating rooms and laboratories spring to mind, but an even larger number of procedure rooms and special spaces exist where lighting requirements are equally critical. Most operating rooms and some procedure rooms, such as dentists' offices, employ specialized task lights that are usually specified by healthcare equipment specialists and supplied by equipment companies rather than lighting companies. But the examination lights in patient bedrooms and many other places are part of the general lighting design.

Healthcare facilities feature spaces where specific aspects of lighting must be controlled especially well. For instance, in radiological suites, low levels of indirect lighting are preferred to prevent exposing X-ray plates to light. In nurseries, newborns' eyes must be shielded from direct light. In magnetic resonance imaging (MRI) suites, lighting must be designed to prevent radio frequency interference (RFI). In dental procedure rooms, lighting should have high color temperature and high CRI to enable accurate color matching of crown work.

The majority of healthcare facilities require conventional lighting as well—for offices, cafeterias, hallways, meeting rooms, lobbies, waiting rooms, and similar spaces that are also found in conventional buildings. Most of these spaces appear to have no special lighting requirements. However, unlike in office buildings, where you can assume that most users are working-age people with normal eyesight, healthcare facilities have a high population of patients who are older or have disabilities, and it is important to remember that they benefit from higher light levels. The key is to increase lighting levels over office building standards, but not so much as to cause glare or discomfort.

Daylighting and views to the exterior are highly desirable in healthcare facilities for several reasons. In addition to the constant importance of energy efficiency, a primary benefit is the strengthening of circadian rhythms, which have been shown to aid the healing process and, in older persons, to aid in overall health and vitality. Not having access to exterior views presents a decidedly negative environment; windows with a city street scene or a natural setting provide a meaningful psychological benefit and should be incorporated wherever possible. Another important attribute of daylight is color rendering, which can be useful in dental procedure rooms and other spaces where color matching is critical. Remember, however, that the color rendering properties of daylight are often lost with the use of glazing systems that are designed for their sun shielding and/or thermal insulating qualities.

The use of decorative lighting in health care historically has been minimal and reserved almost exclusively for waiting rooms. With the growing tendency to de-institutionalize healthcare facilities, there is increased use of decorative lighting, including chandeliers, sconces, pendants, and floor and table lamps. Given that the cost of energy and maintenance are major concerns, compact fluorescents should be used with decorative lighting in healthcare settings whenever possible.

Most ceilings in healthcare institutions employ major use of acoustic tile that permits easy access to the ceiling plenum; with the number of services above the ceiling—plumbing, sprinklers, heating, venting, and air-conditioning (HVAC), medical gases, and data lines—access is a primary concern. Hard ceilings such as gypsum wallboard are rarely used because they require access panels that detract from the appearance of the ceiling, make maintenance access more difficult and time consuming, and add to the cost of construction. Unusual ceiling types are uncommon because of cleanliness and health concerns.

Flexible lighting designs are rarely used in healthcare facilities because lights are not often changed or relocated, with the exception of surgical and exam lights and

lighting for art collections, gift shops, and a few other minor areas. To the contrary, a good healthcare design is fixed and durable, and uses energy efficient light sources that last a long time. Fluorescent lamps are preferred; a good design uses just a few lamp types, which simplifies stocking and replacement. Some healthcare facilities lend themselves to general lighting. Ignoring portable and fixed examination and surgical lights, the following spaces tend to require general illumination: treatment and exam rooms, toilets, working corridors, operating and surgical rooms, scrub-down rooms, kitchens, storage rooms, intensive care suites, procedure rooms, and laboratories. This is because of the relatively large portion of the space in which tasks may occur and, in some cases, the potential for interference with procedures and emergency response.

But a large number of spaces in the healthcare setting can employ layered lighting principles. Because layered lighting permits decorative lighting, it is easy to incorporate simple and effective decorative lighting and still meet overall illumination and energy requirements. This approach works best in offices, lobbies, waiting rooms, patient corridors, nursing stations, and libraries. In fact, a trend in healthcare design is to introduce decorative lighting as a key element in interior design, serving to de-institutionalize by adding sparkle, color, and accent to these spaces.

A major benefit of layered lighting is in allowing different lighting levels by day and night. The general lighting within the nursing environment by day should probably be bright, providing both ample task lighting and a daytime sense of activity. At night, however, bright lights can interfere with the sleeping cycle of patients; by extinguishing ambient lights and dimming task lights, a comfortable night environment for both nurses and patients can be created. The patient bedroom is an especially complex lighting problem. Most of the time, the lighting of the patient room should be as residential as possible. This is particularly important in birthing suites and senior living quarters, where the usual intent is for the space to look and feel like a home. Soft ambient light permits easy movement about the room, and task lights permit reading in the bed and in nearby chairs. At night, a very low light level permits nurses to check on patients but does not interfere with sleep. But during an examination of the patient, high light levels throughout the bed area can be energized at the flick of a switch.

Codes can play a limiting role in healthcare design. Healthcare design regulations, which vary by state in the United States (and elsewhere), require certain foot-candle levels in various facility types. For instance, in Oregon, the laws regulating senior care facilities specify foot-candle requirements for various rooms and spaces. In California, hospitals and senior care facilities must meet the requirements of the Office of the State Architect. It is good practice to contact the regulating authorities before proceeding with a design.

The Americans with Disabilities Act (ADA) specifies critical requirements for lighting, especially in limiting wall-mounted light projections to 4" unless the light is 80" or more above the floor. Furthermore, because the focus of the ADA is accessibility, the healthcare designer should consider every aspect of lighting carefully, keeping in mind the limited eyesight and mobility of many facility users. For instance, locate easy-to-use light switches where they can be reached by people seated in a wheelchair.

The case studies in this chapter represent two of the most common spaces and functions. The examples presented are relatively basic in order to make the lighting design issues easily understood. These lighting design issues are fundamental and can be translated to other settings and to varying conditions.

CASE STUDY 13—Patient Room Lighting

The floor plan for the patient room for this case study is presented in Fig. 15.1. It represents the current practices and trends in current private patient care rooms. The ceilings in the bedroom and the bath are acoustical tile, and the finishes are typical for healthcare facilities, including vinyl wall coverings.

As discussed earlier in this chapter, a residential ambience is sought in patient rooms, but the visual tasks are significantly more demanding than those

Fig. 15.1 Patient Room Floor Plan

in a residence because nursing and treatment needs, as well as the patient's personal needs are specific and complex. Ceiling-mounted and wall-mounted lights can be used extensively, although table lamps and other typical residential fixtures are employed wherever practical, keeping in mind that portable lamps may interfere with patient beds, intravenous (IV) stands, privacy curtains, and crash carts.

The visual tasks in the patient bedroom include the following:

1. Focal light is needed for artwork located on the wall to the west of the patient bed and the south wall beside the patient's personal chest of drawers.
2. Task lighting is required for reading in bed, medical examinations and treatments, grooming at the bathroom lavatory, and writing at the desk.
3. Decorative lighting is desired in the room to reinforce the residential ambience.
4. Ambient lighting is needed at the entry to the room, in the bathroom and in its shower, and in the general area of the patient room; also, a night light is needed by the patient and the nursing staff.

The lighting design solution for the patient room is shown in the lighting plan of Fig. 15.2. A section of that same room is shown in Fig. 15.3.

1. In creating a residential ambience, focal lighting is provided by recessed wallwasher luminaires placed to illuminate the artwork planned for the west and south walls of the room.
2. Multiple levels of task lighting are addressed at the patient bed area. An up/down wall-mounted luminaire is placed directly over the bed to provide light for reading in bed, as well as providing ambient light for the room. The up/down functions can operate separately or together, providing flexibility for the patient. A recessed 2' × 2' troffer is placed directly over the bed to provide task light for medical examinations and treatments. A wall-mounted luminaire is placed over the bathroom mirror for grooming purposes, with the lamp selected for its high CRI rating. A table lamp for the desk provides task light for reading and writing.
3. The table lamp at the desk also adds the desired eye-level glow and a decorative touch.

4. Specific ambient lighting is provided at the entry and in the bathroom with a recessed downlight centrally placed. A recessed "waterproof" downlight is located in the shower stall. In addition, a recessed, wall-mounted night light is placed 18" AFF on the north wall near the patient bed specifically for nursing staff needs during sleeping hours. With the many luminaires in the patient room, both architectural and portable, additional ambient luminaires are not needed.

Switching is made as simple as possible because it is used by so many different people: the patient, nurses, physicians, nursing floor staff, kitchen staff, and the patient's guests. A switch is at the entry door for the downlight in the entry area. A separate dimmer is provided for the wallwashers. The switches for the examination luminaires are also located at the entry. The examination luminaires contain step ballasts providing bi-level control depending upon the needs of the physician and staff. In the bathroom, there is a switch to control all of the three luminaires in the room. The switch for the patient's task light is part of the bed control system. The control of the table lamp is contained in the luminaire.

Luminaire and lamp selections should be based on the following considerations:

- Downlights and wallwashers: Compact fluorescent is the most appropriate, or LED if the budget allows. The lamp should be regressed within the cone so that it is not visible or glaring from normal view. A wide beam spread works well for this ceiling height.

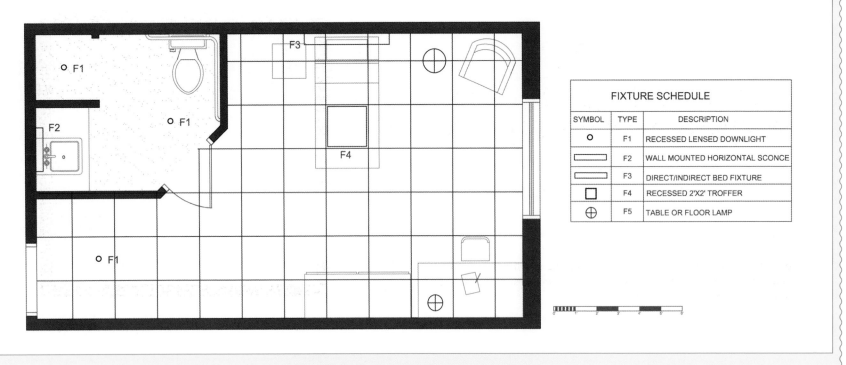

FIXTURE SCHEDULE

SYMBOL	TYPE	DESCRIPTION
○	F1	RECESSED LENSED DOWNLIGHT
▭	F2	WALL MOUNTED HORIZONTAL SCONCE
▭	F3	DIRECT/INDIRECT BED FIXTURE
▢	F4	RECESSED 2'X2' TROFFER
⊕	F5	TABLE OR FLOOR LAMP

Fig. 15.2 Patient Room Lighting Plan

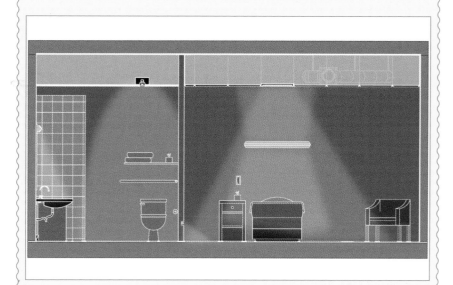

Fig. 15.3 Patient Room Section

- Troffers: Fluorescent lamping is the most common, but now LED could also be considered. Select indirect or high-efficiency troffers for patient comfort.
- Vanity sconce: High-quality CRI and warm color temperature are most appropriate to provide flattering, shadowless light for the user. In this application, fluorescent lamping is most common.
- Table lamps: Size and scale of lamp/shade combination are to be reviewed in elevation. Direct/indirect distribution with translucent shade for eye-level-glow is desired.

Luminaire selection for the patient's task light is typically part of the healthcare furnishings and equipment package. Except for the ones used in the entrance area, the architectural luminaires are generic in nature, have little visual impact on the space, and are selected for their simplicity of design, energy efficiency, and budget concerns.

CASE STUDY 14—Examination Room Lighting

Examination rooms are commonplace in hospitals, clinics, and other medical facilities. They tend to be all-purpose rooms that can be used for a variety of examinations or treatments. Typically they contain an examination table, a work counter and/or desk, a desk chair, and an extra chair. It is unusual for anyone, including the medical professional, to spend an extended period of time in the exam room. Its purpose is purely functional and does not require personalization. Room finishes are similarly utilitarian, with easy to clean surfaces and acoustic tile ceilings for accessibility purposes. While most exam rooms have neutral tone floors and clinically white walls and ceilings, variations in wall colors are possible within the limitations of visual cleanliness.

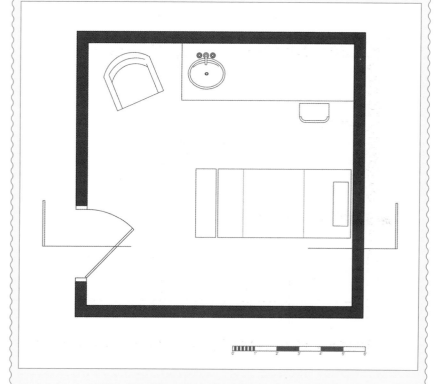

Fig. 15.4 Examination Room Floor Plan

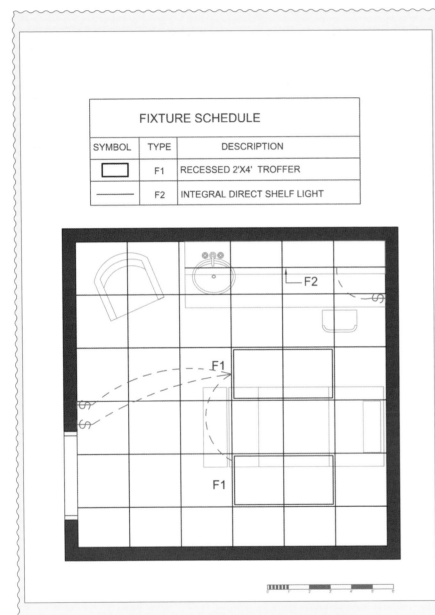

FIXTURE SCHEDULE

SYMBOL	TYPE	DESCRIPTION
▭	F1	RECESSED 2'X4' TROFFER
——	F2	INTEGRAL DIRECT SHELF LIGHT

Fig. 15.5 Examination Room Lighting Plan

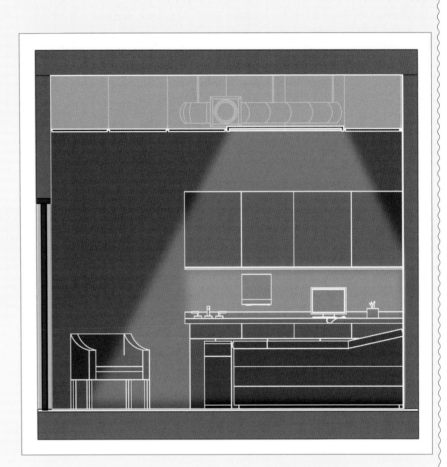

Fig. 15.6 Examination Room Section

The floor plan for the examination room for this case study is presented in Fig. 15.4. The visual tasks in this exam room are primarily functional and are limited to luminaires for task lighting. High-intensity light is required directly over the exam table for detailed inspection and treatment of patients. Reasonably strong task light is required at the work counter/desk for reading, writing, and working with medications and instruments.

The lighting design solution for the exam room is shown in the lighting plan of Fig. 15.5. A section of that same room is shown in Fig. 15.6.

Task lighting for the exam table is provided by two 2' × 4' recessed fluorescent troffers. This low-cost, conventional selection provides ample light for all exam purposes. Bi-level switching of three lamp luminaires (two switches—one for the center lamp and one for the outer lamps of each luminaire) or dimming provides flexibility in light levels. An undercabinet luminaire over the work counter/desk provides appropriate task light for the functions performed there.

Switching control for the exam table luminaires is at the door to the room. Switching for the undercabinet luminaire is on the wall adjacent to the work surface.

Chapter 16 RETAIL LIGHTING DESIGN

Stores use—and their operators appreciate—lighting more than just about any other element of the store's interior. In most cases, brightly lighted stores are more successful and desirable than dimly lighted ones. Lighting in stores not only illuminates products for sale but also plays a major role in store design and style, or theme.

The first and, some say, most important role of lighting in store design is to attract the eye. Lighting naturally does this through the brilliance and sparkle of lighting systems, and this effect is especially significant with stores. For example, in the design of a grocery store, the brilliance of ordinary fluorescent lights attracts the eye and tells approaching shoppers that the store is open for business. In the visually competitive world of the mall, more dramatic lighting effects, such as moving lights, colored lights, and attractive luminaires, must be used to capture the attention of shoppers. Store windows constitute such an important opportunity that lighting them is an art form unto itself and akin to stage set lighting. It should be noted that many mall stores do not have a conventional front window and use the store interior itself to attract and invite shoppers to enter.

The second most important role of lighting in stores is to illuminate the merchandise. The most successful store designs provide illumination for all of the merchandise, not just for highlighting feature displays. This is true whether the store is designed to appear bright, using general illumination, or dramatic, using track or other types of display lighting.

The third most important job of lighting in stores is to excite the shopper. Excitement is part of the theme of the design, and the role of lighting may be substantial. Some ways to excite the shopper include:

1. Dramatically lighting merchandise, especially feature displays
2. Using luminaires whose strong style reinforces the store's theme or the theme of the architecture
3. Using architectural lighting techniques like cove lighting and wallwashing to reveal or reinforce elements of the interior design or architecture
4. Employing highly specialized lighting techniques such as color-changing lights, theatrical lighting, moving lights, fiber optics, and neon to energize the space or produce spectacular lighting effects

The fourth most important role of lighting in stores is to illuminate the work of storekeeping, including stocking, cleaning, and point of sale. For example, a classic solution to many store design problems is to use highly styled pendant luminaires at the point of sale. This technique ensures adequate light for sales work, reinforces the store's theme, and functions as a way finder for shoppers.

The fifth and final role of lighting in stores is to reinforce the shopper's sense of value and price point. This has proven to be a delicate balance. For example, in a discount store, the lighting must appear inexpensive, or the shopper may feel out of place. Many grocery stores use bare-lamp strip lights, both for economy and to suggest that the store merchandise is competitively priced.

Recent research has found that, when used in stores, daylighting dramatically increases sales. If the store design allows, consider adding daylight via simple skylights or more complex architectural expressions. Remember to use many smaller skylights, just as you would use many luminaires rather than one big one. There are some specific situations, such as in art galleries, where the designer must consider the potential of color degradation caused by the ultraviolet content of natural light.

A major difference between stores and other building types is that the merchandise often is displayed in the vertical plane rather than the more typical horizontal plane. As a result, lighting solutions must avoid concentrated downlight—unless, of course, the specific task is in the horizontal plane. General fluorescent downlighting is sufficiently diffuse to create good vertical light, but downlights using incandescent, compact fluorescent, or HID lamps tend to concentrate downlight too much.

Stores are regulated quite heavily by energy codes. In 2011, power density limits for grocery stores and big-box retail stores were about 1.5 watts per square foot (W/sf). The limits for other store types depend on the merchandise, with the highest levels permitted for jewelry stores and the like. The following examples are designed to meet energy codes in most states.

CASE STUDY 15—A Small Boutique

A large percentage of retail lighting is for small and medium-sized stores. In most cases, the store has a rectangular floor plan and is located in a row of similar-sized stores along a street or in a mall.

In most smaller stores, shelving displays are rarely ceiling-high, except at the walls. Instead, displays in the center of the store often consist of short shelving, freestanding merchandise, or flat gondola displays. The focus of the store design depends largely on the type of store. In the three case studies in this chapter, you can see how the store layout and function affect task locations and lighting design.

The lighting design approach in a small store is especially important for store image and appeal. Basic, inexpensive fluorescent lighting and high light levels convey cost-consciousness. Decorative lighting fixtures, especially those with colored glass or other distinctive qualities, tend to give the store an identity. Dramatic architectural and track lighting give the store a sense of mystery and quality. It is critically important to choose the right image in lighting as well as other aspects of store design.

In general, lighting controls should consist primarily of a time clock with manual override switches. In malls, specific coordination must be made with the mall's control systems.

For this case study, a shoe store in a shopping mall illustrates the basic design problems encountered in lighting small stores. The same approach is applicable for any store selling medium-priced general merchandise, such as gifts and cards, clothing, or housewares. The store shown in the floor plan in Fig. 16.1 has a large general display area near the entry to the store, with a long cash-wrap/store-control station in the middle of the store and a large seating/fitting area with display shelves on the periphery at the rear of the store. Stock and work areas lie behind the public areas.

The visual tasks in the store are clearly defined.

1. Focal lighting is required in all areas of the store, focusing light on the countertop displays and peripheral shelving displays of merchandise.
2. Task lighting is needed at the cash-wrap station and in the seating area for sales personnel fitting customers with shoes.
3. Decorative lighting is desired to attract customers at the store's entrance, at the cash-wrap station, and in the seating area.
4. As in most retail stores, where a great deal of light is used for display purposes, specifying particular ambient lighting is usually unnecessary because all of the other lighting supplies more than enough light for navigation and conversational purposes.

The lighting solution shown in the reflected ceiling plan in Fig. 16.2 and the accompanying section in Fig. 16.3 addresses the visual tasks in the following manner:

1. The majority of the focal lighting is produced by the adjustable accent and wallwashing luminaires attached to the track system in the front of the store and those attached to the edge of the dropped ceiling "cloud" in the rear of the store. The adjustable luminaires that are directed at the upper portion of the perimeter walls wash the walls above the display shelves, where there is the opportunity for signage and/or graphics. The remaining adjustable luminaires are selected to accent the shoes in the front window displays and focus on the shoes on the countertop display fixtures. The recessed accent fixtures in the dropped ceiling over the cash-wrap area

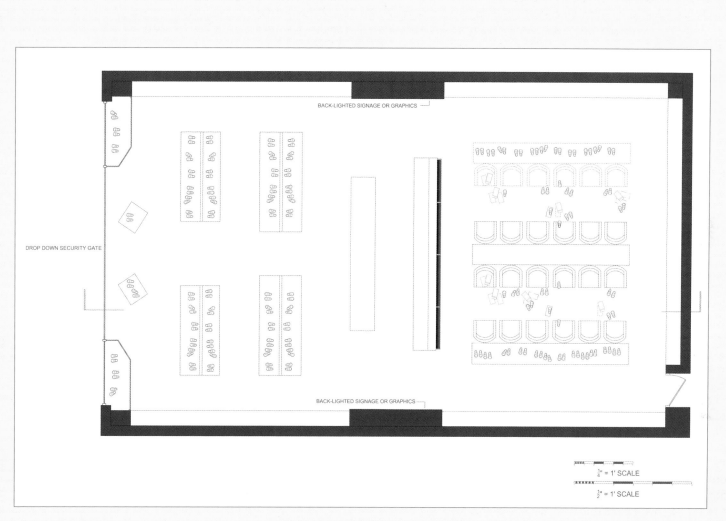

BACK-LIGHTED SIGNAGE OR GRAPHICS

DROP DOWN SECURITY GATE

BACK-LIGHTED SIGNAGE OR GRAPHICS

$\frac{1}{4}$" = 1' SCALE

$\frac{1}{2}$" = 1' SCALE

Fig. 16.1 Small Boutique Floor Plan

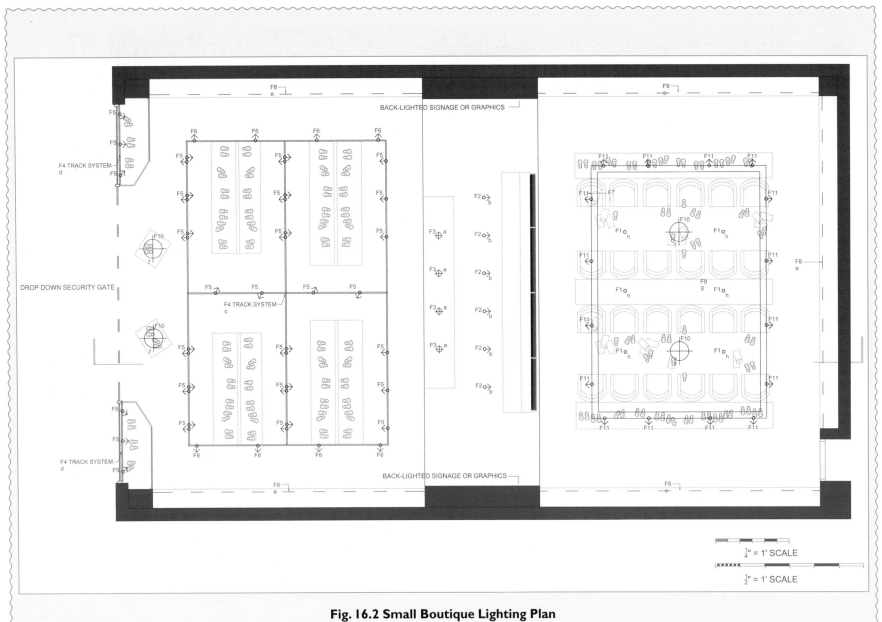

Fig. 16.2 Small Boutique Lighting Plan

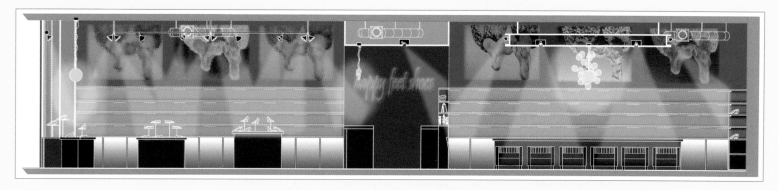

Fig. 16.3 Small Boutique Section

FIXTURE SCHEDULE		
SYMBOL	TYPE	DESCRIPTION
○	F1	RECESSED DOWNLIGHT
⦶	F2	RECESSED ACCENT WALL WASHER
⊕	F3	MINI-PENDANT
—	F4	TRACK SYSTEM
⦶	F5	ACCENT TRACK FIXTURE
⦶	F6	WALLWASH TRACK FIXTURE
— —	F7	INDIRECT COVE
— —	F8	INTEGRAL DIRECT SHELF LIGHT
⊕	F9	CHANDELIER
⊕	F10	PENDANT
⦶	F11	RECESSED COVE ACCENT LIGHT

direct their light on the shoes displayed in the see-through open shelf wall unit behind the cash-wrap counter. The two decorative pendants at the store's entry focus directly on the display fixtures immediately below them. The five long sections of perimeter wall contain display shelving that is uniformly lighted by undershelf luminaires.

2. The two store functions that require task lighting are the cash-wrap area and the seating/fitting area at the rear of the store. The cash-wrap counter is lighted by four relatively small decorative glass pendants that not only give store personnel adequate light for their work task but also serve to identify that function for customers. The grid of recessed downlights in the suspended ceiling "cloud" provide the light needed by both sales personnel and customers for fitting and trying on shoes.

3. The primary decorative lighting is provided by the two large pendants in the seating/fitting area. They will be seen from the store entry, creating a beacon to attract customers to the fitting area, and serve as sculptural accents in an otherwise featureless portion of the store. While their primary purpose is not decorative, the pendants at the store's entry and at the cash-wrap station should be selected for their decorative/sculptural qualities.

Specific luminaire selections were made as follows. With the exception of the several pendants, the luminaires are either recessed or generally not easily seen, so that their appearance or aesthetic qualities are not a significant issue; the criteria for selection is primarily functional.

- *Track system:* The track-mounted accent luminaires must first be easily relocated and highly flexible or adjustable for refocusing.
- *Accent luminaires:* The recessed accent fixtures above the cash-wrap counter must also have the same qualities of flexibility as the track.
- *Pendants:* The pendants at the entry must provide a narrow, concentrated beam and also have a translucent housing or shield to attract the eye of passersby in the mall. The pendant task luminaires at the cash-wrap counter should also have a narrow focus directly on the countertop and a translucent housing or shield so that its location is visible from any point in the store. The primary purpose of the two pendants in the seating/fitting area is to create a visual attraction to that area of the store, subliminally suggesting that customers try on shoes. The luminaires should be large in scale, attract the eye through glowing elements or surfaces, and be uniquely sculptural to offset the otherwise bare simplicity of the space.

- *Undershelf luminaires:* Minimal-scale linear LED strips mounted at each shelf are used.
- *Downlights:* The recessed downlights in the ceiling "cloud" must create a fairly uniform light level in the seating/sales area, with the illumination level to be read at the floor, not at the standard tabletop height. The lamp should be recessed within the cone so that it is not visible or glaring from normal view.

Generally, in retail applications, high-output sources with good color rendering are used. Traditionally, halogen lamps worked well where a point source was required. More currently, LED and ceramic metal halide lamps are preferred for their energy efficiency and longer lamp life. In lower-end environments, where ambient or general lighting is used to provide a blanket of uniform light, fluorescent lamping is the most typical.

CASE STUDY 16—A Small Supermarket

Supermarkets and their lighting techniques have undergone a great deal of change in recent years. It is rare to find a recently built or refurbished supermarket without specialty areas, such as bakeries, delis, and wine shops, and equally rare to find the lighting limited to pendant fluorescent strip lighting and in-case fluorescents. More and more, supermarkets resemble other retail establishments, with lots of focal and decorative lighting and attention to sophisticated marketing detail, including a special concern for color temperature due to the need to make food look appetizing. And all of this is accomplished within the limitations of increasingly stringent energy code requirements.

The floor plan of the relatively small supermarket used in this case study is shown in Fig. 16.4. While it is not an enormous prototype, it has several specialty areas outside of the central bank of gondolas and freezer cases, as well as attempting to enhance the shopping experience. Most of the store has an open (unfinished) ceiling, but the four specialty areas (bakery, deli, wine, and gourmet) and the combined checkout, customer service, and entry vestibule areas all have suspended ceilings. The visual task requirements in the store are as follows:

1. Focal lighting is required in many of the areas outside of the central gondola/ freezer case area such as those featuring produce and flowers, baked goods,

deli items, wine, and other specialty items. The special sale items at the ends of the rows of gondolas also need highlighting, and food seen in display cases, both refrigerated and unrefrigerated, require integral display case lighting.
2. The two primary areas that require task light are the items displayed in the gondola shelves and the checkout area, which has an obvious need for strong light on the checkout counters. The back work counters in the bakery and deli shops also require task light for food preparation. In addition, the customer service counter and the small manager's office require effective task light.
3. Decorative lighting is desired as customers enter the store at the produce section, and at the specialty areas for baked goods, deli items, wine, and gourmet foods.
4. Ambient lighting is required in the store's entrance vestibule and in the exit path after customers have paid the cashiers. The central areas of the bakery and deli shops require ambient light between the front and back work counters.

The lighting design solution for this case study is shown in the lighting plan (Fig. 16.5) and in a section (Fig. 16.6). The placement and selection of luminaires are made with the following design criteria:

1. Most of the focal lighting (produce, specialty shop areas, and ends of gondola rows) is accomplished with the use of track lighting because of its great flexibility and relatively low cost. Wallwashers are employed for a few locations, such as the center space between wine and gourmet foods, and the announcement boards at the customer service counter and entrance vestibule. Specialty in-case luminaires are used within display cases for meats and poultry, as well as bakery and deli counters.
2. Task lighting is provided by pendant-mounted linear direct troffers centrally hung between the rows of gondolas to illuminate the products on the shelves. The checkout area and the customer service counter have recessed downlights to illuminate the visual tasks. The back counters in the bakery and deli shops are provided with effective working-level lighting from a linear direct cove. The manager's area is lighted with recessed troffers for working-level general illumination.
3. Large, decorative glass pendants are hung as a welcoming gesture in the produce area as customers enter the store. More conventionally sized glass pendants are hung in each of the four specialty shop areas as an attraction to their special offerings.

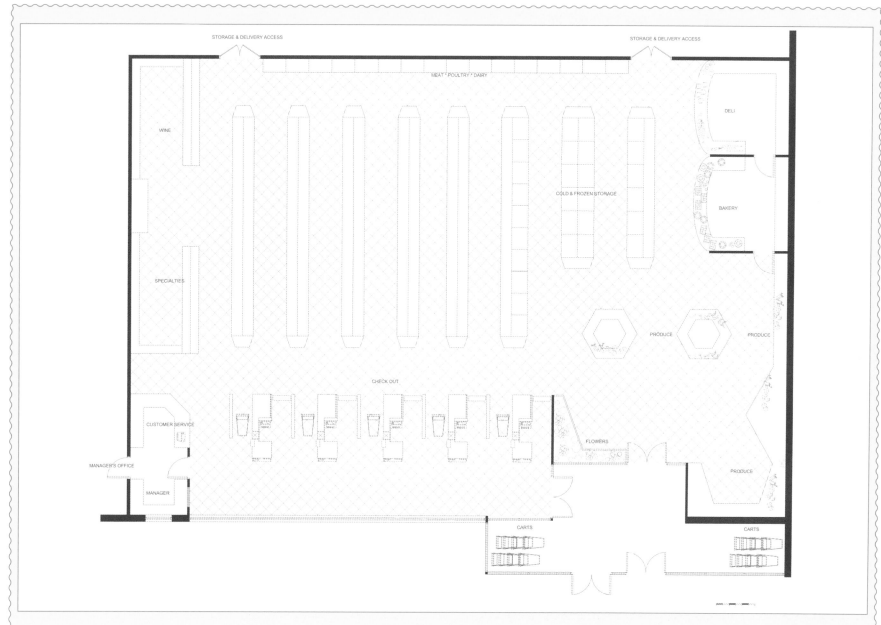

Fig. 16.4 Small Supermarket Floor Plan

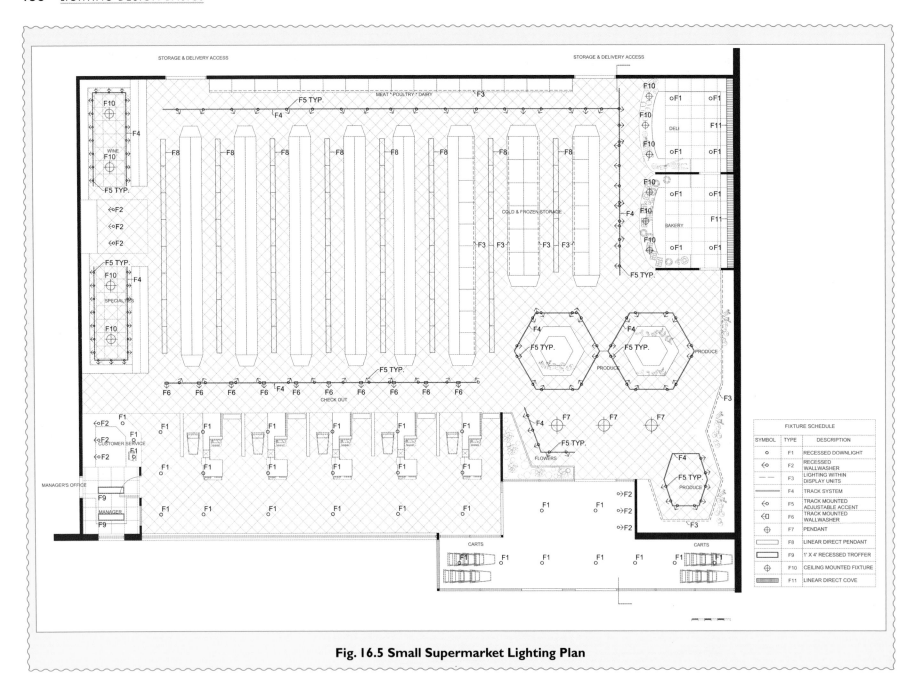

Fig. 16.5 Small Supermarket Lighting Plan

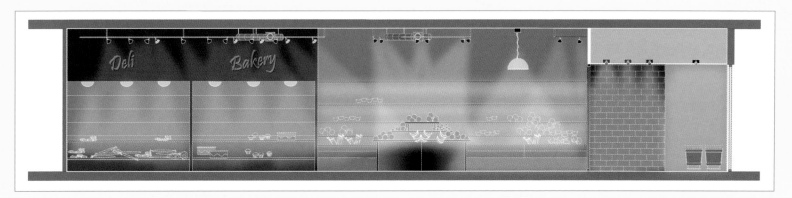

Fig. 16.6 Small Supermarket Section

4. Specific ambient lighting needs are accomplished in the exit path beyond the cashiers' counters, in the entrance/exit vestibule to the store, and in the central areas of the bakery and deli shops with the use of recessed downlights.

Switching in a supermarket generally incorporates a simple, straightforward approach. However, many supermarkets are employing control solutions that assist in saving energy, in turn increasing their bottom line. During the day, the light level in a retail establishment must compete with the brightness of the sun. This necessitates that the interior lighting be at a higher level so the space maintains the cheery, crisp, and clean atmosphere typical of a supermarket. This does not negate the opportunity to incorporate daylight harvesting in zones close to large spans of windows. With this approach, there is an opportunity to reduce the light level at night overall so that the contrast between the exterior and the interior is not so significant. This is especially important in stores that are open 24 hours a day. When there are fewer customers during the late-night hours, it is not necessary to have all the lighting at 100 percent. Furthermore, it is becoming common that integral display case lighting contains occupancy sensors so that it is normally off unless someone is in the aisle.

Luminaire and lamp selections should be based on the following considerations:

- *Lighting within display units:* Traditionally, linear fluorescent luminaires were incorporated into the detailing of the displays, but now LEDs are becoming more common because of their small size and long life. Appropriate ballasts must be specified for coolers and freezers. Care must be taken in selecting color temperature and CRI for each display type.
- *Track lighting:* Because a point source is required and low energy use is preferred, ceramic metal halide has become a popular choice for accent lighting in supermarkets. As LED technology and light quality improve, it is becoming a preferred choice for higher ceiling applications.
- *Downlights and downlight/wallwashers:* Compact fluorescent or ceramic metal halide is most appropriate, or LED if the budget allows. The lamp should be recessed within the cone so that it is not visible or glaring from normal view. A medium beam spread works well for this ceiling height.
- *Linear direct pendant:* Providing uninterrupted, consistent, and shadow-free illumination on the typical shelving is important, and fluorescent lamping is still the most efficient and economical source for this application.

With the exception of the several pendants, the luminaires are either recessed or generally not intended to be seen, so that their appearance or aesthetic qualities are not a significant issue; the criteria for selection are primarily functional.

CASE STUDY 17—An Art Gallery

A gallery is a hybrid between a museum and a retail store. As in a museum, the lighting should display art objects in their best light. Also, as in any store, the artwork is for sale; therefore, creating an atmosphere that is visually and psychologically appealing is of critical importance.

The main lighting task is to illuminate the artwork throughout the gallery. In addition to paintings, prints, and other two-dimensional art, many galleries also display sculpture, glass, jewelry, and other forms of three-dimensional art. Other lighting tasks include circulation of light through the gallery space, the point of negotiation or sale, and task areas such as framing and crating.

In general, galleries should be lighted using a track lighting system. The flexibility of track is unparalleled, and it permits an uncomplicated and quick method of changing the lighting as displays of the artwork are changed periodically. Tracks should be placed parallel to surfaces that display two-dimensional work, and far enough away from those surfaces to permit correct aiming. Refer to Chapter 6 for additional information about placing track and other adjustable accent fixtures. Three-dimensional artwork also requires the same flexibility provided by track lighting, but it is often placed away from wall surfaces, and additional track may be needed to light them for optimal viewing.

In most galleries, ambient light is not specifically designed because the typically strong focal lighting provides more than adequate ambient light for navigation and conversation, even for receptions and event openings. Despite that, many galleries will decide to create, on general terms or for specific exhibits, a dramatic approach to exhibiting a group of artwork and have the focal lighting employ a very narrow focus, creating specifically bright light on the exhibited pieces that potentially can make most of the surrounding space quite dark; in those cases, an ambient light system must be employed for navigational and conversation/reception areas.

An automatic time clock system that turns lights off between closing and opening is the best approach for controlling gallery lighting. It is often desirable to include dimming; however, the intensity of light can also be controlled by varying the wattage or beam spread of the lamp. Undoubtedly there will be some galleries that will require a more complex or detailed approach to lighting controls due to the speciality of their operations. This case study does not address the support spaces of the gallery, such as the office/sales/work areas, because they are so similar to office and other support areas addressed in precious case studies.

The gallery floor plan shown in Fig. 16.7, accompanied by its reflected ceiling plan in Fig. 16.8, and the section in Fig. 16.9, is typical of a modest-size commercial gallery. It is designed to accommodate a wide range of arts media, both two- and three-dimensional, as well as a variety of works at varying scales, including very small items that can be exhibited in the display case on the south wall. The freestanding partitions can be relocated in order to accommodate ever changing exhibits. The entry area contains the gallery's logo and words and/or graphics to let passersby and visitors know about the current work being exhibited. The back wall of that unit will also serve as an exhibit wall. The visual tasks include the following:

1. Focal lighting is by far the dominant concern in designing the lighting for the gallery. The track system is selected for its ability to accommodate adjustable luminaires that can be easily relocated, angled, and relamped for the changing exhibits. The track is located parallel to the north, south, west, and east entry walls where the majority of two-dimensional artwork will be hung. The long, centrally located east-west track and the remaining north-south tracks provide ample flexibility for lighting the freestanding partitions, regardless of their positioning, as well as any freestanding sculpture or other works on pedestals that may be placed in the center spaces of the gallery. Focal lighting for the items in the display case will be placed within the case and concealed from direct view. To provide interest to those passing by and to contrast the artwork, a backlighted translucent wall is incorporated into the entry wall to display the gallery's graphic signage.
2. In general, ambient light is more than adequately provided by the focal lighting that supports the gallery's primary purpose. The one exception is the entry area. The backlighted announcement wall will not provide adequate ambient light in the northeast and southeast corners of the entrance area. Wall-mounted sconces are placed on either side of the entrance wall side lights to brighten the corners and add an element of decoration.

The criteria for luminaire and lamp selections are as follows:

The track fixtures need to contain a point source lamp. Traditionally, halogen PAR and MR16 lamps have been used for the variety of wattages and beam angles that are available. They provide the flexibility that is needed in a gallery where the type and size of art may change frequently. Unfortunately, halogen lamps are not very efficient and emit heat and UV which can damage the artwork through photo degradation. More recently, LED track heads are

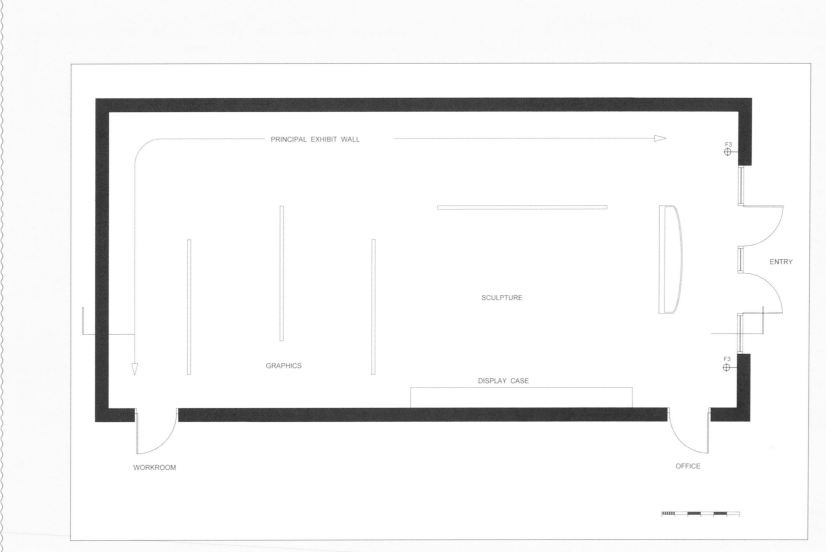

Fig. 16.7 Gallery Floor Plan

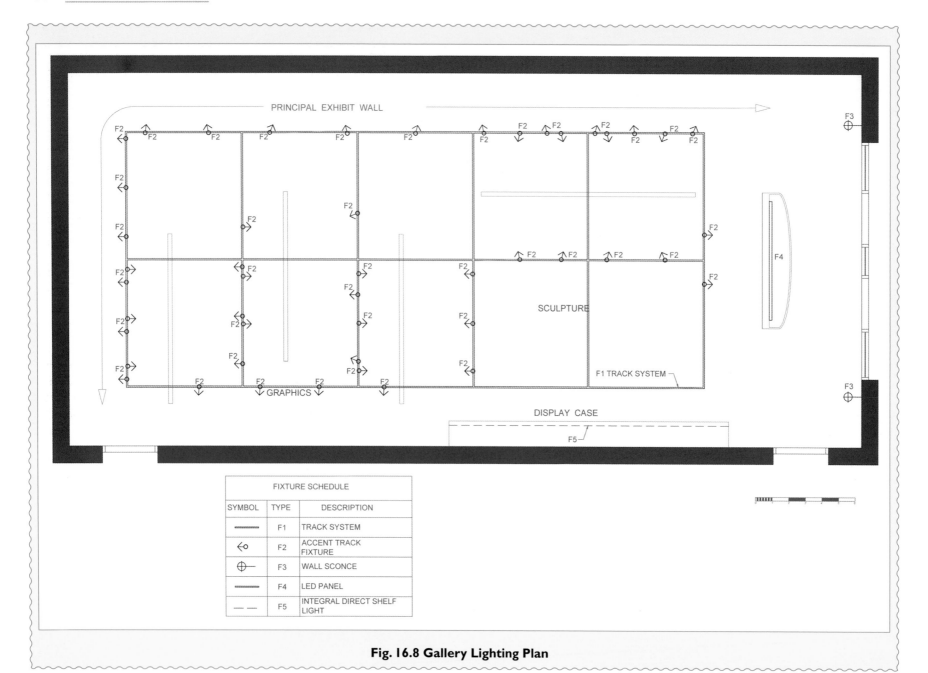

PRINCIPAL EXHIBIT WALL

SCULPTURE

F1 TRACK SYSTEM

GRAPHICS

DISPLAY CASE

F5

F4

FIXTURE SCHEDULE		
SYMBOL	TYPE	DESCRIPTION
	F1	TRACK SYSTEM
	F2	ACCENT TRACK FIXTURE
	F3	WALL SCONCE
	F4	LED PANEL
	F5	INTEGRAL DIRECT SHELF LIGHT

Fig. 16.8 Gallery Lighting Plan

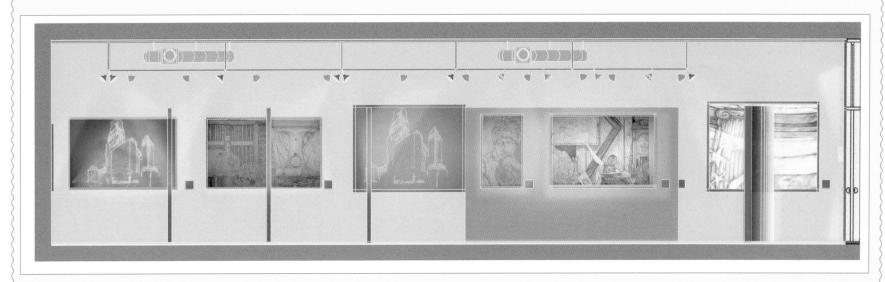

Fig. 16.9 Gallery Section

being considered because of their efficiency and lack of heat and UV emissions. Unfortunately, at the time of this printing, many LED track heads are still cost prohibitive.

The lighting within the display case is intended to be a small profile continuous LED source located at each shelf. This will provide even illumination along the entire display surface.

The backlighted entry wall could be illuminated like a sign. In the past this was achieved by incorporating rows of fluorescent lamps, spaced 12"–18" on center along the entire wall. With the development of LED systems, it is much

more common to use LED strips or LED panels behind the translucent material. Depending on the type of work sold at the gallery, a color-changing LED source could be used. With any type of backlighting application it is critical to view the material with the light source behind it to ensure that the results are acceptable.

The wall sconces should be translucent, providing an eye-level glow to the entry area. The recommended source would be compact fluorescent for its ambient quality and efficiency.

Chapter 17 HOSPITALITY LIGHTING DESIGN

The hospitality business involves serving people and offering them diversion and pleasure. From restaurants to hotels, resorts, and casinos, facilities are designed with the intent of transporting guests from the world of the ordinary to a special time and place.

Lighting design for hospitality projects is, along with retail lighting, the most demanding. Many of the spaces are designed to be visually interesting or intriguing; others are highly themed, more like stage sets than rooms. It is generally important to create drama and sparkle to enhance the effects of the space.

One of the challenges of hospitality lighting is to create adequate task light while achieving the necessary style, theme, and drama. For some demanding tasks, such as gaming tables in a casino, illumination levels must be high and glare control is critical for players, dealers, and video surveillance cameras. It is important to identify the visual tasks, design illumination for them, and then work the task lighting into an overall program of lighting design that meets the requirements of the project. Lighting for these projects employs layered designs out of necessity; the ambient light is the apparent light source, while concealed architectural lighting often provides the task illumination.

Because of the huge variation in options, viable designs are myriad. But, as with offices, the best solution to a particular problem generally flows from the interior design or interior architecture, which sets the style and mood of the space. Layered lighting is best because it builds the design on the decorative lighting selections that are of necessity present from the beginning. The challenge of the lighting design is to add focal, task, and ambient light in a manner that completes the illumination of the space without the design appearing too busy or contrived.

Most hospitality designs rely heavily on decorative chandeliers, sconces, pendants, table lamps, floor lamps, and other highly styled lights that play a critical role in interior design. Because of this, decorative lighting is commonly part of the furniture, fixtures, and equipment (FF&E) budget and is specified by the interior designer, whereas architectural lighting in the same space is part of the construction budget and is specified by the architect, engineer, or lighting designer. Coordination among professionals is critical in these spaces because the actual lighting design is a combined effort, and the whole design must meet the energy code requirements.

Energy code compliance is a challenge in hospitality spaces; the ability to employ fluorescent or LED lighting in nondescript architectural lighting can permit the traditional luminaires to use incandescent lamps and still meet the energy code. The twinkle quality of an incandescent filament and the natural warmth of incandescent lights when dimmed are critical to creating atmosphere and mood. The layered approach to lighting design is essential here. Conserve wherever possible so the overall building design complies with the code.

Most hospitality facilities are designed for specific uses; a hotel lobby will always be a lobby, and a restaurant will remain a restaurant. In some hospitality functions, day-to-day flexibility is needed, as in exhibition halls, ballrooms, meeting rooms, and conference centers, where the capability of rearranging seating, partitions, and lighting systems is important. In general, hospitality facilities are not renovated without a relatively complete replacement of lighting systems, so the long-term flexibility of lighting with respect to reconfiguration is minimal.

Some hospitality spaces, such as conference centers, hotel ballrooms and exhibition halls, restaurants, and bars with stages are designed with both architectural lighting and performance lighting systems. Performance lighting systems are often simple, employing track lighting and separate dimming channels to permit dramatic illumination of a solo performer, small group, or keynote speaker. A few spaces require more complex theatrical systems; these designs generally call for professional entertainment lighting assistance.

A variety of ceiling types are used in hospitality spaces, ranging from ordinary acoustic tile and gypsum wallboard to decorative and ornamental ceilings. Some spaces may not have finished ceilings at all, as when the character of a loft or club is desired. Ceilings are critical to lighting, and it is important that proposed lighting designs be checked for compatibility with the ceiling system. Especially in hotels and other large spaces, the ceiling can become a platform for a multitude of building functions; lighting systems should take precedence to make sure the lighting works properly.

This leads to the following overall approach to solving the lighting design problem at hand. The interior designer and/or architect must first develop a complete design concept, including a well-articulated lighting design criteria matrix, as described in Chapter 10. Next, identify all of the visual tasks. Take into account both guests and staff, remembering that the two groups often have different needs. Then determine whether or not the decorative lighting provides adequate focal illumination, and add it for those situations not properly illuminated. Repeat the process for task lighting.

The case studies in this chapter represent four typical spaces and functions. The examples are relatively basic in order to make the lighting design issues easily understood. These issues are fundamental and can be translated to other settings and to varying interior designs and styles.

CASE STUDY 18 — Restaurant Lighting

The most important attribute that lighting design brings to a restaurant is its ability to create character or ambience. Initially, that attribute is conceived and created by the interior designer or architect, who must accurately convey those ideas and forms to the lighting designer. In turn, it is within the lighting designer's province to translate those concepts using lighting tools and techniques to create a corresponding lighting design solution. A restaurant's atmosphere, or mood, or theme is of critical importance to its success. In some cases, that ambience is subtle or subdued, and in other cases it can be dramatic and even flamboyant. A seafood restaurant, particularly in a seaside location, may borrow images from traditional fishing wharf interiors, while a restaurant featuring steaks and chops may make reference to an English country inn. In any case, the lighting design solution for restaurants often requires the use of decorative fixtures, such as lanterns, pendants, sconces, and chandeliers that reinforce the desired ambience.

The classic lighting design problem in restaurants is illuminating tabletops. Diners musts be able to read the menu, see their food, and see the faces of their dining companions, but not at the expense of the desired ambience. There are several alternative solutions to resolve this problem, such as installing a low-voltage downlight or a pendant over each table, or placing a table lamp on each table, powered by an outlet on an adjacent wall. Because tables can be moved, either periodically or even daily, many restaurants prefer to use a candle or a battery-powered table lamp on each table. Portable solutions like these provide great versatility as well as maintaining the original atmosphere, but neither works as well from a lighting point of view. Banquette seating has a significant advantage in that tables can easily be moved to serve two, or four, or six, and overhead lighting from recessed or pendant luminaires will continue to work well if the luminaires are intelligently placed. Ultimately, the decision about lighting tables should be made jointly with the restaurateurs, who know their customer base and their preferences about seating options.

The bar is an important part of many restaurant operations, often being the most profitable revenue source. Some bars constitute a relatively small part of the restaurant's overall size, while others dominate the space. Frequently, a small bar simply reminds patrons that alcoholic beverages are available, while most of the beverages are sold at the dining table.

There are three quite different lighting tasks involved in lighting a bar. First is creating the lighting atmosphere for customers at the bar; second is lighting the back bar with its colorful display of liquor and wine bottles; and third is providing the bartender with adequate light to work by. It is rare to find bars that are brightly lighted; the general preference is to create an atmosphere that is softly lighted and conducive to intimacy, ranging from a convivial sports bar to a corner for a romantic tryst. Finding just the right light level and color temperature requires an artful decision. The back bar typically calls for attracting and pleasing the eye with the sparkle of glass and colorful liquids and labels, often enhanced by the use of a mirrored surface behind the bottles. Providing enough working light for the bartender is less difficult, but keeping the light source out of sight and avoiding glare from reflections off of stainless steel surfaces and equipment are challenge enough.

It is important to keep in mind that there are generic categories of restaurants that must be understood from the start, taking into account the restaurant's lighting design concept. This includes public expectations for each of the categories. In a restaurant geared to family dining, general illumination is the norm, often employing themed decorative lighting that references the cuisine or the locale and avoiding the creation of areas that are too dimly lit or overly bright. Fine dining demands a quite different approach, typically with a subtle and/or subdued light level and the use of themed decorative luminaires that reference the cuisine and/or the locale, as well as expressing the high quality of the restaurant. At the other end of the scale is the fast-food eatery, where the expectation is a uniformly high lighting level, typically using architectural luminaires only, as opposed to decorative ones, and fluorescent lamps throughout. While some fast-food operations have themed interiors, themed luminaires are uncommon. It is important to make note of the special challenge presented by some hotel dining rooms, where the same space is used for breakfast, lunch, and dinner. The challenge encompasses every aspect of the design, from space planning to furniture selection, color, and lighting. Different lighting systems must be employed to match the changes in food service and time of day, stretching the possible limitations of lamps and luminaires.

Some secondary lighting tasks are still of great importance. The quality of lighting at the point of entry is always of critical importance because it sets the tone for what follows. With or without an entrance vestibule, there should be a carefully planned lighting sequence that carries the eye first to the maitre d' and then to the bar, or possibly first to the bar if that's the sequence the restaurateur prefers. The mood created in the few moments of a patron's entrance can affect how the person spends his or her time and money while there. Service stations for the waitstaff present a special problem because they need relatively bright task light, but the light source should not be visible to diners. Access to restrooms is obviously important, but drawing attention to patrons heading toward the restrooms is not desirable. And finally, the restrooms themselves must be lighted. Chapter 18 addresses the general issues related to public restroom lighting, but only some of the approach presented there is applicable to restaurant restrooms. Many, if not most, high-end res-

taurants do not want the blandness of a typical public restroom for their facilities, preferring to have their restroom décor reflect the status and style of their establishment. Lighting in these restrooms has more in common with the personal qualities of upscale residential bathrooms, where luminaires are decorative in intent.

Because lighting characteristics and design are so critical to the overall design of a successful restaurant, the lighting should be thought of as a specific design medium for creating the lasting atmospheric impression of the space.

The floor plan for the modest-sized restaurant in this case study is shown in Fig. 17.1. This restaurant seats 82 in the dining area and 18 in the bar area. It is situated in a storefront setting and is clearly in the fine dining category. Although it may typically serve weekday lunches and weekend brunches, daylight is not a major factor because the limited window area permits daylight to penetrate only the first 20' to 25' of the space and it does not affect the dining area. The bar is considered to be primarily a dinner and late-night operation. From a lighting design perspective, the only influence that daylight may have can be controlled by separately switching the luminaires in the relatively small area near the storefront glass.

The maitre d' station is strategically placed between the bar area and the dining room so that it is clearly visible when guests enter the restaurant. Placing the bar at the point of entrance may encourage some diners to stop at the bar first for a drink or two, as well as serving as a place for diners to wait until their table is ready. The restrooms are strategically placed in the bar area and deliberately are not located adjacent to the dining area. The doors to the two restrooms are located in a short, recessed corridor so that the opening and closing of those doors will barely be noticed elsewhere. The coatroom, with its pass-through counter, is the one remaining function at the entrance end of the restaurant.

The dining room offers three types of seating for dining: booths on the south wall, banquette seating on the north and west walls, and eight square tables for four in the center of the room. Entrance to the kitchen is in the southwest corner of the dining area. In addition, there are two service stations, one at the entrance to the kitchen and the other, larger station diagonally opposite, in the northeast corner.

The restaurant design presents the following visual tasks to be accommodated:

1. Focal lighting is required in several places, including at the artwork in the entrance vestibule, in the short corridor leading to the restrooms, on the

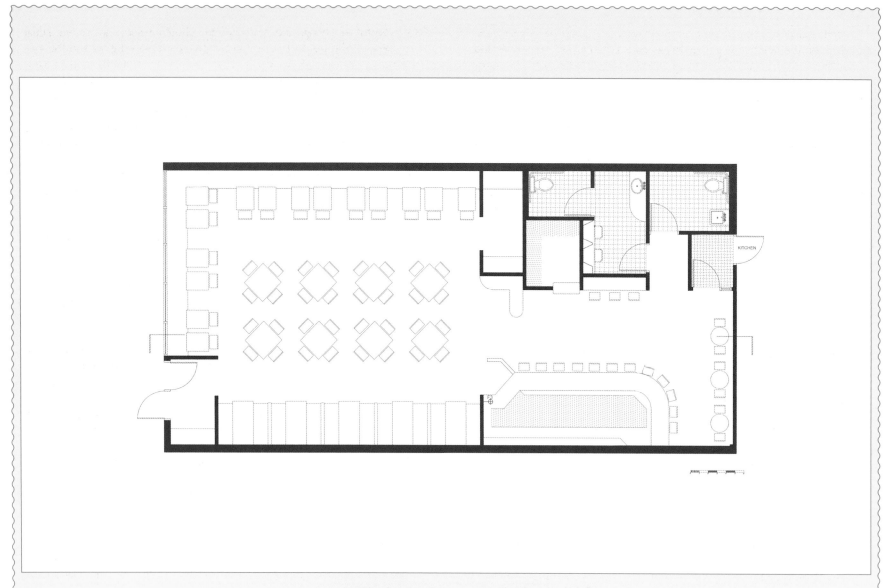

Fig. 17.1 Restaurant Floor Plan

north wall at the side of the maitre d' station, and along the series of art-work on the north wall of the dining room. Focus is also needed on the bottles at the back bar and the vertical front face of the bar, which features a special finish.

2. Task lighting is required at the bar top for the patrons and the bartender. The freestanding and permanent booth tables require adequate illumination for dining and conversation. The servers need task lighting within the wait stations that doesn't interfere with the dining experience. Additionally, the lavatory and vanity counters require shadowless task lighting while maintaining the restaurant's overall aesthetic.

3. Decorative lighting, always an important element in restaurant lighting, should be incorporated to reinforce the restaurant's design, while also typically providing eye-level glow and warmth.

4. Ambient lighting is generally in ample supply in most of the areas of the restaurant because of the previously described layers; however, adjusting the ambient level can greatly influence the atmosphere.

The lighting design solution for this restaurant is shown in the lighting plan in Fig. 17.2 and the section in Fig. 17.3.

Clearly identifying the lighting solution in the restaurant is deceptively complex, because many luminaires serve more than one purpose.

1. Focal lighting is provided for the artwork on the north wall of the dining room by adjustable accent fixtures mounted to a suspended track. The remaining art locations and the bottles behind the bar are highlighted by recessed adjustable accent fixtures. The front of the bar is illuminated by a low-profile linear fixture mounted to the underside of the bar top.

2. At the bar, task lighting for the patrons is supplied by small pendant luminaires. The bartender is provided with additional working light by a concealed undershelf luminaire. As permanent seating, the booths are also illuminated by pendants over each table. The banquette tables at the north side of the dining area are lighted by luminaires mounted to the same track that illuminates the artwork. The track fixtures are focused downward and contain a wide beam to provide a continuous level of light no matter where the tables are positioned. Additionally, the loose seating in the center of the dining room is illuminated by a regular pattern of downlights that provide a uniform blanket of light. The task lighting at the lavatory and vanity in the restrooms is produced by wall sconces flanking the mirrors.

3. Decorative lighting is incorporated throughout the space and serves a dual purpose. The pendants over the bar provide eye-level glow and the intimacy that is typically desired at a bar. The sconces at the bar and adjacent drink rail provide a decorative companion to the pendants, vertical brightness, and low-level task lighting for the servers and guests. The table lamp at the host stand not only provides identification for the patrons entering but also offers task lighting for the host. The decorative pendants at the booths help provide a private and focused light for parties seated at those tables, while also providing a focus to that side of the dining room.

4. Ambient lighting is necessary in areas surrounding the bar, where one approaches the maitre d' from the entry vestibule, and along the east glass wall, where three cocktail tables are placed. The recessed downlights in this area must be separately zoned because the level of illumination will probably vary for different hours of operation. The remaining locations where ambient lighting must be placed are in the coatroom, in the service station at the entry to the kitchen, and in the toilet stall in the women's restroom, where additional recessed downlights will provide the desired light. The indirect cove lighting above the booths provides a soft, low-level ambient light, while also leading guests into the dining room.

Lighting control is very important in restaurants because, typically, the atmosphere changes significantly throughout the day. Most moderate to high-end restaurants incorporate a preset lighting control system, which allows scenes to be established for the various meals and times of day that are required. Because of the high turnover of staff in the restaurant industry, a system like this is advantageous, since it allows the restaurateur and designer to maintain the preferred look without relying on the staff to individually adjust the zones. During the design process, it is important to appropriately and adequately zone the lighting so there is enough flexibility to produce the desired effect.

Luminaire and lamp selections should be based on the following considerations:

- *Downlights:* Point source with high CRI and medium spread of light to focus on the table surface. The lamp should be regressed within the cone so that it is not visible or glaring from normal view. Halogen or high-quality LED would work well.
- *Adjustable accent fixtures:* Recessed with internal aiming mechanism. A point source is required; either low-voltage halogen or LED would be appropriate.

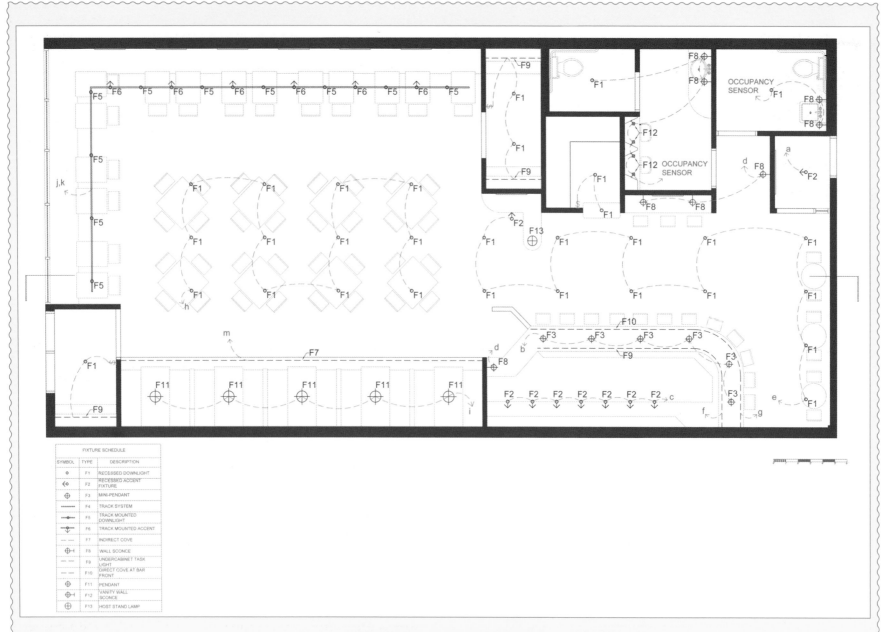

Fig. 17.2 Restaurant Lighting Plan

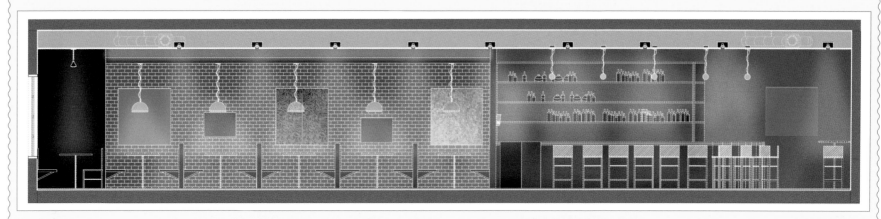

Fig. 17.3 Restaurant Section

- *Track system:* The quality and source of light should be similar to those of the recessed downlights and accent fixtures. The track system provides additional flexibility. Because it is being used for both focal and task lighting, a two-circuit track should be considered.
- *Undershelf fixture:* Fluorescent or LED with direct light focused on the length of the bar work surface; light source concealed to prevent glare.
- *Indirect cove and bar die lighting:* Continuous low-profile LED luminaire is most appropriate for its size and cool operating temperature.

- *Pendants and sconces:* Direct-indirect distribution with eye-level glow and/or sparkle determined by the degree of translucency of the shade and user preference.

Specific luminaire and lamp selections are as critical as their placement. For intensely themed restaurants, the search for specialty, antique, and/or custom luminaires can be both time consuming and challenging. As in all aspects of lighting design, the ability to make artful decisions is part of the job.

CASE STUDY 19—Hotel Lobby Lighting

A hotel lobby gives a first impression about the hotel. Style, appearance, and aesthetics are dominant considerations. Decorative and focal lighting are usually critical in the success of a hotel lobby, even for a modest hotel.

The lobby also presents several visual tasks. The most important of these is generally the illumination of the service desks, including registration, concierge, and bell station. The service desks employ computers, making the lighting at these locations similar to that of a computer workstation. Relatively high light levels must be provided locally, while the balance of the lobby must be warm, friendly, and welcoming.

The other major visual task in a lobby generally involves seating areas, where casual reading and socializing occur. In addition, the gift/sundries shop, a conventional but low-key retail operation, must be inviting and produce sales. The entrance vestibule, although a transitory function, must be an appropriate introduction to the lobby environment, and the luggage storage room at the bell captain's desk requires simple, functional lighting.

The floor plan of the boutique hotel lobby for this case study, shown in Fig. 17.4, includes all of these elements. The design intention in this lobby is to create a decidedly warm, inviting, and contemporary space, using form, color, textures, and lighting as the design tools to accomplish this. As guests pass through the vestibule and enter the space, the registration desk is in direct view, and the lobby space is generous in terms of circulation and access to the elevators. The lounge/seating area to the far right uses a fireplace as the primary visual attraction, with comfortable seating arrangements for waiting, lounging, and conversation. The bell captain's station is conveniently adjacent to the vestibule, with the door to the luggage storage room a step away. The gift shop will be fully open (except for a curved locking security screen for nonoperating hours), with an open display of merchandise and a cash/wrap station in its southeast corner. The specific visual tasks in the lobby are as follows:

1. Focal lighting is required for the wall behind the registration desk containing mailboxes, notices, and a counter that requires illumination. Also, the wall provides a backdrop for the staff and generally includes a decorative quality worthy of lighting. The front face of the desk is made of rich materials that should also be highlighted. The floral arrangement to the west of the registration desk is in direct view of the point of entrance and is meant to be dramatically lighted, creating a focal point and leading guests into the space. The framed artwork in the lounge area, including the work over the fireplace mantle, requires accent lighting. The merchandise in the gift shop requires typical retail accent lighting, as well as undershelf lighting for the perimeter shelving. The graphic work on the sides of the entrance vestibule requires accent lighting in order to announce specific hotel features and events.
2. Task lighting is needed for the registration transaction counter for guests checking in and out. Lighting is required for the staff side of the registration desk as well. The bell captain's desk needs task lighting, along with adequate light in the luggage room to allow for selection of the correct items. A specific task light is needed at the gift shop's cash/wrap station.
3. Decorative lighting reinforces the hotel's overall design theme or concept and is critical in hotel spaces. Opportunities to incorporate decorative lighting should be reviewed at all scales, from large chandeliers to pedestrian-scaled wall sconces as well as personal table and floor lamps.
4. While the lobby may contain a significant amount of focal, task, and decorative lighting, additional ambient lighting is important in a hotel lobby. It enables the space to change throughout the day. During the early hours, the ambient light is typically set higher, providing a brighter and livelier space. During the evening and late at night, the ambient layer is reduced, allowing the focal and decorative lighting to pop and provide more drama.

The lighting design solution for a hotel lobby is seen in the reflected ceiling plan (Fig. 17.5) and in the section through the space (Fig. 17.6). Luminaire placement and selection were made with the following design criteria:

1. Recessed wallwasher luminaires are used to provide focal lighting and brighten the wall behind the registration desk. A continuous low-profile strip is incorporated in the detailing of the desk to illuminate the vertical face. Recessed accent luminaires are used to highlight the flowers on the semi-circular table to the west of the reception desk, as well as the wall-hung paintings in the lounge area (including the painting over the fireplace mantle) and the announcement posters on the side walls of the entrance vestibule. The track-mounted, adjustable, accent luminaires are used to highlight the displayed merchandise on the gift shop's center table and perimeter shelving.
2. The six pendant luminaires over the registration desk's transaction counter provide task light for guests reading and signing, and the decorative glass housings also provide glow to signal the desk's location when guests enter the lobby. Undershelf luminaires on the staff side of the transaction counter are provided with good, screened working light for those behind the desk. The cash/wrap station in the gift shop will also be provided with more than adequate task light from an undershelf fixture just above the station.
3. Chandeliers in the central lobby are the primary decorative luminaires. As is typically the case, their main function is to provide sparkle and glow to the central space. In addition, a smaller pendant is placed over the large circular seating element in the southeast corner of the lounge, not only to provide glow but also as the main visual identification of the lounge function at the east end of the lobby. The sconces at the elevators are designed to comfortably accompany the large chandeliers in the central lobby and help direct the guests.
4. While the primary ambient lighting is provided with the use of a large grid of downlights throughout the central lobby and lounge areas, many other elements contribute to the ambient lighting. The downlights will cover the overall space with a soft and warm blanket of light. The three sconces and two recessed downlights at the elevators project a warm and subtle glow reflected from the satin-finished metal doors and wall panels. The two ceiling areas in the central lobby are raised 12" above the normal ceiling, providing vertical space for these raised ceiling areas to be rimmed with soft cove lighting. The round raised ceiling area in the lounge portion of the lobby is treated in the same manner, with a rim of cove lighting. Finally, the floor and table lamps in the lounge area will be selected primarily for their eye-level-glow quality.

Lighting controls are very important for hotel lobbies. The desired ambience needs to change significantly from morning to evening and then again

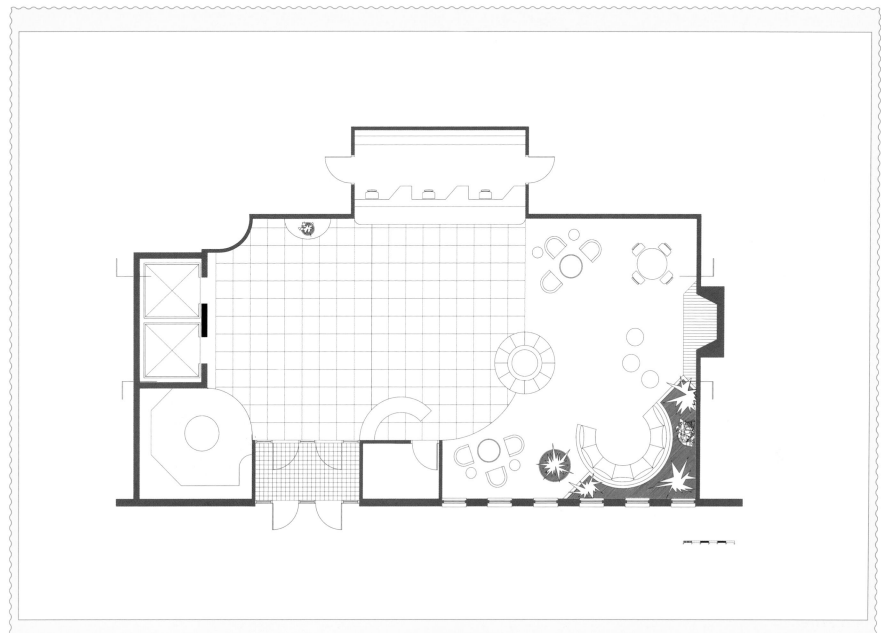

Fig. 17.4 Hotel Lobby Floor Plan

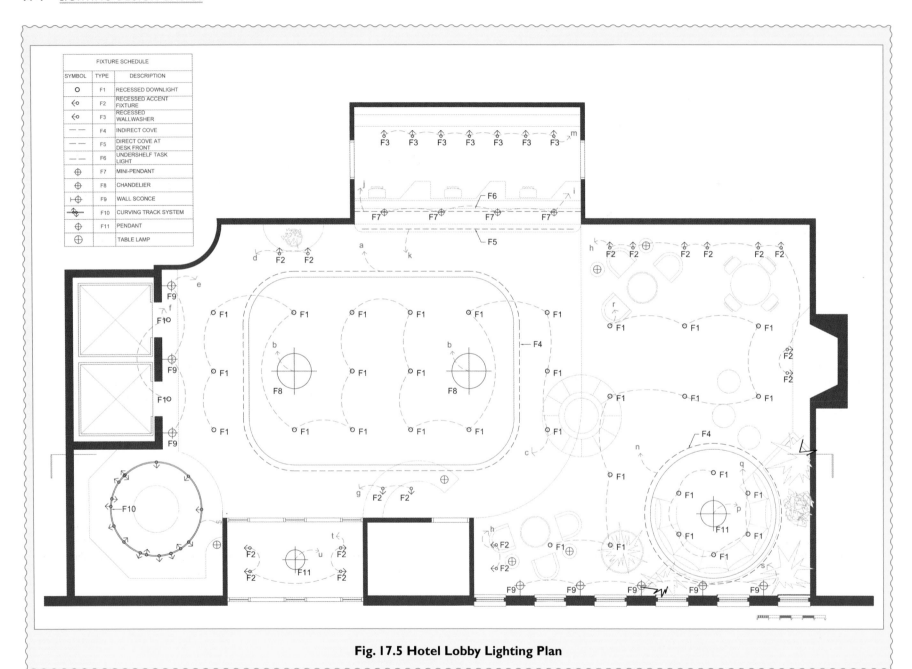

Fig. 17.5 Hotel Lobby Lighting Plan

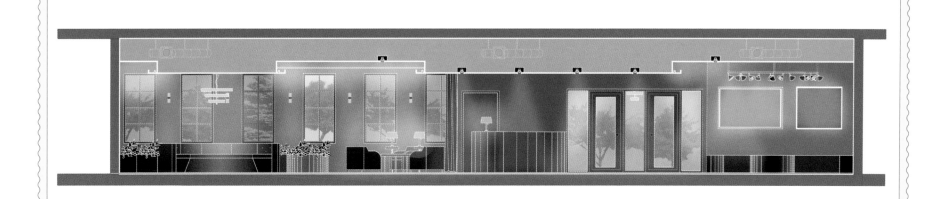

Fig. 17.6 Hotel Lobby Section

during the late-night hours. Providing dimming capability allows the hotel staff to adjust the lighting to create these different atmospheres. Preset systems are used most often, so the scenes can easily be changed throughout the day. Time clock control is also common, enabling these changes to occur automatically.

The criteria for luminaire and lamp selections are as follows:

In general, the quality of light in a hotel should replicate the comfort and warmth of residential lighting. In the past this was achieved by using primarily incandescent lighting; however, energy codes and maintenance costs have limited its use. In more upscale hotels, halogen lamps are still often used for accent and downlighting, with LED lamps and fixtures becoming more common as costs come down. Moderate to lower-end facilities may use compact fluorescent lamps to reinforce their brand's sense of economy.

For decorative and portable fixtures, when translucent fabric, acrylic, or glass shades are used, compact fluorescent lamps can be installed, and most

guests will not know the difference. In this hotel lobby, the chandelier that was selected contains reflective materials that best react to a clear lamp, which will create sparkle. Traditionally, this was achieved by using incandescent or halogen lamps. More recently, many LED sources can mimic this quality and result in significant energy savings and reduced maintenance.

LED and fluorescent strip fixtures are typically used for cove and task lighting, with the selection dictated by the intensity required and budget available.

The design quality or style of the selected luminaires will be determined primarily by the quality or style of the architectural and interior design detailing and materials, from traditional cut glass (sconces) and fringed shades (portables) to contemporary woods, plastics, and metals and high-tech materials. This aspect of luminaire selection is difficult to articulate because it concerns the elusive elements of aesthetics, style, and taste. Only long experience in a trial-and-error process over the course of many projects will sufficiently inform the designer to make intelligent aesthetic decisions.

CASE STUDY 20—Hotel Guest Suite

Over the past couple of decades, the hotel industry has been increasing the number of small guest suites, rather than exclusively providing standard single room accommodations. While small guest suites occupy more square footage, as well as requiring more furnishings, and consequently cost more to produce than single rooms, there has been major public acceptance of this trend and its increased room rates. The standard single room and the typical suite share an important quality: The architectural configuration is rectangular and straightforward, without a suspended ceiling and with basic finishes for floors, walls, and ceilings. This generally precludes ceiling-mounted or recessed fixtures in the bedroom and living room. However, the entry and bathroom areas typically have somewhat lowered dropped ceilings in order to accommodate mechanical services, permitting the use of ceiling fixtures in these limited areas.

Guest accommodations are designed to convey a residential ambience, but they must also be designed for easy maintenance and loss caused by damage. Because ceiling-mounted fixtures cannot be used in the two major spaces, table lamps and sconces are common solutions. The challenge is in providing enough luminaires with enough light output to satisfy the visual tasks in the rooms and to provide sufficient flexibility for many different types of users.

The floor plan for the guest suite in this case study is shown in Fig. 17.7; it presents the following visual tasks to be resolved:

1. Focal lighting is required for the artwork in the entrance area. The remaining artwork is purely decorative and does not require more light than it receives from the ambient light in the living room and bedroom.
2. Task lighting is required at the kitchen counter, over the living room desk, for in-bed reading, and by the reading chair in the bedroom, as well as for grooming at the bathroom lavatory. The need for light for reading and dining tasks in the living room and other areas of the bedroom is incidental and is adequately accommodated by the ambient light.
3. Decorative lighting in guest rooms plays an important role in reinforcing the design of the space. All of the table lamps in the living room and the bedroom have decorative potential. A collaborative effort between the lighting designer and the architect/interior designer is required to satisfy the combined decorative and ambient lighting needs and desires.

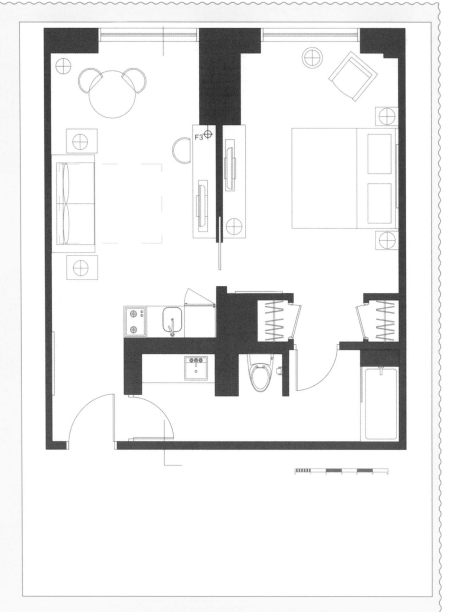

Fig. 17.7 Hotel Guest Suite Floor Plan

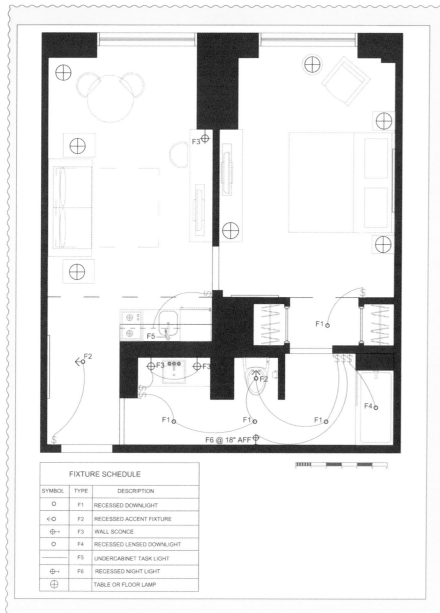

FIXTURE SCHEDULE

SYMBOL	TYPE	DESCRIPTION
O	F1	RECESSED DOWNLIGHT
←O	F2	RECESSED ACCENT FIXTURE
⊕⊣	F3	WALL SCONCE
O	F4	RECESSED LENSED DOWNLIGHT
—	F5	UNDERCABINET TASK LIGHT
⊕⊣	F6	RECESSED NIGHT LIGHT
⊕		TABLE OR FLOOR LAMP

Fig. 17.8 Hotel Guest Suite Lighting Plan

4. Ambient lighting is required throughout the guest suite. Where specific luminaires have not been selected for focal, task, and decorative purposes, additional lighting must be provided, as in the bathroom, adjacent to the closet, and in the seating and dining areas of the living room.

The lighting design solution for the guest suite is shown in the lighting plan (Fig. 17.8) and the section (Fig. 17.9). Luminaire placement and selection were made using the following design criteria:

1. Focal lighting to highlight the artwork is provided by the recessed accent fixture in the entry area, but, more important, the resultant reflected light will provide welcoming and navigational light for that area.
2. Task light for the kitchen is provided by an undercabinet luminaire. A direct/indirect sconce on the wall adjacent to the living room desk provides adequate light for reading and writing, as well as providing some soft ambient light for that corner of the room. In the bedroom, the table lamps for the night tables and the small table adjacent to the reading chair have been selected with shades or shields specifically for reading in those locations. The sconces on either side of the bathroom lavatory have translucent lenses selected to provide shadowless light for grooming.
3. As noted, the selection of decorative luminaires is ideally accomplished through a collaborative effort between the lighting designer and the architect/interior designer in order to satisfy the combined lighting and aesthetic needs of the space.
4. Navigational ambient light is provided by three wide-beam recessed downlights over the length of the bathroom. A light-sensitive nightlight is placed 18" AFF in the center of the bathroom. A wide-beam downlight is placed between the two clothes closets. The two table lamps and the floor lamp along the west wall of the living room are needed for conversation and casual dining. The table lamp on the drawer unit on the west wall of the bedroom is needed to softly illuminate that area of the room.

Switching should be kept as simple as possible because the hotel guests must feel comfortable with the placement of the switches within a very short period of time after their arrival. A switch immediately inside the entry door is essential for lighting the recessed accent luminaire in the entrance hall. Three-way switches are needed at both entry doors to the bathroom to activate the three recessed downlights. A wall-mounted switch must be

Fig. 17.9 Hotel Guest Suite Section

placed adjacent to the two clothes closets. All other lights are switched at the lamp.

Luminaire and lamp selections should be based on the following considerations:

- *Downlights:* Compact fluorescent is most appropriate, or LED if the budget allows. The color temperature should be warm, with a high CRI to mimic incandescent. The lamp should be regressed within the cone so that it is not visible or glaring from normal view.
- *Adjustable accent fixtures:* Recessed with an internal aiming mechanism. A point source is required; either low-voltage halogen or LED would be appropriate.
- *Table and floor lamps:* Size and scale of lamp/shade combination to be evaluated in elevation studies. Direct/indirect distribution with translucent shade for eye-level glow desired. Generally, compact fluorescent lamping is used because of long life and energy savings.
- *Sconce at desk:* Direct/indirect distribution providing task (reading) light for the adjacent desk; eye-level glow and/or sparkle determined by the degree of translucency of the shade and user preference.
- *Undercabinet fixture:* Fluorescent or LED with direct light focused on the length of the work surface; light source concealed to prevent glare.

- *Vanity sconce:* High-quality CRI and warm color temperature most appropriate to provide flattering, shadowless light for user. In this application, fluorescent lamping is most common because of maintenance.
- *Downlight for shower area:* Recessed luminaire with lens rated for shower/bath use; with halogen, compact fluorescent, or LED lamp; medium beam spread.
- *Nightlight:* Recessed with asymmetric distribution; light source concealed from direct view. LED or halogen lamping is most common.

The design quality of the selected luminaires must be determined by the quality or style of the architectural and interior design detailing and materials, from traditional silk shades to contemporary natural woods and high-tech materials. It is rare for the room's detailing and materials to be determined by the lighting design solution, including the selection of luminaires. This aspect of luminaire selection is difficult to articulate because it deals with the elusive elements of aesthetics, style, and taste. Only long experience in a trial-and-error process over the course of many projects will sufficiently inform the designer to make intelligent aesthetic decisions.

CASE STUDY 21 — Hotel Ballroom

A ballroom in a hotel is a multipurpose room; it serves as a banquet hall, exhibit hall, convention hall, meeting room, recital room, theater, showroom, classroom, reception hall, church, studio—and, on occasion, it actually serves as a ballroom. The types of events are limited only by the size of the room and the height of the ceiling. Most ballrooms can be divided into segments, in which different functions can occur simultaneously. It is not possible to identify all of the potential visual tasks, nor is it possible to illuminate all of them correctly. The best approach is to determine the visual tasks common to ballroom functions and make both permanent and flexible provisions to illuminate them.

The ballroom floor plan for this case study is shown in Fig. 17.10. This modest ballroom in a contemporary style is designed as four equal modules, or quadrants, and with the use of two movable partitions the room can be divided into two small one-quadrant rooms and one larger two-quadrant room. The high suspended ceiling is geometrically soffited to permit the use of many kinds of luminaires to serve the constantly changing functions of the space. Chandeliers, coves, downlights, sconces, and adjustable accent luminaires work in preset combinations for the many hotel functions in the space. This ballroom presents the following visual tasks that require resolution:

1. Focal lighting is needed to focus on a speaker's table (as the floor plan suggests) or a small stage for an ensemble or musical group at the western end of the room.
2. Task lighting is required to permit the use of all or sections of the ballroom as a meeting room, conference room, or classroom, as well as accommodating more specialized uses, such as trade shows, exhibits, and other purposes for which temporary focal lighting can be added.
3. Decorative lighting helps set the decorative tone of the room. It needs to serve this purpose both when the room is undivided and when it is sectioned off by the movable partitions. In addition, chandeliers and sconces provide eye-level glow and the opportunity for design consistency.
4. To provide adequate flexibility to the room, ambient lighting is required to help reduce or increase the overall light level and modify the ambience in the space for the various functions.

The lighting design solution for the ballroom is shown in the lighting plans (Figs. 17.11 and 17.12) and the section (Fig. 17.13). Luminaire placement and selections were made with the following design criteria:

1. The adjustable, recessed, narrow-beam accent luminaires are placed in relation to the expected location of a speaker's/panel's table, presenter's lectern, or raised music/performance platform. The typically high ceiling in the ballroom must be taken into account so that the angle of the beam is effective for accenting the speakers or performers.
2. The downlight luminaires are evenly spaced to provide a consistent blanket of task-level light over the entire space. A medium-beam fixture is needed to provide the intensity required for meetings, but it must be spaced appropriately to avoid the pooling effect at the floor or table level.
3. Because they play such an important design role in the ballroom's ambience, the size and scale of the chandeliers are as critical as their lighting quality. In addition to providing a low to medium level of nondirectional ambient light, the chandeliers are expected to provide glitter or sparkle through the reflective quality of their materials. While the sconces at the ballroom's perimeter do not play as important a role in the ambient lighting, they are selected to provide some needed eye-level glow, as well as some sparkle or glitter that is consistent with those qualities of the chandeliers.
4. The cove uplight luminaires at the perimeter of each quadrant are selected to provide a soft, even wash of ambient light for the entire space. The centrally placed chandeliers and the perimeter wall sconces provide another layer of ambient light that permits several alternatives to the ballroom's ambience. While the downlight's primary role is to provide task light, it offers still another layer of ambient light potential.

Usually, ballrooms have sophisticated dimming systems that permit each group of lights in each bay to be dimmed independently of other bays and fixtures. Some ballrooms even have control rooms, where the architectural dimming controls can be managed from a console that also controls theatrical lighting. In simpler ballrooms, a preset dimming system permits the choice of four or more scenes, or an "off" setting, in each partitioned space. These systems have separate control circuits for each layer.

The dimming and control system must be designed and circuited so that it can operate the lights correctly in each partition setting. Modern dimming systems have partition switches that automatically reconfigure the dimming system depending on the partition arrangement. In addition, the dimming system is usually connected to an emergency generator source; in the event of a power failure, some lights will automatically come to full brightness relatively quickly under emergency power.

Luminaire and lamp selections should be based on the following considerations:

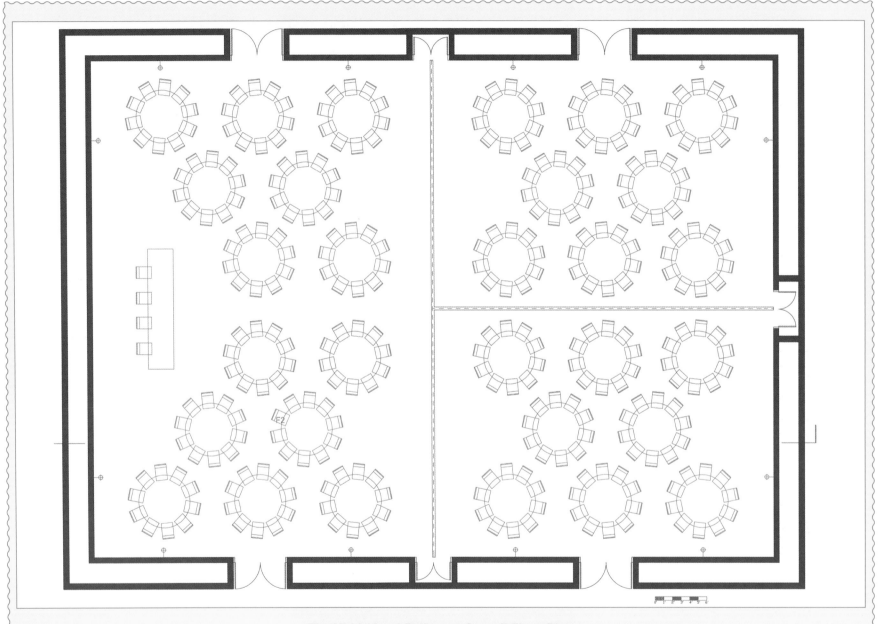

Fig. 17.10 Hotel Ballroom Overall Floor Plan

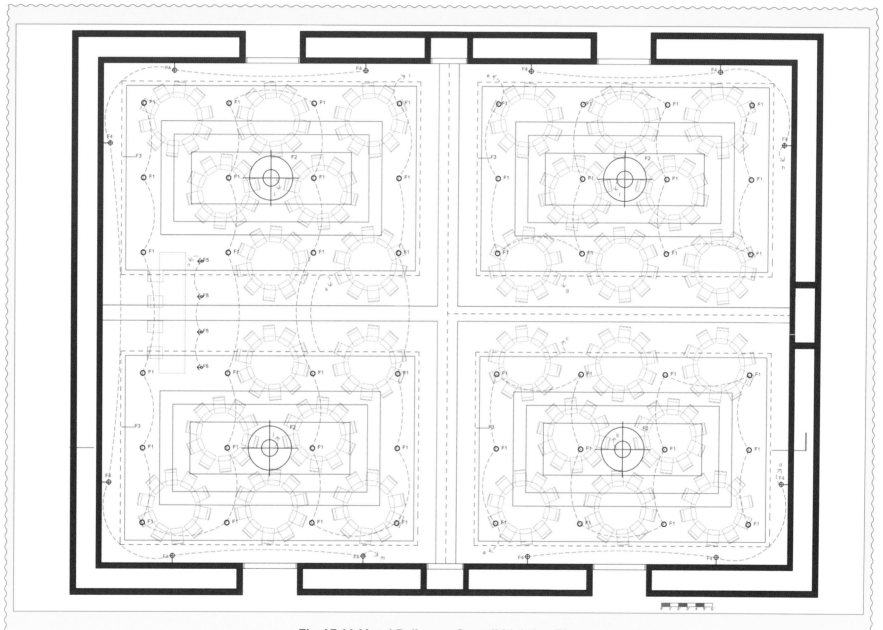

Fig. 17.11 Hotel Ballroom Overall Lighting Plan

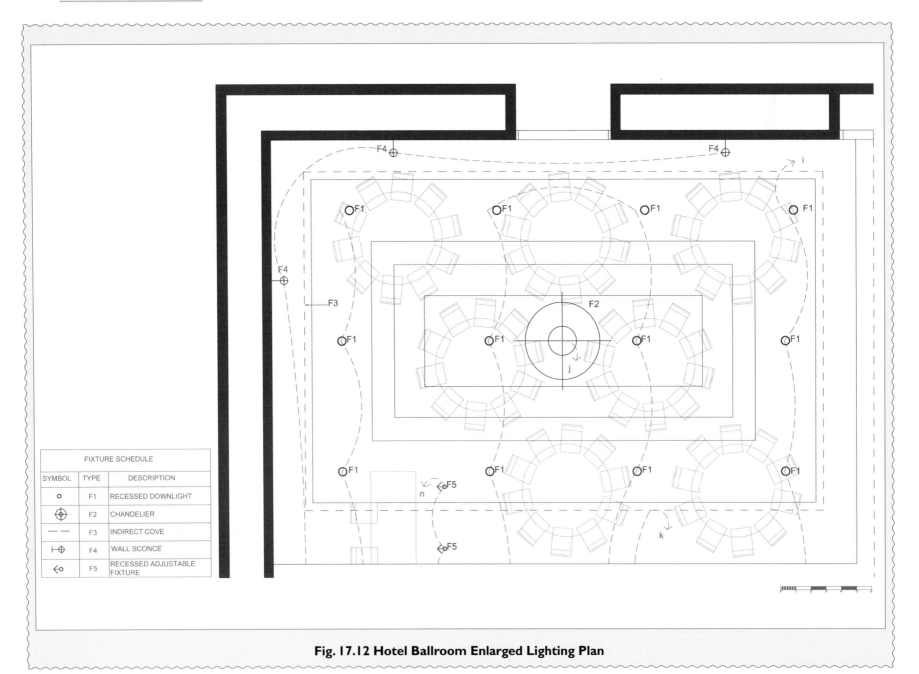

FIXTURE SCHEDULE

SYMBOL	TYPE	DESCRIPTION
o	F1	RECESSED DOWNLIGHT
⊕	F2	CHANDELIER
– – –	F3	INDIRECT COVE
⊢⊕	F4	WALL SCONCE
←o	F5	RECESSED ADJUSTABLE FIXTURE

Fig. 17.12 Hotel Ballroom Enlarged Lighting Plan

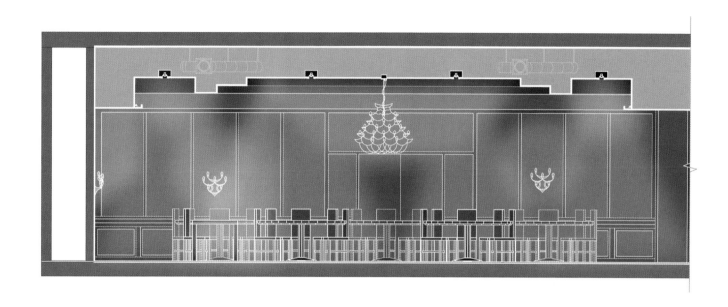

Fig. 17.13 Hotel Ballroom Section

- *Downlights:* Halogen PAR or MR lamps are traditionally common because of the punch they provide on a table to highlight tableware or meeting materials. LED is now being considered because of energy code restrictions. The color temperature should be warm, with a high CRI to mimic halogen. The lamp should be regressed within the cone so that it is not visible or glaring from normal view.
- *Cove:* Linear fluorescent is typical when functional light is desired. Care must be taken to incorporate an appropriate warm color temperature. Linear LED cove fixtures are common because of their ease of installation, energy savings, and long life. Many hotel ballrooms incorporate color-changing LED coves as an added selling feature for parties and weddings.
- *Chandelier and sconces:* Direct/indirect distribution with glow and/or sparkle is determined by the degree of translucency of the diffusers and user preference.

The design quality of the selected luminaires must be determined by the quality or style of the architectural and interior design detailing and materials, from traditional silk shades to contemporary natural woods and high-tech materials. It is rare for the room's detailing and materials to be determined by the lighting design solution, including the selection of luminaires. This aspect of luminaire selection is difficult to articulate because it deals with the elusive elements of aesthetics, style, and taste. Only long experience in a trial-and-error process over the course of many projects will sufficiently inform the designer to make intelligent aesthetic decisions.

Chapter 18 LIGHTING FOR COMMON SPACE

Almost all buildings have one or more of the spaces that are here defined as common spaces. Clearly, halls, corridors, and stairs fall into this category. Public or common-use restrooms are found in almost every nonresidential building. Large, general-use public spaces, such as malls, airport waiting areas, and atria, also are in this category.

Although common spaces are found in all building types, they present different lighting design requirements and considerations. In residences, corridors and stairs are treated as a part of the personal environment, while in nonresidential buildings they are public domain and often quite anonymous in character. Public restrooms, while always personal in their use, can vary tremendously from strictly utilitarian to decorative and even luxurious. Creating a personally tolerable environment for large public waiting areas, like those found in airports, is a particularly challenging design problem. Shopping malls, with the constant movement of people and the efforts of individual stores to vie for shoppers' attention, present still another common lighting design challenge.

The techniques for solving these common-space lighting design problems vary as widely as their uses. Their one shared characteristic is that lighting requirements are generally fixed and need not be adjusted to changing conditions; once set in place, the lighting condition usually remains constant. Otherwise, however, every type of luminaire and light source is used in common spaces, from fundamental to complex and from utilitarian to ornamental.

Except for residential settings, code compliance plays a significant role in the lighting of common spaces because so many of them are, directly or indirectly, part of a building's egress system and must provide safe paths of evacuation in emergencies. Energy consumption code factors are usually not an area of concern because critical visual tasks are normally not performed in these spaces and high levels of illumination are not needed. Nevertheless, minimally adequate vision to find one's way out of a building when power is cut off due to a fire or other crisis situation is clearly essential and required by all building codes. An emergency lighting system, employing accepted industry techniques, must be an integral part of every nonresidential building's overall lighting system. All common spaces that are part of a building's means of egress, including corridors, stairs, lobbies, and malls, must incorporate emergency lighting that is powered by battery and/or emergency generator methods.

Some standard techniques for lighting fire stairs and utilitarian corridors are sensible and acceptable because they are used infrequently. But beyond these purely utilitarian spaces, most common spaces deserve (and sometimes demand) creative lighting design attention. Corridors are rarely thought of as interesting spaces, but they can be saved from their usual pedestrian quality with thoughtful lighting design solutions. This is the case in countless office, apartment, hospital, and hotel buildings. Atria, lobbies, monumental stairs, and other major entrance or gathering spaces typically receive a great deal of design attention, including lighting design attention, and significant budget is applied to make them special. Entrances, in particular, are symbolic spaces, creating the visitor's first impression and setting the tone for what lies beyond. These special spaces typically require extensive collaboration between the architect and/or interior designer creating the space and the lighting designer responsible for a successful lighting design solution.

It should be obvious that the lighting of common spaces runs the gamut from purely functional to dramatic. The case studies in this chapter identify the most frequent of these lighting design problems, expecting that the concepts employed are translatable to a wide range of design conditions.

CASE STUDY 22—Public Restroom Lighting

The character and quality of public restrooms vary from utilitarian and bare-boned to lavish and decorative, depending on the setting and budget. Size and the number of people to be accommodated also range from an uncompartmented two-fixture facility to large-scale men's and women's rooms geared to serving large numbers of people, as at airports and sports stadiums. Most people have experienced the vast difference in design intent between restrooms in fast-food chain restaurants and those in expensive and elaborate restaurants. Obviously, lighting design solutions must be consistent with the design intent and quality of the restrooms they serve.

The restrooms shown in the floor plan (Fig. 18.1) are in the middle range with respect to both size and elaborateness; they are the kind of facility one might find on a typical floor of a large office building or adjacent to the lobby of a museum. Except for the grooming area provided in the women's room, the lighting requirements of both rooms are identical.

1. Focal light is required for the signage indicating gender so users approaching the restrooms can comfortably identify.
2. A somewhat greater concentration of light is needed at the lavatories, but washing hands and some perfunctory grooming at the mirror above do not require much more than the ambient light level of the remainder of the room. The one critical visual task occurs at the vanity counter in the women's room, where high-level and properly positioned light is needed.
3. A patron entering one of these rooms needs comfortable navigational ambient light for finding his or her way into the main space. In the urinal area and all of the toilet stalls a general wash of ambient light is needed.
4. Decorative lighting is desired to provide a less utilitarian approach.

As discussed in Chapters 12 (residential) and 17 (hospitality), evenly distributed and relatively shadowless light are best for combing hair and applying

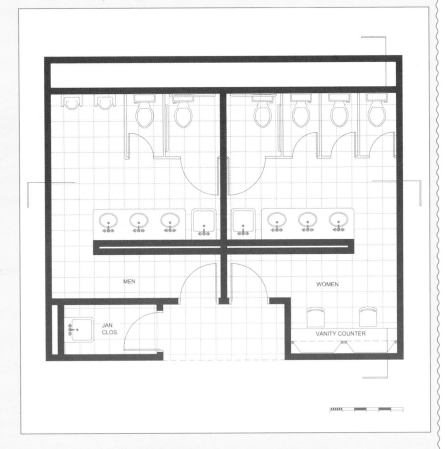

Fig. 18.1 Public Restroom Floor Plan

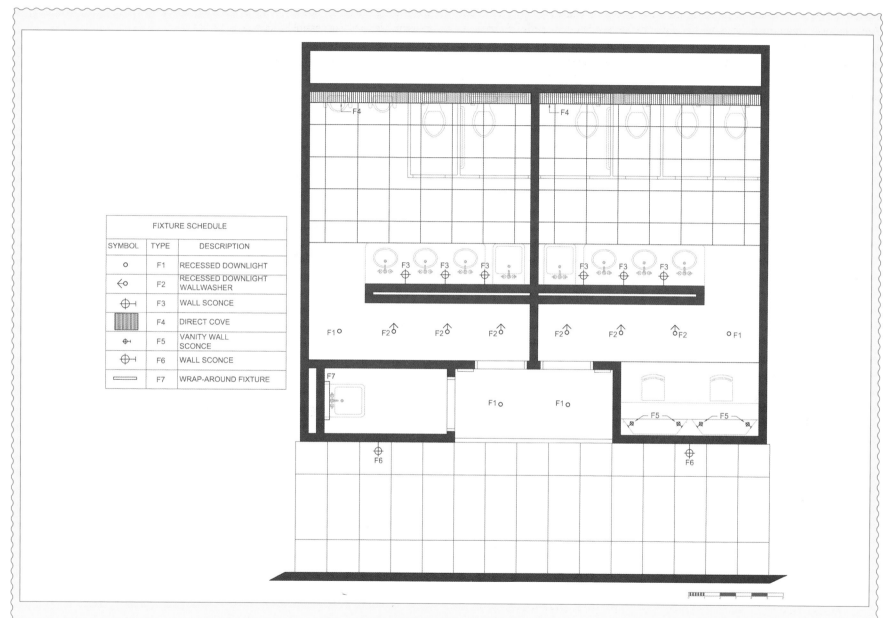

Fig. 18.2 Public Restroom Lighting Plan

FIXTURE SCHEDULE

SYMBOL	TYPE	DESCRIPTION
o	F1	RECESSED DOWNLIGHT
←o	F2	RECESSED DOWNLIGHT WALLWASHER
⊕⊣	F3	WALL SCONCE
▦	F4	DIRECT COVE
⊕⊢	F5	VANITY WALL SCONCE
⊕⊣	F6	WALL SCONCE
▭	F7	WRAP-AROUND FIXTURE

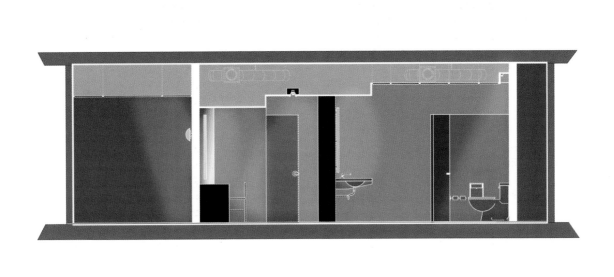

Fig. 18.3 Public Restroom Section

makeup. Note that the ADA compliance issues of these restroom facilities do not place special demands on the lighting solution.

The lighting design shown in the reflected ceiling plan (Fig. 18.2) and the section (Fig. 18.3) addresses the visual tasks in the following manner:

1. In the recessed corridor area, two recessed downlights are adequate for lighting the necessary signage that identifies the respective facilities for men and women. Note that the ceiling height has been raised 4" so a drywall ceiling may be placed in that small area, and the luminaire can be placed without having to conform to the corridor ceiling grid pattern. Under other corridor conditions, the drywall ceiling in the recessed area could be lowered by four or more inches.

2. In the lavatory areas, a vanity luminaire is placed between the mirrors located directly above each lavatory; they should be designed and placed to cast nonglare illumination on users' faces, as well as to provide adequate light for hand washing. Unlike the surfaces in most interior spaces, wall and floor surfaces in restrooms tend to be relatively permanent, such as ceramic tile or stone, resulting in equally permanent reflectance values. Because of this, long-term lighting results can be counted on. At the vanity counter, two vertically mounted fluorescents with wraparound translucent shields are placed to provide high-intensity and shadowless light for each of the two grooming stations. Unlike the grooming light indicated in the residential and hospitality case studies (Chapters 12 and 17), where lavatory use also had to be accommodated, the users' func-

tions and positions are fixed and known, and a "perfect" lighting solution can be achieved.

3. In the toilet stall and urinal areas, a continuous recessed direct cove is used, providing an even wash of ambient light for those areas of both restrooms. In the entrance area to each restroom, three downlight-wallwashers have been used to provide a bright wall leading one into the space. The wall sconces at the lavatories provide the desired decorative lighting and a more welcoming ambience.

Switching in public situations of this kind is usually controlled at a locally central panel box, with the power on during all operating hours and, when needed, time clock operated. Occupancy sensors are also often used in public restrooms; however, care must be taken with selection and placement so that the lights do not turn off prematurely.

Luminaire and lamp selections should be based on the following considerations:

- *Downlights and downlight-wallwashers:* Compact fluorescent is most appropriate, or LED if the budget allows. The lamp should be recessed within the cone so that it is not visible or glaring from normal view. A wide beam spread works well for this ceiling height.

- *Lavatory wall sconces:* Equal direct/indirect distribution with a translucent shield or shade, and lamped with compact fluorescent containing a high CRI and warm color temperature.
- *Direct cove at stalls:* Continuous architectural pocket in ceiling containing linear fluorescent strips with a baffle or lens flush with the ceiling plane to conceal the lamps.
- *Vanity sconce:* Fluorescent vertical sconces of appropriate length placed directly adjacent to the sides of the two mirrors. High-quality CRI and warm color temperature are most appropriate to provide flattering, shadowless light for users.

Design character and style are determined primarily by the quality and style of the architectural and interior design detailing and materials that are being used in the space. In this case study—and this is true for most public restrooms—luminaire selection is limited by the impersonal nature of the space and the narrow range of materials, finishes, and toilet stall and plumbing fixture colors and finishes that are normally employed. There are the occasional decorative restrooms, usually in restaurants and other hospitality settings, which permit and call for a much wider range of luminaire selections.

CASE STUDY 23—Corridors and Stairs

We encounter corridors and stairs just about everywhere. Except in single-story buildings, which do not require stairs, they are a necessary element of every building. They range from utilitarian to decorative and are, on occasion, monumental in character. Critical safety issues are always related to them because they are the means by which we get out of buildings at times of emergency or panic. Stairs present the additional danger of people tripping and falling. These safety issues have made corridor and stair design, including their lighting, a major element of all building codes.

Corridors range in width from the typically narrow halls in residences to quite wide corridors in places of heavy pedestrian traffic, such as schools and assembly buildings. They often dominate the design character of a building, particularly in the case of hotels, apartment buildings, and office buildings.

Many corridors feel lifeless because the pedestrian traffic is occasional or sporadic. Long corridors present difficult visual problems; their length should be deemphasized.

The design character of stairs ranges from rarely used fire stairs to grand stairways that are the central feature of an elaborate lobby or entrance. In residences, stairs take on a personal character and fuse with other architectural and interior elements. On occasion, stairs become a traffic hub, as in an interconnecting open stairwell between the floors of a single tenant in a high-rise office building. In all cases, stairs present an unusual design challenge because of their dynamic volumetric configuration.

The visual tasks in corridors and stairs are primarily navigational and usually not critical. Lighting levels are conventionally low to moderate, similar to those required for casual conversation or other situations in which vision is not vital. Occasionally, a corridor or stairway is part of a larger space, such as a lobby or

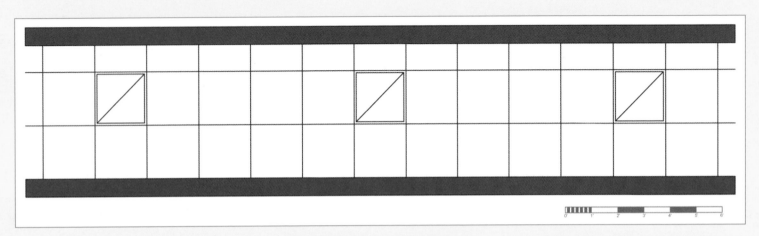

Fig. 18.4 Corridor A Lighting Plan

exhibit area, where higher levels of illumination are required—for example, at a bulletin board or display panel in a school or hospital corridor. Lighting on stairs must provide a clear view of treads and risers to minimize the inherent dangers of tripping and falling. Generally, the visual tasks in corridors and stairs that are related to safety are critical. More specifically, lighting is critical when providing for safe passage out of a building when a fire or other emergency, or just the fear of such a crisis, creates the need to get out quickly. Because electrical systems often fail at such times, building codes require that auxiliary or emergency lighting be provided in corridors and stairs. While this lighting requirement is minimal in terms of illumination level, emergency lighting must be properly incorporated into every nonresidential building.

This case study is unlike all of the others because it presents generalized lighting solutions for several corridor and stair conditions rather than an in-depth solution for a single example. In the diagrammatic reflected ceiling plans, the corridor width is drawn at 5'-0''. The purpose of this approach is to provide a needed range of solutions for the many corridor and stair conditions found in buildings.

Corridors
Corridor A, shown in the reflected ceiling plan (Fig. 18.4), indicates the typical corridor lighting solution found in nonresidential buildings. Because major mechanical and electrical lines and equipment are often in the corridor ple-

num, lay-in acoustic tile ceilings are employed to provide easy access. Recessed fluorescent troffers are placed at intervals of about 10', resulting in alternating dark and light areas as one traverses the length of the corridor. All of the light is downlight, resulting in a particularly flat or unmodulated appearance. The use of a dropped lens or, better still, a surface-mounted luminaire with translucent sides, will provide some horizontal light and result in a less flat or better modulated appearance.

Instead of the 2' × 2' luminaires shown in Fig. 18.4, 1' × 4' or 2' × 4' units can be used, being careful to place the long dimension across the width of the corridor in order to deemphasize the corridor's length. Luminaires do not have to be placed in the center of the corridor, and ceiling tile patterns can be adjusted to provide an eccentric or asymmetrical arrangement. However, luminaires should not be placed adjacent to the corridor wall, which may cause hot spots on the wall. Lamps must be selected to produce the desired level of illumination directly under each luminaire as well as at the midpoint between two luminaires. Emergency lighting can be provided by supplying emergency power to designated luminaires or by installing wall-mounted battery pack units at the required intervals.

The **Corridor B** reflected ceiling plan (Fig. 18.5) shows a common solution found in both residential and nonresidential buildings, although the acoustic tile ceiling is rarely used in residences. It presents the same disadvantages of alternating dark and light areas and a flat appearance. Luminaires can be

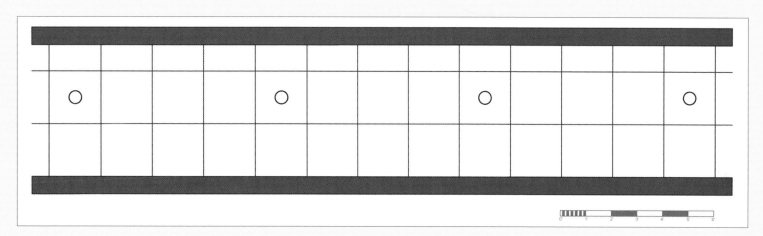

Fig. 18.5 Corridor B Lighting Plan

placed off center for an asymmetrical appearance, including placement close enough to one wall to create a scalloped light pattern on it, if desired. Lamping can be easily adjusted to produce the desired level of illumination. Emergency lighting can be provided by an emergency generator tied to selected luminaires or by battery pack units at the required intervals.

The **Corridor C** reflected ceiling plan (Fig. 18.6) demonstrates the use of sconces as the primary approach to lighting corridors. Their advantage in corridors is that they produce both direct and indirect light as well as the potential for eye-level glow and a decorative quality, depending on the luminaire(s) selected. Their disadvantage is that they must coordinate with door openings, corridor recesses, and intersecting corridors. To compound this disadvantage, sconces should be placed at fairly regular intervals to avoid creating a visually chaotic vista down the length of a long hallway.

Sconces can be effectively used in apartment buildings, hotels, and other settings where corridor door locations are not subject to change. However, particularly in office buildings, where door locations are subject to frequent change, sconces are impractical.

When they are used in corridors, sconces usually represent a major design element, and their design characteristics should be carefully selected to complement the architectural and interior design characteristics of the corridor. Lamp selection should be based on the levels of illumination desired at the luminaires and at the midpoint between luminaires. ADA compliance requires

that they not project more than 4" from the wall or that the bottom edge be at least 80" AFF. Emergency lighting can be accomplished with an emergency power system tied to selected luminaires or with battery pack units at the required intervals.

The **Corridor D** reflected ceiling plan (Fig. 18.7) illustrates a solution often found in hotel corridors, where doors to guest rooms are at quite regular intervals. From a lighting design point of view, this is an opportunity to create a visually interesting result not often found in long, uninterrupted corridors. As a design approach or concept, it is sometimes applicable to other building types in which the recessed doorways occur at irregular intervals. As illustrated here, the recessed doorway areas are lighted with a centrally placed recessed downlight in a slightly raised gypsum wallboard ceiling, so that ceiling tile patterns do not have to be considered. In most hotels, paired recessed doorway areas occur every 25' to 30' and require a wall-mounted luminaire at the midpoint between the recessed doorways, as shown in the reflected ceiling plan.

If a wall-mounted luminaire is used, its design characteristics and style are visually important and must be consistent with the architectural and interior design elements of which it is a part. This lighting solution, in addition to providing a visually interesting alternative to conventional corridor lighting, also supplies the minor task light needed by people looking for where to place the plastic key card. Lamp selection is based on the levels of illumination desired

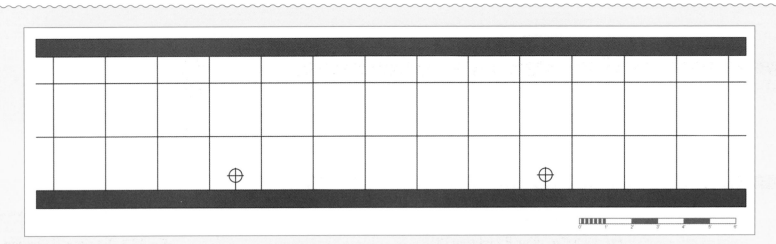

Fig. 18.6 Corridor C Lighting Plan

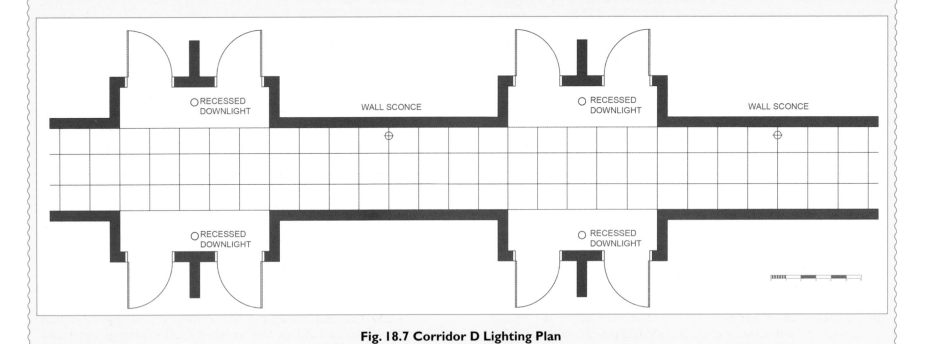

Fig. 18.7 Corridor D Lighting Plan

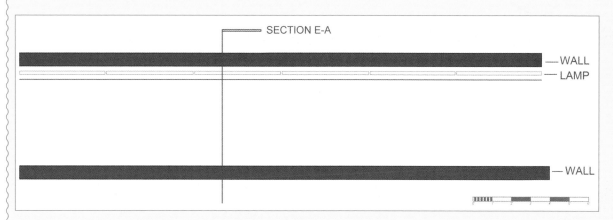

Fig. 18.8 Corridor E Lighting Plan

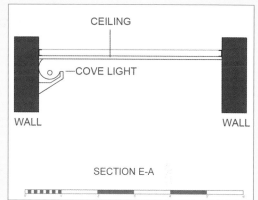

Fig. 18.9 Corridor E Section

in the recessed doorways and in the areas between the doorways. Emergency lighting can be accomplished with emergency power supplied to selected luminaires or with battery pack units at the required intervals.

The **Corridor E** reflected ceiling plan and section (Figs. 18.8 and 18.9) illustrate the use of cove lighting, a technique that has many possible applications. It provides an uninterrupted and relatively shadowless quality of light. The cove can easily be detailed to ride above door heads, but this approach may be impractical in corridors interrupted by recesses or intersecting corridors. Unless the cove is used on both sides of the corridor, one side of the corridor will be appreciably lighter than the other, although it is possible to detail the valence or cove to project its light toward the other side. In particularly wide corridors, especially in hospital or geriatric care settings, the use of cove lighting on both sides of the corridor will provide a desirably even wash of light that will not produce visually disturbing glare on smooth, shiny floor surfaces.

A continuous line of light is needed to produce the desired effect of cove lighting, so lamp selection is limited to readily available straight lengths of fluorescent or LED lamps. In carefully detailed construction of this kind, lamp ends are staggered, or a reflector is incorporated in the fixture design in order to avoid the minor unevenness of light that occurs between lamp ends. Emergency lighting can be accomplished with emergency power supplied to selected luminaires or with battery pack units at the required intervals. It is important to note that, even though this lighting approach may be desirable,

by itself it will not meet the energy code. If using the space-by-space method, described in Appendix B, it may be possible to trade this overage with a space that is under the code requirements.

The **Corridor F** reflected ceiling plan and section (Figs. 18.10 and 18.11, respectively) describe a variation on cove or valence lighting that is particularly applicable to long, uninterrupted corridors and can be installed quite economically. It also has the advantage of visually breaking up a dauntingly long vista of corridor ceiling. The section illustrates how a direct view of the fluorescent or LED lamp is avoided when corridor doors are opened. Also note in the section that enough space is provided between the lamp and the ceiling surface to permit easy relamping by maintenance personnel. Materials for the long central element and the repeated cross-members must meet building code flammability requirements; chemically treated noncombustible wood or formed sheet metal are two obvious choices. An extremely basic industrial channel can be employed for the luminaires. One or two lamp luminaires can be used, depending on the spacing of the luminaires and the level of illumination desired. Emergency lighting can be accomplished with emergency power supplied to selected luminaires or with battery pack units at the required intervals.

Stairs

The enclosed stairwell is found in almost all multistory buildings other than residences. In many buildings, such as high-rise office buildings, hotels, and

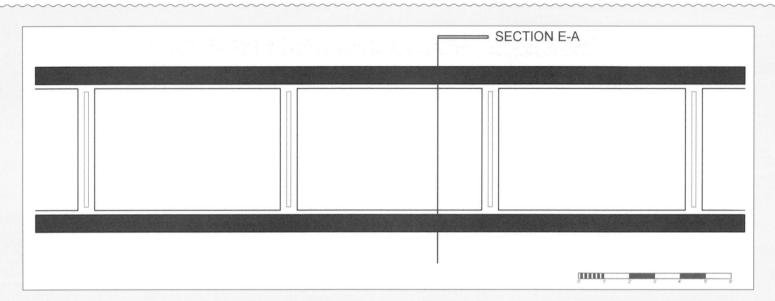

SECTION E-A

Fig. 18.10 Corridor F Lighting Plan

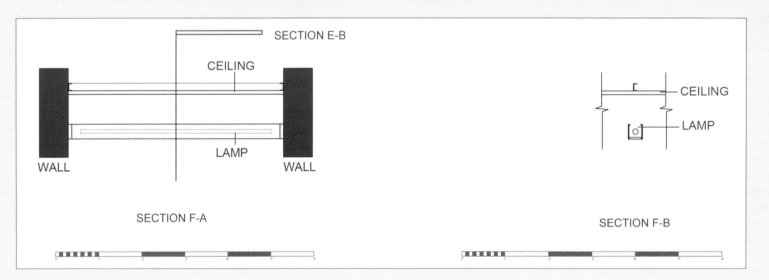

SECTION E-B

CEILING

WALL   LAMP   WALL

SECTION F-A

CEILING

LAMP

SECTION F-B

Fig. 18.11 Corridor F Section

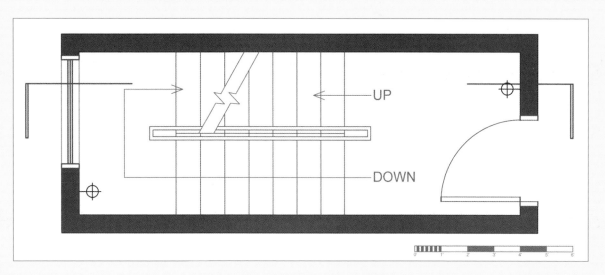

Fig. 18.12 Stair Lighting Plan

apartment houses, the stairwells are used only in emergencies. However, in many other buildings, particularly smaller multistory buildings, stairs are the primary means of interfloor circulation. Obviously, regularly used stairs must receive more detailed design attention.

One approach to designing the lighting of typical enclosed stairwells uses wall-mounted fluorescent or LED luminaires with both direct and indirect light distribution at each landing, providing appropriate and safe lighting. Depending on the luminaire selected, this technique can add to the design character of the space. A ceiling-mounted fluorescent luminaire with both down- and side-light distribution can be equally effective. Avoid luminaires that provide downlight only because they will be less effective, and therefore less safe, in lighting the treads and risers of the adjacent runs of stairs.

For the rarely used fire stair, lighting levels can be at minimal navigational intensity, while for stairs that are regularly used, lamp selection should be geared to the same level as a normally traveled corridor. When windows bring natural light into a stairwell, luminaire placement may have to be adjusted to accommodate the architectural condition as well as the daytime lighting condition. When emergency power is available, all stairwell luminaires are tied to that power system; otherwise, battery pack units are employed.

The stair lighting design solution illustrated in plan and section (Figs. 18.12 and 18.13, respectively) is quite basic. It places a translucent, shielded, wall-mounted luminaire at each landing, high enough to be out of reach and located to direct its beam on the rising flight of steps so that each riser is seen without shadow. The level of illumination must be great enough to provide good ambient light throughout the stairwell. During the heart of the daylight hours, the large windows at the noncorridor end of the stairwell will provide adequate navigational light. If this stairway is expected to be used as a regular means personnel traffic, a more decorative approach would be desired, employing more highly styled luminaires and possibly a more sculptural approach to enhancing the space.

In the case of an unusually long floor-to-floor run of stairs with a sloped ceiling or soffit following the stair slope, it is often best to use downlights placed directly in or on the sloped ceiling surface. Attention should be given to luminaire selection so people descending the stairs need not look directly into the light source. This architectural condition tends to occur more frequently in residences, where luminaire selection may have to be particularly well integrated with surrounding interior design detail.

Several techniques for lighting stairs involve installing the light source close

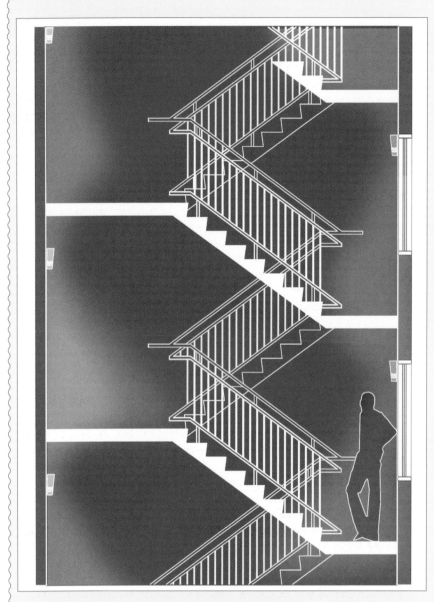

Fig. 18.13 Stair Section

to and directly focused on the treads and risers. While these techniques are ideal for generating safe lighting conditions, they do not provide adequate ambient light for most situations and must be supplemented with ambient light for the overall stairwell. One possible solution is the use of fluorescent lamps or continuous LEDs incorporated into the stair handrail, which casts light directly on the treads and risers.

Another option is the use of small luminaires recessed into the stairwell's side wall, usually placed every two or three treads and lamped with halogen, compact fluorescent, or LEDs. For a dramatic effect, the use of a linear LED placed under each tread nosing is a technique that yields excellent illumination for safe passage. This approach is obviously expensive to construct, install, and maintain, but in special situations where dramatic effect is desired, it may be appropriate.

Switching and Controls

A commonsense understanding of how people enter and exit rooms and other spaces, including halls and stairs, is a good guide to switching in residential settings. Dimmers should be approached in the same commonsense manner. Three-way switches are particularly useful at the opposite ends of hallways and at the top and bottom of stairs.

Switching for corridors and stairs in nonresidential buildings is typically controlled in centrally located panel boxes that prevent users from arbitrarily turning lights off in critical paths of egress. Timing devices often control switching patterns in which minimal corridor lighting is employed during low-use hours in office buildings and other settings where use patterns are highly predictable.

Emergency Lighting

Building codes require that all nonresidential buildings provide emergency lighting when normal power service fails. Simply, occupants must be able to safely see their way out of a building at times of emergency or crisis. Additional requirements for emergency lighting pertain in other specialized building types, such as hospitals and large open work areas. Generally, a minimum lighting level of 1 fc is required, and sources may not be more than 50' apart in corridors and other horizontal exitways. The same 1-fc minimum requirement must be maintained in stairwells.

Power for emergency lighting is accomplished in two very different ways. Remote emergency generators can provide power to designated luminaires.

This approach is generally reserved for fairly large buildings, where economy of size makes it practical.

In smaller buildings, the one-, two-, or three-headed battery pack unit is the preferred approach because the installation of an emergency generator system is economically prohibitive. From an aesthetic standpoint, designers usually prefer to avoid battery pack units because they so often appear to be an uncoordinated afterthought, but construction cost economy typically is the deciding factor.

Luminaires and Lamps

Luminaire and lamp selections have generally been addressed in the corridor and stair solutions previously described. Almost every luminaire type is employed in corridors and stairs. Lamping is generally dictated by the desired illumination level for each interior condition. Luminaire design character and style should be consistent with the building's architectural and interior design qualities. But corridors and stairs, so often thought of as anonymous or uninteresting spaces, present many opportunities for creative and unusual lighting solutions. They are spaces in motion, and stairs in particular have an inherently dynamic spatial character. When budgets permit, corridors and stairs are good and appropriate places for customizing luminaires and the housing or integration of conventional luminaires. Sometimes, in highly repetitive situations, customization can favorably compete with standard products and solutions.

CASE STUDY 24—Waiting Room Lighting

Waiting rooms are a common space type in many public buildings, including airports, malls, hospitals, train stations, and government buildings. Many waiting rooms are designed for more than 100 people, while others accommodate just a few. Waiting room spaces vary from very modest rooms, such as the reception room described in Chapter 13, to large and even vast volumes, such as airport holding areas. The visual tasks that are common to most waiting rooms involve providing adequate light for: (1) navigating through the space, (2) casual conversation with others who are waiting, and (3) casual reading. In addition, some waiting rooms require focal lighting to help visitors locate a receptionist or greeter.

The floor plan for the modest-size reception/waiting room used for this case study is shown in Fig. 18.14. It provides examples for most of the visual tasks and concerns related to lighting design problems of this kind that might be found in a medical clinic or a large law firm. Visitors enter the space from the exterior into an enclosed weather-break vestibule. They then enter a symmetrical center space, where they immediately encounter a two-person reception desk. On either side of the central space are two identical seating areas, each accommodating 10 to 12 people. The visual tasks to be resolved in this space are as follows:

1. Focal lighting is required for the logo display wall behind the reception desk and for two of the four artwork locations in the seating areas.
2. Task lighting is required at the reception desk for the receptionists and at the transaction counter for visitors who will be reading and/or filling out forms.
3. Decorative lighting is desired in the reception desk area, as well as in the two seating areas in order to enhance a welcoming ambience.
4. Ambient lighting is required throughout the space, from the entrance vestibule to the reception desk, including the short corridor behind the logo display wall, and obviously in the two large seating areas.

The lighting design solution for this case study is shown in the lighting plan and section in Figs. 18.15 and 18.16, respectively:

1. *Focal lighting:* A direct downlight cove luminaire placed on top of the 80"-high logo wall behind the reception desk illuminates the company logo and immediately attracts visitors to the reception desk. Recessed accent fixtures are focused on the artwork above the 2 two-seaters on the south walls.
2. *Task lighting:* An undershelf luminaire is placed under the transaction counter to provide high-quality working light for the receptionists. In addition to serving a decorative/welcoming function, the two desk lamps placed on either side of the transaction counter provide light for visitors to read and fill out forms or other paperwork.
3. *Decorative lighting:* The major decorative lighting is provided by the two translucent shielded pendants in each of the two seating areas. The two desk lamps on either side of the transaction counter will also add a decorative touch to the entry area.

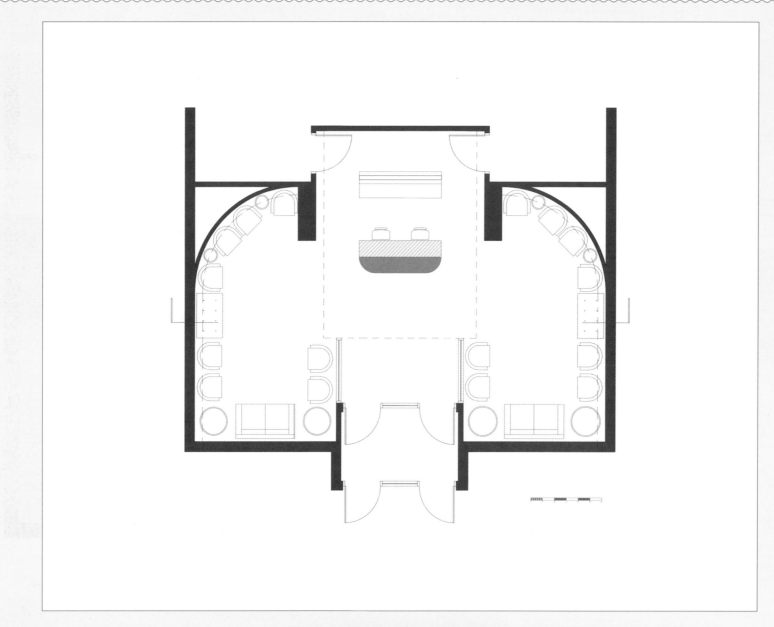

Fig. 18.14 Waiting Room Floor Plan

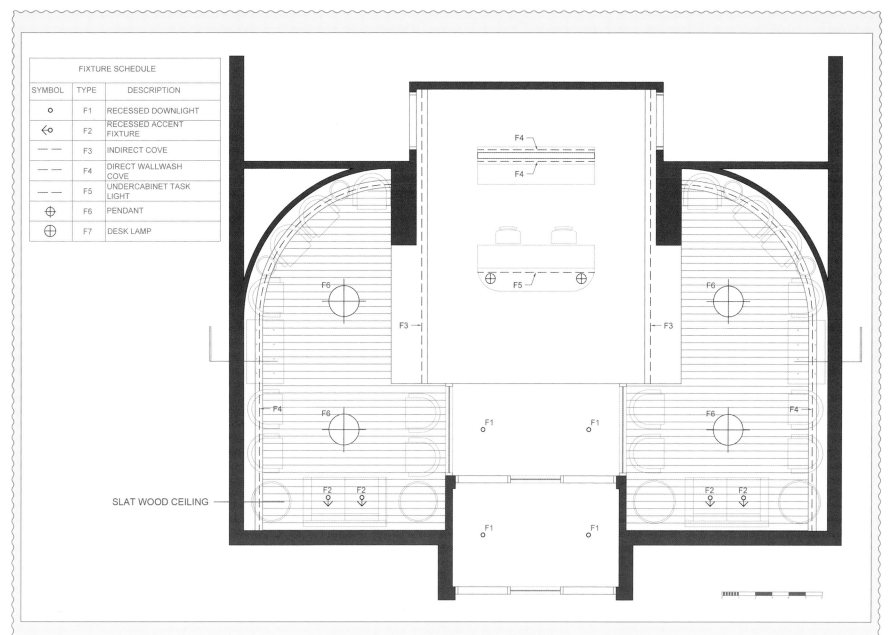

FIXTURE SCHEDULE		
SYMBOL	TYPE	DESCRIPTION
o	F1	RECESSED DOWNLIGHT
⟜o	F2	RECESSED ACCENT FIXTURE
— · — ·	F3	INDIRECT COVE
— — —	F4	DIRECT WALLWASH COVE
— — —	F5	UNDERCABINET TASK LIGHT
⊕	F6	PENDANT
⊕	F7	DESK LAMP

SLAT WOOD CEILING

Fig. 18.15 Waiting Room Lighting Plan

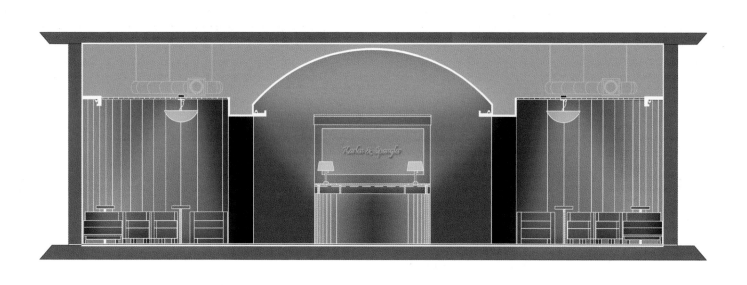

Fig. 18.16 Waiting Room Section

4. *Ambient lighting:* The four wide-beam downlights in the vestibule and entrance area provide a soft ambient quality as visitors enter the facility. The short passageway behind the 80"-high logo wall is illuminated by a direct wallwash cove that provides a lower intensity of light than the cove on the opposite side of the wall. The two large seating areas are provided with a wash of soft light by the continuous direct wallwasher cove fixtures.

Luminaire and lamp selections are based on the criteria of functionality, energy consumption, aesthetics, and budget. The two luminaire types that have significant impact on the design quality of the space are the four pendants and the two transaction counter lamps. The pendants have a translucent shield that provides visible sparkle and direct and indirect illumination; the up/down ratio is to be determined by the type of lamp, the degree of translucency of the shield, and the color/material of the ceiling finish. The two lamps on the transaction counter also have translucent shields or shades to act as beacons for the incoming visitors and direct enough of their light to the countertop to serve as task light for reading and signing forms and documents. The cove luminaires are an integral part of the interior construction; their fluorescent or LED lamps are selected to provide a soft wash of light on the walls below them, with careful selection of color temperature that is consistent with the palette chosen for the space. The recessed, wide-beam downlights in the vestibule and entry area, and the recessed accent luminaires focused on the artwork on the south walls, are selected for their unobtrusive appearance, functional appropriateness, and attention to budget concerns.

All switching is contained in a nearby electrical panel and is programmatically controlled with the use of timing devices.

CASE STUDY 25 — Shopping Malls

The mall spaces within shopping center complexes are pedestrian thorough-fares or indoor streets designed to provide access to the retail tenant spaces as well as generate an atmosphere that stimulates an interest in shopping. (Stimulating an interest in buying is the retailer's job.) For many shoppers, the attraction of the mall is also the opportunity for social experience, albeit a passive one—to get out of the house and see, hear, and even make casual social contact with other people. Successfully creating this kind of complex environment—which is a mix of practical planning, simulation of interesting street vistas, the infusion of a sense of theater or entertainment (sometimes including a space for planned or impromptu performance), an audio experience of canned music and/or splashing fountains and/or wind chimes, and even subliminal olfactory awareness via food vendor stands and/or piped-in aromas—has a great deal to do with the success or failure of a shopping mall enterprise.

The primary task of the lighting designer is to support the mall's commercial purpose. The important visual focus must be the retail stores. The mall space and its contents should not compete for visual attention. This is rarely a problem, as the mall space itself rarely sports major attractions. Low to modest levels of navigational light are the primary lighting requirement. Even specialty sales carts, often found within the mall space, normally provide their own focal lighting. The exception to this general rule for navigational light is the presence of a central or spectacular visual attraction unrelated to the tenant spaces, such as a large fountain, waterfall, or electronic display, that becomes the complex's identifying feature or sense of place. When these feature attractions are present, their lighting breaks all the rules and requires an individual lighting design focus.

It is necessary to note one more generality concerning mall lighting: the use of daylight through major skylights. Most mall spaces are two or three stories high, with the upper level(s) having balconies overlooking the central mall. It is common to find these mall spaces daylighted by large steel-and-glass skylight roof structures that flood the mall space with natural light during the day. The integration of natural and electric light must be carefully calculated and designed, including the phasing for diminishing natural light as night approaches. Night-time shopping is of major importance to mall complexes, and the effects of the full electric lighting system are critical, even when large skylights are incorporated into the overall building design.

The floor plan for the shopping mall for this case study is shown in Fig. 18.17. Only one wing of the entire mall is used for the case study, because this wing identifies all of the lighting design issues that are common to mall planning and lighting. It is fairly typical of modest-size malls with a three-story-high skylighted promenade atrium space and retail shops on both sides. The second- and third-story pedestrian walkways overlook the central mall space. The barrel-vault skylight that runs the length of each wing of the mall is a major architectural feature. The visual tasks that require resolution are as follows:

1. *Focal lighting:* As noted, the retail stores demand the primary focus. However, to provide a pedestrian scale to the atrium, the trees in the several planters can be enhanced in the evening with focal light on them.
2. *Task lighting:* There are no critical visual tasks in the mall space.
3. *Decorative lighting:* This is required to enhance the desired ambience that stimulates the visitors to window-shop and enter the retail stores. That includes enhancing the passive social experience that is critical to attracting shoppers to the mall.
4. *Ambient lighting:* This is the primary lighting task that makes navigating one's way through the mall an enjoyable experience. The focal and decorative lighting make a major contribution toward creating the desired ambience.

The lighting design solution for this case study is shown in the lighting plan (Fig. 18.18), the key plan (Fig. 18.19), and the section (Fig. 18.20) and is explained as follows:

1. *Focal lighting:* Two uplights are placed in each planter to highlight the beautiful natural qualities of the trees in contrast to the architectonic nature of the building's structure.
2. *Task lighting:* This is not required and is not provided.
3. *Decorative lighting:* The four large translucent and sculptural pendants suspended from the glass barrel-vault skylight cast their light both up and down, making them a major contributor to the mall's decorative quality. The decorative sconces in line with the storefronts are translucent, creating a rhythmic sense of eye-level glow without competing with the retailers' need to attract customers; the sconces are repeated on the second- and third-floor levels. The marquee-style lights that are strung

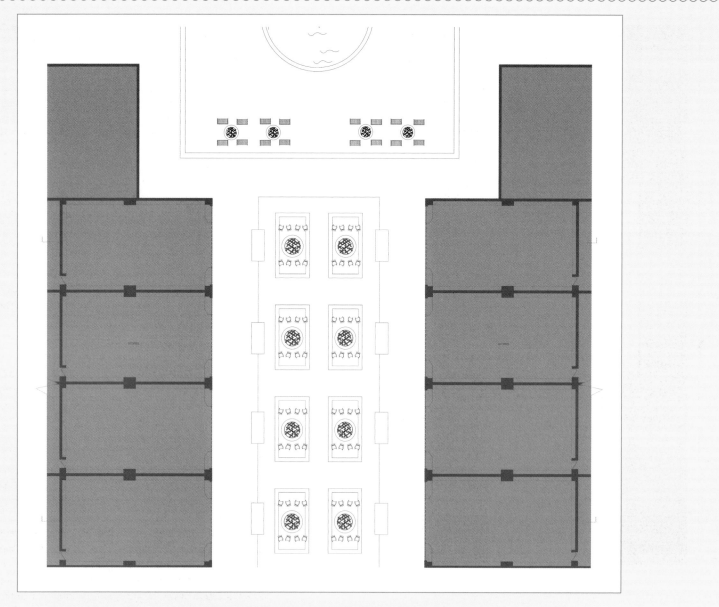

Fig. 18.17 Shopping Mall Floor Plan

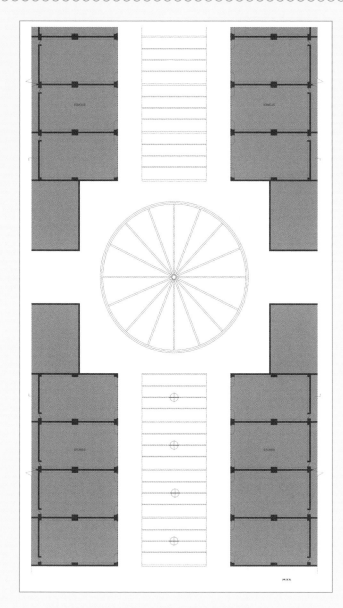

Fig. 18.18 Mall Lighting Plan

along the radial ribs of the large, central dome skylight enhance that major architectural element of the overall mall structure, enhancing the skylight's form and adding a decorative touch reminiscent of the theatrical world.

4. *Ambient lighting:* The long lines of recessed downlights in front of the storefronts provide the primary navigational light for walking the mall; they are lamped specifically not to compete with the lighted storefronts. Additional ambient light in the central dome area is provided by an indirect uplight cove luminaire that follows the circumference of the dome, illuminating the dome's surface during evening hours and enhancing the form of the dome. The recessed adjustable downlights, two for each pie-shaped segment of the dome, follow the curve of the dome and provide ambient light at the floor level in the central mall area below the dome.

Controls

All switching is contained in a nearby electrical panel and programmatically controlled with the use of timing devices. The abundant amount of daylight also allows the use of photocell control to turn off a significant amount of the lighting during the daytime hours.

The criteria for luminaire and lamp selections are as follows:

- *Downlights:* Because dimming is not required, compact fluorescent or ceramic metal halide is typical, depending on the ceiling heights. LED is also now being considered, to improve energy efficiency and reduce maintenance. The lamp should be regressed within the cone so that it is not visible or glaring from normal view.
- *Tree uplights:* Can be recessed in the soil or surface mounted, but in either case lamp shielding is important to avoid glare. A point source is needed to highlight the sculptural quality of the trees, so halogen, ceramic metal halide, or LED is preferred and should be selected based on budget and size of tree.
- *Pendant:* Although decorative, this particular fixture contains many functions. The uplight will illuminate the barrel-vault skylight at night. This could incorporate white or colored light depending on how thematic the intent is. The downlight portion will need to provide functional light on the floor below. Because of the height, ceramic metal halide may be the only viable source, with LED becoming possible in the near future. The shape and

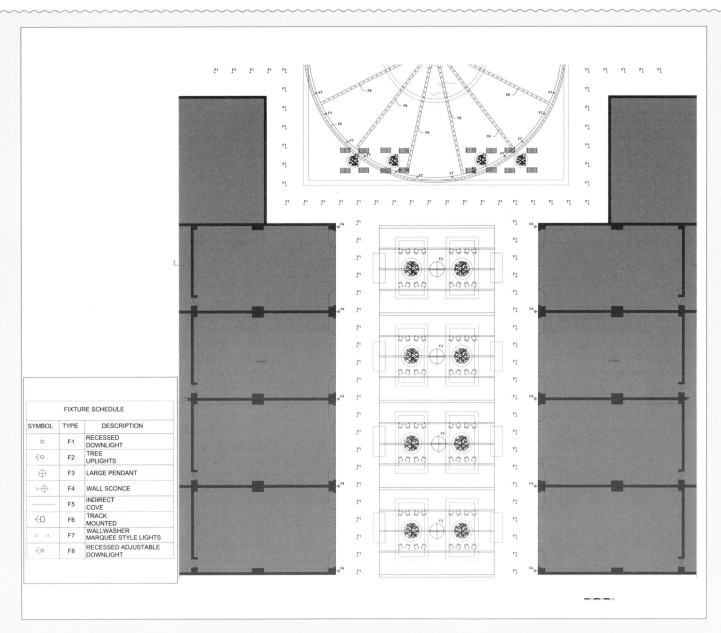

SYMBOL	TYPE	DESCRIPTION
		FIXTURE SCHEDULE
○	F1	RECESSED DOWNLIGHT
←○	F2	TREE UPLIGHTS
⊕	F3	LARGE PENDANT
⊢⊕	F4	WALL SCONCE
—	F5	INDIRECT COVE
←▢	F6	TRACK MOUNTED
○ ○	F7	WALLWASHER MARQUEE STYLE LIGHTS
←○	F8	RECESSED ADJUSTABLE DOWNLIGHT

Fig. 18.19 Mall Lighting Key Plan

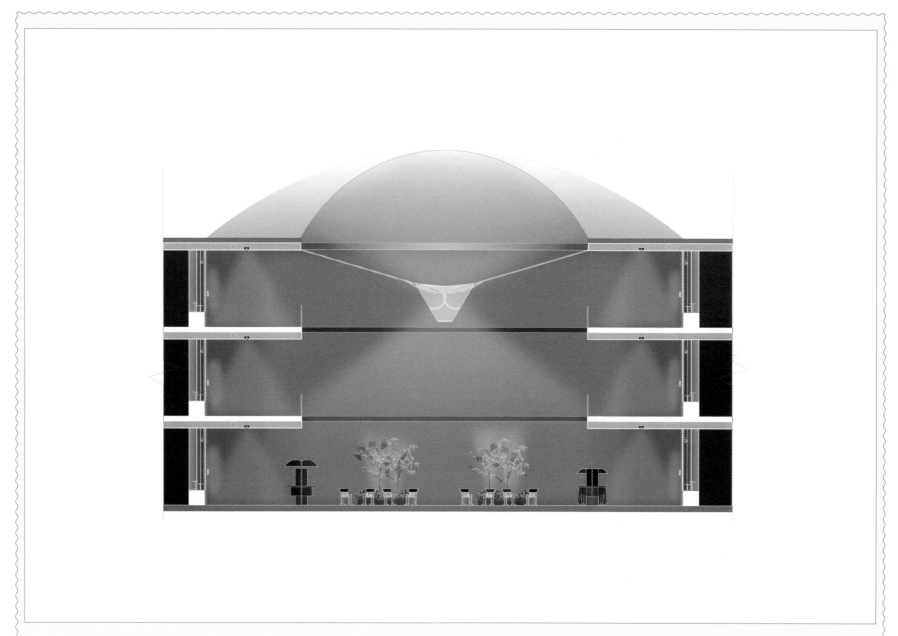

Fig. 18.20 Mall Section

material of the pendant is dictated by the aesthetic of the mall design; however, a translucent material is ideal to provide a luminous decorative element in the space.
- *Sconces:* Direct/indirect distribution with glow and/or sparkle determined by the degree of translucency of the diffusers and user preference.
- *Indirect cove:* Linear LED cove fixtures are preferred because of their ease of installation, energy savings, and long life.

- *Marquee lights at dome:* Traditionally, this was completed with incandescent globe lamps, but with this height and operation schedule, it would not be practical. There are LED replacement lamps or complete LED systems that can mimic this festive approach.

Chapter 19 OUTDOOR LIGHTING DESIGN

Although an entire book could be dedicated to the methods and applications of outdoor lighting design, this chapter provides an introduction to exterior lighting and focuses mainly on how interiors can be impacted by the lighting outside of a building.

APPROACH TO OUTDOOR LIGHTING DESIGN

The process behind exterior lighting design does not differ greatly from interior lighting; however, the means to achieve those effects does vary. Referring back to the design approach discussed in Chapter 10, the same steps can be applied:

DESCRIBE
LAYER
SELECT
COORDINATE

With outdoor lighting it is still necessary to determine the design concept and quality of light, develop the layers of light, select the appropriate light sources and luminaires, and coordinate the design. Exterior lighting does require some specific considerations, including the contrast between the lighted nighttime and daytime environments, safety and security, and respect for nature and human surroundings.

The biggest difference between interior and exterior lighting, quite obviously, is that exterior lighting does not have an enclosure to contain it, so generally it should be minimized as much as possible. Decreasing the amount of exterior lighting reduces light pollution into the nighttime sky, saves energy, and provides a cost-effective solution for the client. In addition, because exterior lighting often does not benefit from walls and other surfaces to minimize unwanted glare and brightness, luminaire selection and location are very important.

QUALITY OF LIGHT

Historically, with exterior lighting, color temperature and CRI have not been as important as efficacy and lamp life, which is why there are so many parking lots, garages, façades, and landscaped areas using sodium and mercury vapor lamps. With the improvement and development of sources like metal halide, fluorescent, and LED, the quality of the light is improving and designers generally pay closer attention to these attributes. In addition to improving the aesthetic effect, the better color quality improves visibility and color recognition, which also increases a person's sense of safety.

Fig. 19.1 Example of High-Contrast Exterior Lighting

QUANTITY OF LIGHT

When beginning an outdoor lighting design, it is important to use the layering approach to determine exactly what areas need to be addressed, and avoid providing a uniform blanket of light whenever possible. As with interior lighting, the focal and task layers take the lead, and many times are not supplemented with any ambient light. Because of the darkened environment, features are often in much higher contrast than what would be typical for an interior, adding to the dramatic effect often contributed to exterior lighting (see Fig. 19.1). Although this effect may be desirable, it is important to not overlight these features, as the wasted light will contribute to the unwanted sky glow associated with highly illuminated areas.

APPLICATIONS

Accent Lighting

Like the focal layer for interior lighting, accent lighting for exterior areas provides vertical brightness that can create hierarchy, visual interest, and intuitive way-finding through an area. While every design will differ, architectural features like sculptures (see Fig. 19.2), and natural settings such as fountains or trees (see Fig. 19.3), often provide interesting lighting opportunities. When architects, interior designers, landscape

---

Electrician's Notebook

The IESNA also indicates exterior light level recommendations; however, they differ from interior recommended levels because they relate to the surrounding ambient light and the impact the added light will have on the existing environment. The IESNA has developed zones based on the area type and the ambient light level. The zones are:

- LZ4: High ambient lighting—Includes areas where there is frequent human activity and the occupants have adapted to higher, more uniform light levels. Lighting could be reduced after hours when usage reduces.
- LZ3: Moderately high ambient lighting—Includes areas where there is still regular human activity, and the users are accustomed to a higher level of light. Lighting could be reduced in most areas after hours.

- LZ2: Moderate ambient lighting—Includes areas where there is some human activity; however, users have adapted to lower, less uniform light levels. Lighting could be reduced in most areas after hours.
- LZ1: Low ambient lighting—Includes areas where lighting may negatively impact plants and animals. Lighting may only be provided for safety and convenience. Lighting should be reduced or turned off in most areas after hours.
- LZ0: No ambient lighting—Includes areas where lighting would have an adverse effect on plants and animals, or where lighting is generally less important to enhance appreciation of the outdoor environment for humans. The users have adapted to the low light levels. Lighting is only needed for safety and security and should be turned off when not needed.

Refer to the *IESNA Lighting Handbook*, tenth edition, for additional information about specific light level requirements for each zone type.

architects, and lighting designers work collectively, there may be an opportunity to tie exterior and interior design concepts together. The outdoor space becomes an opportunity to introduce the interior design. Or, on the other hand, the interior designer may choose to be influenced by the concepts outside of the building.

Façade Lighting

Façade lighting improves a building's visibility from a distance, and can enliven a neighborhood. Often the approach to façade lighting is greatly influenced by the type and style of the building. There are generally two methods:

1. Provide an even wash of light on the building (see Figure 19.4).
2. Highlight specific architectural features.

Of course, it is possible to combine the two, but each approach has its advantages and disadvantages. An even wash of light works well for buildings that contain very little detail; however, care must be taken to not overlight the façade relative to its surroundings. Also, it is typically not appropriate to wash glass or specular façades as

Fig. 19.2 Sculpture Focal Lighting

Fig. 19.3 Fountain Focal Lighting

Fig. 19.4 Example of an Evenly Illuminated Façade

Fig. 19.5 Example of a Façade with Architectural Elements Featured

Electrician's Notebook

All exterior luminaires contain an Ingress Protection (IP). The IP rating is indicated by two numbers. The first number specifies how well the fixture will be protected from hazardous access and dust intrusion. The second number denotes how well the luminaire is protected from water. Table 19.1 provides a summary of the ratings:

Table 19.1 IP Rating Summary

Solids Level	Object Size Protected Against	Protection Against
0	—	No protection
1	>50 mm	Any large surface of the body, but no protection against deliberate contact with a body part
2	>12.5 mm	Fingers or similar objects
3	>2.5 mm	Tools, thick wires, etc.
4	>1 mm	Most wires, screws, etc.
5	Dust protected	Ingress of dust is not entirely prevented, but it must not enter in sufficient quantity to interfere with the satisfactory operation of the equipment; complete protection against contact
6	Dust tight	No ingress of dust

Liquids Level	Protection Against
0	No protection
1	Vertically dripping water
2	Dripping water when tilted up to 15°
3	Spraying water at any angle up to 60°
4	Splashing water from any direction
5	Water jets from any direction
6	Powerful water from any direction
7	Immersion up to 1 meter for 30 minutes
8	Immersion beyond 1 meter (conditions specified by manufacturer)

the light will reflect into the sky and contribute to light pollution. Generally, lighting specific architectural features is more efficient and provides a more dramatic result. It is important to study the elevations and details to develop a composition of light that will enhance the building façade without overlighting or disconnecting the features.

Building Entries

When an occupant or visitor is ready to enter a building, there are a few factors that should be considered. The entry can act as an introduction to the interior space. If there is an opportunity, the interior designer should work with the architect to provide a coordinated entry point that speaks to both the inside and outside of the building.

From a technical standpoint, the entry and vestibule space provide a transition between the exterior and interior. This is important during both the day and night. To

Fig. 19.6 Landscape Lighting

Fig. 19.7 Concealed Pathway Lighting

Fig. 19.8 Decorative Pathway Lighting

allow enough time for the user's eyes to adjust during the day, the vestibule should be at a higher level, since the brightness of the interior lighting will be much less than daylight. Inversely, at night, the vestibule lighting should be lower to allow adjustment from the darkened exterior to the much brighter interior.

Landscape and Pedestrian Paths

Lighting of paths and landscapes generally produces a lower level of light at a pedestrian scale, often contributing to eye level glow. Frequently, the uplighting of trees provides a backdrop to other lighted features, or if the trees are unique in shape, they become the actual feature. Smaller shrubs and plants can also be lighted, but they are typically not illuminated uniformly (see Fig. 19.6).

Path lighting can be achieved in many ways, often greatly influenced by the architectural opportunities available. The approach can be very architectural, carefully integrated into a wall, bench, or railing (see Fig. 19.7) or from a simplistic lower height fixture. In contrast, the same path could be illuminated with highly decorative pole luminaires or sconces on a nearby building (see Fig. 19.8).

LUMINAIRE SELECTION

As expected, luminaires for exterior installations need to be rated for outdoor use, which includes consideration for low and high temperatures and water and dust protection.

In addition, it is imperative that the mounting of the fixture be coordinated with the surface on which it is mounted. Often, ground-mounted fixtures require concrete foundations to ensure they remain stable through temperature changes, and protected from wind and other environmental and human factors. Wall-mounted luminaires need to be coordinated early so that conduit and wiring can be installed before the wall is complete. Luminaires mounted near or in trees or plant materials should be located to minimize damage during installation and as the plants mature.

Chapter 20 BASIC LIGHTING RETROFITTING

In the design and construction industry, providing an energy efficient lighting solution is not only a code requirement but also the socially responsible approach. Decreasing the amount of energy used by a lighting system can provide a considerable impact, since globally lighting encompasses almost 20 percent of the electricity used. Additionally, building owners and tenants can achieve significant energy savings that translate into long-term cost savings.

The efficiency of lighting systems has improved quite drastically in the past few years. This coupled with the changing needs of end-users, who require less light for many tasks and realize that spaces may have been overlighted, provides an opportunity to upgrade aging, inefficient systems. Also, there are many government and utility company programs rewarding energy efficient designs with rebates and tax savings.

The extent of the change required depends on several factors, including the age of the system, what types of fixtures and lamps are installed, the desired payback period, and, of course, the client's initial budget. It's important to note that even though an upgrade may appear costly, the energy consumed represents a majority of the total costs accrued through a lighting system's lifespan. To begin the process of upgrading or retrofitting an existing project, it is important to understand exactly what is installed and how much energy is being used. This will require a thorough survey of the lighting in the facility that takes note of the horizontal and vertical foot-candle levels, and the type of control that is being used. It is also very helpful to find out how and when the spaces are used, and whether there are any complaints about the current lighting. Although the main goal in a retrofit is to save energy, the quality of light should be equal to or better than what exists.

After surveying the existing conditions, the scope of the lighting upgrade can be determined. It could range from a simple lamp change to a complete lighting system redesign.

RETROFIT SOLUTIONS

Lamping

The simplest form of a retrofit is to upgrade the lamps in a fixture to a more efficient source. There are many halogen, compact fluorescent, and now LED lamps that have been designed with a medium base socket to directly replace incandescent lamps. Because of legislation that will be banning certain incandescent lamps in 2012, this approach will become even more relevant. However, care must be given when taking this approach, so the quality of light is maintained or improved. It is important to review the output, color temperature, and color rendering of the new lamp to ensure it will meet the requirements of the space.

Halogen lamps typically use the same bulb shape as incandescent, so switching them is very simple, but the energy savings is minimal. Many compact fluorescent and

LED lamps are designed to replace incandescent lamps; however, the technology is quite different and the envelope is generally not identical. This can be problematic because the existing fixture is designed around the optical performance of the original lamp. The new lamp may perform poorly, provide unwanted glare, or fail to fit physically in the existing fixture. Also, many retrofit lamps do not dim, or they require a specific type of dimmer. This will also need to be coordinated if dimming is needed. It is always recommended to perform a mock-up prior to ordering a large quantity to test all these factors in comparison to the original.

With the continual improvement of LED technology, there are now many opportunities to use LED lamps to replace halogen PAR and MR lamps. Because the LEDs are so small, the shape is typically very close to the lamp it is intended to replace; however, they are usually surrounded by finned heat sinks. To allow for airflow, LEDs generally cannot be installed in a completely enclosed fixture. It is important to completely understand the installation requirements of an LED lamp prior to using, so the long life and energy savings that are claimed can be achieved.

In older commercial and industrial settings it is still common to find linear fluorescent T-12 lamps. It is possible to retrofit these lamps with more efficient T-8 lamps since the length and sockets are the same; however, the ballast will also need to be replaced. Again, a mockup should be completed, since the original fixture is designed around the T-12 lamp, which is 50 percent larger in diameter.

Ballasts

Changing the ballast is necessary when retrofitting from T-12 to T-8 fluorescent lamps; however, even in an installation of older T-8 lamps, there may still be an opportunity for energy savings. Switching from magnetic to electronic ballast makes significant improvements. Additionally, if during the initial survey it was found that the light levels were much higher than current recommended practices, an energy saving lamp and ballast combination could be employed to reduce light levels. Also, for a minimal cost increase, a stepped ballast could be used to provide two or three light levels within a space.

Older metal halide systems can also be retrofitted with new lamps and ballasts to provide energy savings. Typical by-products are improved color quality and consistency.

Luminaires

Within many standard commercial and industrial fixtures, it is possible to replace or add new reflectors and lenses to increase the light output. Often this type of change can impact the distribution of the light as well, so it is critical to review a mock-up

to ensure it is acceptable in the space. When the fixture becomes more efficient, it may be possible to reduce the number of lamps. Most luminaire retrofits also require lamp and ballast replacements as well.

Recently, there has been quite a bit of research and development of LED retrofit kits for interior and exterior fluorescent and High Intensity Discharge (HID) luminaires. The obvious difference in technology requires a complete kit including the LEDs, driver, reflectors, and other optics that will replace the internal components of the existing fixtures. Because the LEDs are inherently a point source, again it is important to view the retrofit kit installed to verify that the distribution, visual brightness, and possible increased glare are acceptable. This solution is attractive because it not only provides energy savings, but reduces maintenance with the LED's long life.

As previously mentioned, the energy savings that can be achieved by replacing aged systems quickly pays for a retrofit; therefore, when a system is 20+ years old, providing new fixtures often makes the most sense. This is especially true when simple retrofits are not yet available, the luminaire housing and components have been damaged, or the installed system no longer meets the needs of the user. When a new design is pursued, investigating new circuiting and control opportunities will also improve energy efficiency.

Lighting Controls

Whenever a lamp or luminaire retrofit is taking place, the lighting controls should always be reviewed because there are very simple, low-cost solutions that can be incorporated. For example, in a small space, a wall switch could be replaced with an occupancy sensor, or a time clock could be installed at the electrical panel to turn large banks of lights off at a designated time.

On a larger scale, ceiling-mounted occupancy and daylight sensors could be incorporated. These typically are wired back to a power pack, which contains a relay to control the circuitry. Many manufacturers now have wireless sensors that are powered by a battery instead of being hardwired. They then communicate to the power pack via a unique wireless signal.

In addition to local controls, incorporating an energy management system or a digital lighting control system provides the most opportunity for savings, but as expected, also has the highest up-front costs. With a complete building or space control system the user has the opportunity to track and report the energy being used throughout the day. This allows the user to locate possible inefficiencies, while also incorporating load shedding during peak hours.

The key to incorporating new energy saving controls is the commissioning at the end of the installation. It is critical that the controls are set up properly so the savings anticipated can be realized.

Chapter 21
PROFESSIONAL LIGHTING DESIGN

Lighting design is a relatively new part of the process of building construction. Many of the principles and standards needed for lighting come from architecture and engineering, and for good reason—architects and engineers are the licensed professionals who design buildings. However, because of the rapid changes in lighting technology and design technique, the lighting designer must address some unique lighting issues.

DESIGN DOCUMENTATION

General Information

During the process of design, it is important to record project criteria, decisions, and other information so the data can be reviewed and checked as the project advances. For each space being designed, it is a good idea to record:

- Area and dimensions of the space
- If available, room elevations and sections
- Finishes on all surfaces
- Furniture
- Visual tasks and locations, including focal tasks
- Architectural or interior design concept

- Light level(s) selected, including task, ambient, and focal
- Light color temperature and CRI
- Control requirements
- Cost budget
- Power or energy budget
- Code requirements
- Additional requirements specific to the project

Recording this information serves the project in a number of ways. First, it ensures that you are reasonably thorough in collecting the information needed to properly execute your work. Second, it challenges you to identify the design problems and how you might solve them. Finally, it provides a paper trail for liability protection. For this reason alone, many designers keep every sketch or red-lined plan they produce during the design phase.

Calculations

Some type of calculation is required on almost every commercial project. Even when the lighting design is intuitive and artful, as for the design of a restaurant or hotel lobby, many cities now require point-by-point lighting calculations for emergency and path-of-egress lighting.

As a practical matter, most architects and interior designers (and many electrical engineers and lighting designers) have calculations performed for them by manufacturers or agents. While there is nothing wrong with this, you should be familiar with the input data as well as the output reports so you can make sure the right luminaire, lamp, and room finishes have been used. The results of all calculations actually used in the design should be retained and labeled for future retrieval.

Conflicts and Issues

Lighting can be a touchy subject with many opinions about a particular design. It is not uncommon for a preferred lighting design to be altered or rejected for many reasons, including personal preference, cost, energy use, and interference with pipes or ducts. Often these changes compromise the integrity of the lighting design.

While lighting is generally more forgiving than, say, structures, the failure of a lighting design to be correctly implemented can have major implications such as:

• Insufficient light levels for the tasks to be performed
• Unattractive luminaires or layouts
• Systems that use too much energy
• Systems that are expensive to maintain
• Potentially unsafe conditions for people or vehicles

Good lighting is often considered frivolous and dispensable, particularly when building costs are over budget. It is common to change the design, reduce the number of lights, or change the type of light without performing new calculations or considering the impact. The most common reason is value engineering, whereby the contractor proposes cost-cutting measures to the building owner. The lighting design may be changed without the designer's knowledge. Having good records of your design and decisions is important in protecting yourself from liability in case the changes don't work.

Potential liabilities in design make recording and resolving design criteria especially important. For instance, the rising costs of energy and new energy codes tend to decrease lighting levels. But the growing population of aged persons requires more light and more energy to see. This is a classic conflict, of which many more involving light will emerge. By properly documenting your decisions, you can appeal to authorities and perhaps resolve problems more quickly. Again, you will be protected from liability.

Products of Design

Tables 21.1 and 21.2 list what is needed for the documentation of a lighting design.

Table 21.1 Lighting Documents for Review and Reference

Lighting Plans	Lighting designs shown in plan form using base floor plans and/or reflected ceiling plans (see Chapter 11). The lighting plan is not a contract document until it is used by a licensed professional or contractor (see below). It is common to draw a lighting plan because it is important in showing the complete lighting design. But the lighting plan is often only an intermediate step in developing a suitable electrical drawing.
Cut Sheets	A collection of the product cut or tear sheets corresponding to the lighting schedule. The cut sheets sometimes can be used in place of a lighting schedule if the project is easily understood. Cut sheets permit detailed examination of the intended lighting equipment, often for the benefit or approval of the client or other team members.
Narrative (optional)	A written document describing the lighting design and how it will work.
Design Sketches	Drawings, often hand-drawn, that illustrate lighting design concepts or details in the context of the project.
Calculations	Hand calculations and computer printouts containing the input data and results of calculations used in the design.

Table 21.2 Documents for Bidding or Construction

Contract Document Drawings	Electrical lighting plans that are drawn by the architect, engineer, or other licensed professional or contractor to establish the scope of the contract work with respect to lighting. While these plans are often based on the lighting plan (see above), they include additional information such as branch circuit wiring.
Lighting Schedule	The schedule or list of luminaires listed by tag. The schedule should include all information about each luminaire, including tag, description, operating voltage, connected power (watts), number and type of lamps, number and type of ballasts, mounting, finish(es), and approved manufacturer and model number (see Chapter 11).
Details	Drawings indicating specific details of luminaire attachment. These are especially vital to coordination of cove lights and similar applications.
Lamp Schedule (optional)	The schedule or list of lamps by type. This is especially useful on very large projects or projects with an unusual number or type of lamps.
Written Specifications (optional)	The specifications for lighting, typically in the electrical section of the project manual. Written specifications are required for major projects. Describes lighting and lighting control equipment and requirements for procurement, installation, adjustment, and programming the operation of all lighting systems.
Isocandle Plots (when required)	For some types of lighting, authorities require isocandle plots on floor plans or site plans. Exporting a calculation plot file to the appropriate plan drawing generally does this.
Control Riser Diagram (when required)	Indicates the components and suggests the operation of a lighting control or dimming system.

Seldom are lighting documents used without review and approval by an electrical engineer. As a minimum, an engineer must design branch circuits to power the lights. Both the lights and the circuits must appear on the engineer's electrical drawings for the project. If the engineer is also the lighting designer, the point is moot; but if the lighting designer is independent of the electrical engineer, conflict or coordination issues may need to be solved.

Phases of Design

A lighting design is part of the building design. Historically, the engineer added lighting during later design phases. However, due to increasing demand for energy efficiency, daylighting, and better integrated lighting in the overall design process, lighting design should begin early in the project.

In accord with the standard phases of the American Institute of Architects (AIA), the following text as·well as Table 21.3 detail the lighting design activities that should occur as the project progresses.

Programming Phase

Ideally, the lighting design is reviewed early in the project's development. A good time to start thinking about lighting is shortly after the design programming is complete and the first physical plan arrangements can be seen. The architect or interior designer should review all of the expected spaces in the project and record his or her preliminary thoughts and expectations concerning lighting results for each space, including issues related to practical functions, intensity of light, color effects, special effects, code concerns, budget, emergency lighting needs, aesthetics, and unusual architectural features. One good technique for concisely recording these lighting design thoughts is to use the matrix format included with this book. In a larger or more complex project, a lighting designer is often brought into the picture at this point. The matrix format can be used to easily convey those thoughts to the lighting designer.

Schematic Design Phase

At this point, a preliminary lighting design solution should be developed for review with the project team and client. This stage is set for dialog to ensure that the architect's or interior designer's thoughts and intentions concerning lighting are appropriately understood and preliminarily resolved.

Design Development Phase

As with any design process, it is likely that the review and discussion of the preliminary lighting design schemes by the project designer and/or the lighting designer will result in a need for revisions, and an interactive process is set in motion. In the case of large and complex projects, this review process can involve many of the professionals working on the project's design. After basic lighting design issues are resolved, the review process will move on to the details of luminaire and controls selections and placements, until the lighting design process is completed.

During the latter phase of design development, the lighting design process usually reaches completion; however, the design must be coordinated with the other project consultants, such as the electrical and mechanical engineers and landscape architect, to ensure that the lighting design works within the context of the balance of construction. Critical activities include checking ceiling plenum depths, coordinat-

Table 21.3 Project Phases and Products of Lighting Design

AIA Design Phase	Activity	Products
Programming	Determine what role lighting and daylighting are expected to play in the project. Establish appropriate budgets.	Narrative and budget line items
Schematic Design	Assist in developing a daylighting strategy. Assist in conceiving spaces, especially those requiring specific lighting performance or aesthetics. Establish an energy budget and strategy, if needed. Develop lighting concepts using preliminary plans, sketches, or other illustrations. Perform preliminary calculations. Identify products for possible use. Test the concepts for budget compliance.	Narrative with cut sheets, sketches, and preliminary plans. Budget line items. Results of preliminary calculations of critical lighting systems. Renderings, if developed.
Design Development	Assist in developing plans, sections, and details, especially reflected ceiling plans. Complete lighting concepts and begin lighting plans and details. Begin lighting schedule. Identify lighting controls equipment and devices. Perform final calculations and layout lighting on plans. Confirm budget and energy compliance. Begin lighting specifications.	The following should be at least partially complete: lighting plans and details, lighting schedule with cut sheets, specifications, code compliance documents. Also provide controls narrative.
Contract Documents	Design and engineer lighting controls and add circuits to the drawings. Complete all documents. Make final adjustments as required. Confirm budget and energy compliance.	All of the following should be complete: lighting plans and details (turn over to engineer for branch circuit design), lighting schedule, lighting and controls specifications.

ing duct sizes and locations, developing and checking mounting details, confirming ceiling and soffit heights, and coordinating with fire protection needs.

If a lighting designer is hired, his or her work is mostly completed by the end of design development. Because the lighting designer's drawings often do not serve as contract documents, the architect, interior designer, and electrical engineer must use them to produce actual working drawings.

Contract Documents Phase

Many details of coordination are required in this phase, such as working with the electrical engineer on issues related to providing power, checking with the mechanical engineer on the availability of plenum space, and working out ceiling and other construction details and the compatibility of finishes.

Bidding and Negotiation Phase

When contract documents are complete, some form of construction cost bidding or negotiation typically takes place. Quite frequently, the bidding or negotiation process reveals significant cost overruns, requiring design revisions to reduce overall project cost. Except where overruns are so great that overall project size must be reduced, the details of finishes and installed products, including luminaire and lighting controls, are targeted for cost reductions. Unfortunately, it is not uncommon for lighting design quality to be significantly compromised in this cost-cutting process.

Contract Administration Phase

During the construction phase of a project, the lighting designer is often called in to advise on a variety of details, from the precise focusing of accent lighting to the fine-tuning of complex control systems. Unexpected problems inevitably require expert troubleshooting, such as plenum space conflicts with ductwork or sprinkler runs or last-minute luminaire substitutions created by the late shipment of specified items.

Once construction is complete, the lighting designer should help commission the building by doing the following:

1. Walk through the building and make sure that the lighting is installed correctly and without defects. A list of defects, called a punchlist, is turned over to the contractor for repairs.
2. Adjust or direct the adjustment of lighting systems that are aimed, such as track lighting and accent lights. Add filters, lenses, and other accessories.
3. Check the operation of controls systems and set dimming systems.
4. Instruct the owner's personnel in using the lighting systems.

These steps are especially important if the lighting design is sophisticated, creative, or unusual in any way. It is impossible to specify and then expect a contractor to complete the artistic vision of a highly creative lighting design. On a more mundane level, many lighting controls systems, especially motion sensing, daylighting, and preset dimming systems, are not set up and calibrated properly. This results in energy waste and, worse, the disconnection of the system by frustrated occupants.

Post-Occupancy Evaluation

For projects in which post-occupancy evaluation services are provided, the contributions of the lighting designer can be extremely valuable. Often, small adjustments made to luminaires and lamps can have major positive results. Of equal importance is the mutual learning process involved in discovering what works well and what doesn't—not only so mistakes in design judgment are not repeated but also to gain new insights and innovative ideas for future projects.

DESIGN INTEGRITY AND COST MANAGEMENT

Every lighting design relies heavily on the appearance and performance of the lighting equipment. When the designer specifies lighting equipment, the specified equipment usually will meet the project needs. If more than one product will do the job, the lighting schedule should list as many options as possible.

The electrical sales industry, however, does not always fully respect the specification. Electrical distributors compete for projects. Distributors in turn receive pricing from manufacturers' representatives (or reps). The trend in the industry is for each rep to offer a package in which he or she represents one major manufacturer that makes a wide range of common luminaires and, in addition to the major manufacturer, a number of specialty manufacturers. Thus every project will face competing packages, and often the specified product is only part of one package.

Substitutions are products the rep feels are the same as the specified product. This is often true, and designers should review substitution requests and accept them if possible. Most designers today require substitution requests to be made early in the project. It is a good idea for the lighting designer to review and approve substitutions rather than find them installed without his or her knowledge.

The evolution of the package began with government work. Government agencies generally build ordinary buildings and want to ensure they receive competitive pricing on all materials. The standard requirement became to list three manufacturers for every product. This requirement persists today for both government and private work, although designers are permitted to specify particular products (and one manufacturer) if the design requires specific performance and the product is unique in the market. With the more frequent use of LED products and the industry's attempts to standardize the products and literature, it is not unusual for designers to specify a single manufacturer for LED luminaires.

Uniqueness in the lighting industry is rare. As in the furniture industry, some members of the lighting industry have little respect for the ownership of intellectual property, including designs and patents. Most reps have one or more copy companies in their package, enabling them to furnish every luminaire on the project by substituting the unique products with knockoffs—blatant copies of otherwise unique products. Most knockoffs violate patents or design style protection, but the cost of litigation generally prevents action being taken against the copy company.

Recently, a few companies have fought back, but the situation is impossible to police, and manufacturers have turned to professional designers to help prevent the copying of lighting equipment. Professionals, in turn, can do a great deal to protect intellectual property through specifications and subsequent actions, including:

1. Write specifications and lighting schedules with packaging in mind. As often as possible, list three manufacturers of acceptable, if not equivalent, products. Avoid the phrase "or equal" in specification writing; if the specification must be general in nature, use the phrase "or as approved."
2. Isolate unique products in the specifications and schedule. Make it clear that these products are not part of bid packages and that the products will be individually priced and purchased.
3. Require contractors to submit a unit price schedule so you can check for unusual pricing or gouging.
4. Require contractors to submit substitution requests and receive approval prior to bid. Remember that the drawings, schedules, and specifications form the contract, and the contractor is legally required to provide the specified products unless a substitution is permitted.

Unfortunately, reps having the unique product in their package often use this to their advantage by not selling the unique product to other reps at a fair price. This practice is common despite being a violation of federal antitrust laws. One way to control pricing is to actively work with reps, distributors, and the contractor to manage pricing. Another approach is to work closely with the owner to purchase (or threaten to purchase) unique lighting products separately.

Value engineering is often seen as a chance to substitute lighting systems carelessly. Contractors and reps work together to reduce the scope and quality of the design, but seldom does the owner receive the full financial benefit of this activity. The normal result is that the owner pays a little less for the lighting and gets a lot less.

Protecting the design is critical to the success of the project, and designers must play an active role in cost management if they want their projects to come out well. Protection of the intellectual property of others is important because most inno-vations come from the smaller and more creative companies. If the industry does not respect their property, they won't stay in the business. For more information, contact the International Association of Lighting Designers and read the Specification Integrity document.

AVOID TYPICAL LIGHTING DESIGN PROBLEMS

Lighting designers encounter many problematic conditions and situations when attempting to create high-quality lighting design solutions. Be sure to examine your preliminary solutions for these common problems:

- *Excessive energy consumption*: Use energy efficient lamps and don't overlight. In nonresidential situations, energy code limitations place a not-to-exceed control on wattage use, but the spirit of energy consumption and staying within dollar budget constraints should be added incentives for being economical with energy use.
- *Direct glare*: Use luminaires that shield the eye from direct visual contact with lamps or built-in reflectors. This is sometimes accomplished as much through luminaire placement as by luminaire selection. When eye-level glow is desired, make sure the selected luminaire does not create offensive glare.
- *Veiling reflections*: Place luminaires in nonoffending positions in situations where visual task and user positions are relatively fixed. The classic example is the freestanding desk, but many other work situations are prone to conditions involving veiling reflections.
- *Light source reflections in computer screens*: With the advent of flat screen monitors that typically do not contain a glossy surface, this historically common problem generally has been resolved. However, reflections in other glossy surfaces, like tables, glass walls, and other features, can cause discomfort from the reflections. The employment of a combined task/ambient system still significantly reduces the severity of the problem. Even in small work settings, attention should be given to avoiding this situation, which can negatively affect work production.
- *Problematic lamp color selections*: These have an adverse visual effect on materials and colors used in a particular room or space. Typically, this is a complex and interactive process. Lamp selections often are made before material and color selections are known, in which case the materials and colors must be selected with the light source in mind. However, it is not uncommon for basic architectural materials and colors to be chosen prior to lamp selection, in which case the lamp color should accommodate them. In general, being aware of the lamp spectrum relationship to finishes and colors helps avoid a multitude of potential color problems in the finished interior.

COLLABORATING WITH LIGHTING DESIGNERS

Architects and interior designers typically are responsible for lighting design within their building and interior projects, and, in all likelihood, continue to provide those services for the many basic spaces they design. Quite often, the assistance of sales representatives, lighting showroom personnel, and electrical engineers and contractors is sought to help complete a lighting design solution. Because lighting design technology has expanded and become more complex, and because many building owners and managers have become knowledgeable about the growing capabilities of lighting effects, a new kind of professional (the lighting designer) has emerged over the past few decades to solve the lighting design problems in special or atypical spaces. Lighting design is integrally involved with architecture, interior design, and electrical engineering; this integration has yielded the ability to achieve significant and often dramatic improvements in performance and aesthetics over the basic lighting of a space.

Typically, the lighting designer works as an independent consultant on a contractual basis with and for the architect and/or interior designer. The services of a lighting designer are most often sought when projects require specialized lighting in places where aesthetics, drama, and mood are critically important, as in the case of restaurants, hotel lobbies and function rooms, casinos, art galleries and museums, and high-end retail stores. As the importance of lighting has become more explicitly understood, particularly in terms of its effects on day-to-day activities, lighting designers are more frequently retained for the lighting design in office, healthcare, educational, and other institutional settings. It should be obvious that special lighting design consultation is essential in the design of uncommon or one-of-a-kind building types such as zoos, performance spaces, and exposition and convention centers.

While this book instructs in lighting design for basic interior spaces that architects and interior designers may often perform without the assistance of a lighting designer, it is becoming more routine to retain a lighting designer for the overall lighting of large projects that, in addition to many basic interior spaces, contain visually demanding spaces such as lobbies, atria, performance spaces, and malls that require the attention of a specialist. In these cases, a lighting designer may also be called upon for knowledgeable judgment related to code compliance and budget constraints.

When special effects are appropriate, the lighting designer can be of particular help. Special effects can be for a wide variety of purposes, such as the display of artifacts in a lobby or living room, the lighting of exotic plants, or creating an evening view of exterior sculpture or flora. Situations of this kind are usually found in projects for high-end clients, as in the case of an executive's penthouse office, an extremely elegant boutique, or an extravagant house. When budgets permit, the lighting designer can create strikingly unusual and dramatic results.

Collaborating with a lighting designer confers a wide range of benefits. The most obvious of these is their depth of experience in lighting from both aesthetic and technical perspectives; it is the rare architectural or interior design practitioner who has had the time to focus in an in-depth manner on lighting, considering the broad range of their responsibilities. The lighting field is constantly and rapidly undergoing technological change and has become the province of the specialist, not the average design practitioner. The introduction of new lighting product lines is equally difficult to stay in touch with; again, most architects and interior designers have neither the time nor the inclination to develop adequate knowledge about that complex marketplace.

One of the most valuable aspects of service provided by the lighting designer is coordination with the project's electrical engineer who designs the electrical power system; that coordination is essential for a professionally managed project and saves countless hours of on-site problem solving. Code compliance, if dealt with intelligently, is a complex issue requiring the detailed attention of a specialist; again, the lighting designer brings that expertise to a project by providing techniques for getting the greatest lighting value from the fewest watts. Budget issues can be among the most demanding design problems; as with code compliance, getting the greatest lighting value from limited budget dollars is an art. In addition, the lighting designer can bring a fresh, other-directed, and valuable point of view to many aspects of architecture and interior design that are indirectly related to lighting design.

Because lighting designers are relative newcomers to environmental design teams, it is not uncommon to work with clients who are unfamiliar with the special value they bring to a project and may subsequently be reluctant to incur the additional cost of still another specialist or consultant. In these situations, it is entirely appropriate for the architect or interior designer to persuade the client that the lighting designer's value to their project is of major importance. It is becoming a more widespread practice for architects and interior designers to routinely include the cost of a lighting designer's services in establishing an overall compensation package for a proposed project.

The process of selecting a lighting designer is like selecting any of the other consultants normally engaged to work with an architect or interior designer, such as mechanical and electrical engineers and foodservice consultants. Some design firms routinely work with the same group of consultants on all of their projects, preferring to work with a familiar personality or professional firm. Other design firms vary the consultant group based on the nature of the project at hand and the specific project backgrounds of the consultants. More specifically, the design firm may wish to use a lighting designer with extensive experience in shopping mall design for a project of that kind. Regardless of these issues of familiarity or specialization, the generally accepted methods for selecting a professional consultant include:

- *Referral*: Seek the recommendation of other architects or interior designers whose opinion is respected.
- *Evaluation of previous project results*: Travel to, observe, and talk to users of those facilities. Note that simply looking at photographic results provides limited and sometimes misleading information regarding the success of a lighting design project.
- *Credentials/experience*: Investigate educational background, previous employment experience, and membership and activity in professional organizations; this is a conventional and sometimes useful aspect of the selection process. Special note is made at the end of this chapter concerning the professional organizations related to the lighting field and a relatively new certification process for the lighting industry.
- *Working methods and philosophic compatibility*: Assess the many important issues in this aspect of consultant relationships:

  - At what stage of the project does the lighting designer enter the process?
  - What tasks will be performed, and at what stage of project development?
  - What does the lighting designer expect from the architect and interior designer?
  - Is there basic philosophic compatibility about major professional and design concepts?

- *Contractual relationship*: Discuss in depth the details of the work process, compensation, professional liability insurance, involvement in the bidding and negotiation processes, and involvement in contract administration, including on-site presence.

These thoughts on selecting a lighting designer purposely have been kept quite basic. Working with consultants generally entails complexities that are not discussed here because they go far beyond the intent of this book, including core issues of trust and working rapport that apply to all consultant relationships.

Professional Design Organizations

Special note should be made of the professional organizations in the lighting design field. Similar to the qualifying examination process for both architects and interior designers, the lighting industry, through the National Council for Qualifying Lighting Professionals (NCQLP), has an examination-based certification process. Certified individuals—those who pass the NCQLP exam—have demonstrated that they possess minimum qualifications in the field of lighting technology and are called Lighting Certified (LC). The NCQLP lighting certification program encompasses a broad range of people working in the lighting industry, including those connected with manufacturing, sales, and other business and professional relationships in the field of lighting. The International Association of Lighting Designers (IALD), active in North America and much of the world, focuses much more specifically on people involved in lighting design and requires its professional members to pass a review of their design portfolios and to then practice according to strict ethical standards.

Appendix A COMPUTERS IN LIGHTING

Since the early days of personal computing, lighting computer programs have enabled relatively accurate predictions of light levels for both interior and exterior lighting. Today, these programs determine light levels at specific locations in a space. They can also predict the brightness of room surfaces and give the patterns of light on the ceiling, walls, and floor. Some programs can generate perspective renderings as well, producing a realistic representation of lighting in the space. However, lighting software cannot choose an appropriate lighting system based on the designer's requirements. The designer must develop a design approach first, then analyze it with the computer.

TYPES OF PROGRAMS

Most current programs designed for everyday use in lighting design employ radiosity, a type of calculation that is relatively fast, especially on a modern personal computer. A simple calculation and rendering for an empty room can be generated in less than a minute, making this type of program highly effective as a design support tool. Radiosity's primary drawback is that the calculation assumes that all room surfaces have a matte finish, so renderings lack a lifelike quality.

To create more realistic images, a few programs use a far more precise form of calculation called *ray tracing*. By tracing each ray of light from each source, surfaces of any texture and finish can be accurately depicted. These programs, however, require considerable computer resources, and the analysis for a simple room could take hours on a personal computer. Sophisticated analysts using graphics workstations can use this type of program effectively, but it is not typically an everyday tool for the designer.

Some programs use a combination of radiosity and ray tracing to provide more realistic images while operating at reasonable speed on an ordinary personal computer. The results of this type of calculation can be improved by permitting longer computer execution times. As long as an experienced operator uses the program, this is a powerful presentation tool that is practical to own and use.

At the time of writing this edition, the North American industry standard lighting software is AGI32, a stand-alone program for computer lighting and daylighting performance and for rendering illuminated environments. It is able to import buildings drawn in AutoCAD, SketchUp, and other 2-D and 3-D software, and with the addition of daylighting data (latitude, rotation, climate, etc.) and electric lighting data (luminaire types, locations, etc.), it performs both radiosity and ray tracing calculations.

The current trend with architects and interior designers is to use Building Information Modeling (BIM) software. BIM software enables the entire project team to collaborate in creating an intelligent 3-D model of the building or space with additional tools to analyze the function of the systems. Many BIM software solutions have the ability to calculate light levels and produce accurate photorealistic renderings with artificial and natural light. BIM software has become a helpful tool in "test-driving" lighting concepts and effects during the design process, while also providing real-time information for coordination prior to construction.

The biggest problem with using computers to depict and present lighting is that a practical amount of understanding of illumination and photometric technology is needed. Nothing replaces seeing fixtures and spaces firsthand to understand how light interacts with materials. However, computers and basic calculations help designers ensure their designs will meet basic lighting guidelines and recommendations.

INPUT DATA

To use a computer lighting program, you must first enter the data needed to perform the lighting analysis. All programs, even the most basic radiosity programs, require the following input data:

- Room dimensions, work plane height, and luminaire-mounting height (for pendant-mounted luminaires).
- Room surface reflectance, including inserts—portions of room surfaces that may reflect differently.
- Detailed luminaire photometric data in IESNA format. Photometric data files for interior and exterior luminaires are typically supplied by manufacturers in IESNA format via their website.
- Precise location and orientation of luminaires using *x, y, z* coordinates or an interface with computer-assisted drawing (CAD) programs.
- Light loss factors and any other multiplying factors to adjust the lamp and ballast output from the assumptions used in the luminaire photometry.

For a basic radiosity program, data entry can be rapid. Using CAD-like commands, a simple room can be described in a few minutes, ready for analysis.

Some radiosity programs also permit the use of objects in space, which include tables, partitions, chairs, ductwork, and other items present within the room's volume. Objects in space help improve the realism of the analysis and rendering; however, the same objects can considerably increase analysis time as well.

A few programs also calculate the effect of daylight. To analyze daylighting effects, it is necessary to enter information about windows and skylights, including coordinates and characteristics, and choose the time of day, date, and weather conditions. This increases the calculation time of a radiosity program.

Input data for ray tracing programs can be significant. Most programs accept three-dimensional CAD data, including objects in space. However, the operator must describe the finish and texture of every surface of all room finishes, including the furniture, and must enter the three-dimensional data file for each piece of furniture or furnishing. Daylighting data may also be added; the most photorealistic images require that site and landscaping information be added as well.

INTERIOR LIGHTING CALCULATIONS

Lighting calculation programs calculate the lighting effects caused by specific luminaires in specific rooms at specific points. Output includes:

- Illuminance (lux or foot-candles) on a horizontal work plane at selected points in the room; summary statistics such as average, maximum, minimum, and standard deviation of illuminance values.
- Room surface luminance (candelas per unit surface area) or exitance (lumens per unit surface area). These results are based on the assumption that room surfaces have a matte, not shiny, finish.
- Lighting power density (watts/m^2 or watts/ft^2).
- Visibility and visual comfort metrics. UGR (uniform glare rating), ESI (equivalent sphere illumination), RVP (relative visual performance), and VCP (visual comfort probability) are the principal metrics computed by these programs. They are calculated for a specific location in the room and for a specific viewing direction.

Output from these programs is usually a chart of calculated values, an isolux (isofoot-candle) plot, or a shaded plan with gray scales representing a range of light levels. All programs print results, and most display the results directly on the screen.

Some programs offer three-dimensional black-and-white or color-shaded perspective views of the room showing light patterns produced on the room surfaces by the lighting system. Ray tracing programs produce exceptionally realistic renderings.

EXTERIOR LIGHTING CALCULATIONS

Exterior lighting programs are used for parking lots, roadways, pedestrian paths, and special situations such as airport aprons, car sales lots, and sports fields. Exterior lighting calculations are similar to interior calculations except that they are simpler, as no light reflectance from room surfaces is calculated. Input data typically include the following:

- Plan dimensions of the site to be studied, usually entered in *x, y* coordinates or through a CAD interface.
- Points on the site where illuminance is to be calculated. Some programs permit blocking out the printing of light levels on areas of the site where light levels are not critical, or where buildings or trees would block the light.

- Luminaire photometric file in IESNA format.
- Mounting heights, site locations, orientations, and tilt of luminaires.
- Lumen output of the specified lamp.
- Light loss factors due to lamp aging, ballast factor, and luminaire dirt accumulation.

Appendix B ENERGY CODE CALCULATIONS

Energy codes establish a minimum level of energy efficiency or product performance for lighting systems installed in buildings. The wide variety of energy codes and standards ranges from national model energy codes, which must be adopted by a state or local jurisdiction to have the force of law, to locally developed and adopted standards.

As lamps and luminaires have become more efficient, energy codes have followed and become more stringent. The latest national model code is ANSI/ASHRAE/IESNA 90.1–2010; however, at the date of this printing no states have adopted its more stringent requirements yet. The American Recovery and Reinvestment Act of 2009 requires that states adopt the ANSI/ASHRAE/IESNA 90.1–2007 standard as a minimum to receive federal assistance funds. The International Energy Conservation Code (IECC) adopts the ASHRAE/IESNA 90.1 code by reference. Remember, however, that these are just model codes. In order for them to be legally required, they must be adopted into law by a city or state. In adopting model codes, cities and states sometimes add local amendments or changes, so it is important to read the local energy code carefully.

Some states have developed their own lighting efficiency codes. Because of the state's large population and construction volumes, California's Title 24 Building Energy Efficiency Standards have produced substantial energy savings over the years and have led to relatively energy efficient lighting design norms compared to many other regions of the country. Other states, including Washington, Oregon, Minnesota, and New York, have also developed their own energy codes, in some cases from scratch and in others creating local variations of energy codes developed elsewhere.

The current energy code of every state can be found at http://www.energycodes .gov/.

In addition to state energy codes, a number of other energy codes may apply to any given lighting project. For instance, on federal projects, the Federal Energy Standards, which are similar to ASHRAE/IESNA 90.1, must be used instead of a local code. Likewise, countries other than the United States have energy codes that apply to projects located in their jurisdictions. However, whenever you use ASHRAE/IESNA 90.1 or a similar standard, your design will probably be considered sufficiently efficient.

You can order the lighting portion of the ASHRAE/IESNA Standard from the Illuminating Engineering Society of North America (IESNA) as LEM-1, or you can obtain the entire standard from ASHRAE.

ENERGY CODE STRUCTURE

Energy code requirements for lighting may be grouped into several broad categories.

Lighting Power Limits

Lighting power limits establish a maximum allowable installed lighting power level, typically expressed in watts per square foot (W/ft^2); the value is multiplied by the area of the space to determine the overall limit. This may be given for a whole building, with a single W/ft^2 number specifying a limit applied to all the spaces in it. Limits may also be established by space category, with higher values allowed for spaces with more demanding visual tasks and lower values for spaces where visual demand is less.

For buildings with special lighting needs, neither the whole building nor the space category method may produce a fair lighting power limit—that is, the limit may be too low to adequately serve the needs of the building. In these cases, energy codes may provide special lighting power allowances for special purposes. An example is the tailored method under California's Title 24 energy standards. Some energy codes also provide extra lighting power allowances for special applications on a use-it-or-lose-it basis. These allowances may be applied only to the specific lighting equipment used to illuminate the special application; they may not be used as general allowances to boost the whole building lighting power limit.

Most energy codes also provide a whole building performance-based method for setting an overall building energy budget. Such a method may allow users to obtain higher lighting power allowances by trading off energy with other building components. For example, installing a high-efficiency air-conditioning or heating system could yield an energy credit that allows for a less efficient lighting system (more lighting power).

Outdoor Lighting Power Limits

A few energy codes extend requirements for lighting efficiency to the building's outdoor lighting, such as façade lighting, overhead canopy lighting, walkway lighting, and even parking lighting. These requirements seldom extend to roadway lighting or other types of outdoor lighting that are not powered from the building's electrical system.

Calculation of Installed Lighting Power

All energy codes that specify limits on installed lighting power also include rules for how the installed lighting watts are calculated. These rules require that the types and quantities of lamps, ballasts, and fixtures be called out and that the wattage of lamp-ballast combinations be identified. The rules may also provide default lamp-ballast wattages, which typically are conservative for a given type of equipment but which may be used when the make and model of the equipment are unknown. These rules encourage lighting designers to select more efficient lamp-ballast fixture

combinations because they yield lower installed wattages, but they also require the designers to document the better performance of the equipment. Energy codes may also provide rules for calculating the installed wattages for tricky situations, such as track lighting or screw-in compact fluorescent lamps, which might be easily replaced with higher-wattage alternatives after the compliance-checking process is completed.

Mandatory Switching Requirements

Most energy codes include mandatory requirements for lighting controls; these requirements typically are independent of the lighting power limits. Mandatory control requirements may include requirements for independent light switches in every room, bi-level switching and/or separate switching for areas with daylight, and time clocks or photocell controls on outdoor lighting. Many of the energy codes include a requirement for automatic sweep controls that shut off building lighting during typically unoccupied hours, such as nighttime and weekends. Also, in many codes, lighting that has been exempted or categorized as an additional allowance must be controlled separately from the general lighting.

Mandatory Control Specifications

Energy codes also typically set minimum performance requirements for automatic lighting controls to ensure that they are likely to function as intended and not cause user dissatisfaction. These requirements include such things as time delays for occupancy sensors and sensitivity adjustments for photocell controls.

Compliance Documentation

Most of the advanced energy codes provide standard forms for designers to use in demonstrating that their lighting designs comply with code requirements. The intent of these forms is to make it easier for both designers and code enforcement officials to verify that a given lighting design falls within the lighting power limits and includes the mandatory control requirements. Because these forms can become rather long and cumbersome for large buildings, some jurisdictions provide lighting code compliance software tools so the documentation may be prepared electronically and with a minimized chance of calculation errors. The compliance forms are then printed out and submitted along with the electrical plans. The codes may also have requirements for the level of specificity of lighting system elements and controls that must be shown on the plans. All of these requirements can make for more successful enforcement of code requirements, leading to a higher level of achieved energy savings.

IMPORTANT POINTS TO REMEMBER ABOUT ENERGY CODES

- Codes vary from state to state and, sometimes, from city to city. Always check with local authorities. The U.S. Department of Energy website given above is generally current and useful; it often lists the URL (Web address) of the state code office. Some states publish their energy codes on the Web.

- Some states require that calculations be submitted with plans for permit approval. Other states require little or no documentation.
- Many states do not require compliance except for state or local government projects.
- The federal standards usually apply to federal projects or those undertaken on federal land, including military bases in other countries.

Appendix C LIGHTING IN LEED

Designing a sustainable building has long surpassed the perception of it as a fad, and is more frequently becoming the norm in new construction. Many designers consider this a social and environmental responsibility. Not only is this design approach more sensitive to the environment and its occupants, but it repeatedly makes long-term financial sense for owners. To assist designers, builders, and owners in quantifying and validating their sustainable efforts, the U.S. Green Building Council (USGBC) developed the Leadership in Energy and Environmental Design (LEED) rating and certification system in 2000. LEED is designed to accommodate all building types including commercial and residential, both new construction and major renovations.

LEED has created a point system on a 100-point scale with credits under a variety of categories. For a building to become LEED certified, it must meet all the prerequisites and earn a minimum number of points. Buildings that achieve higher levels may be awarded Silver, Gold, or Platinum recognition. The categories include:

- Sustainable Sites
- Water Efficiency
- Energy & Atmosphere
- Materials & Resources
- Indoor Environmental Quality
- Locations & Linkages
- Awareness & Education
- Innovation in Design
- Regional Priority

Lighting plays an important role in achieving LEED certification, primarily through saving energy. The criteria use a holistic approach, considering both short- and long-term effects. It encourages and rewards the use of efficient lighting systems, but also recognizes the importance of minimizing the time that lights are on. This can be realized by ensuring lights are off when spaces are unoccupied or by reducing or turning off artificial lights when adequate daylight is available. Lighting control is key to providing lasting energy savings for the end user.

In addition to energy savings, the design of sustainable buildings attempts to minimize the negative impact on the surrounding environment, including the nighttime sky. Because of this, LEED requires that exterior lighting be reduced and that light pollution be eliminated.

Generally, LEED-certified buildings lower operating costs, reduce waste both during and after construction, conserve energy and water, and provide a safer and healthier environment for their users.

BIBLIOGRAPHY

Benya, Jim, and Deborah Burnett. *A Prescription for Daylight.* 2010.

DiLaura, David L. *The Lighting Handbook: Reference & Application.* 10th ed. New York, NY: Illuminating Engineering Society of North America, 2011. Print.

Gordon, Gary. *Interior Lighting for Designers.* 4th ed. New York: John Wiley & Sons, 2003. Print.

Russell, Sage. *The Architecture of Light: Architectural Lighting Design Concepts and Techniques: A Textbook of Procedures and Practices for the Architect, Interior Designer and Lighting Designer.* La Jolla, CA: Conceptnine Print Media, 2008. Print.

Steffy, Gary R. *Architectural Lighting Design.* 3rd ed. Hoboken, NJ: John Wiley & Sons, 2008. Print.

INDEX